The Ten Legal Cases That Made Modern Britain

The Ten Legal Cases *That* Made Modern Britain

INIGO BING

\B^b\
Biteback Publishing

First published in Great Britain in 2022 by
Biteback Publishing Ltd, London
Copyright © Inigo Bing 2022

Inigo Bing has asserted his right under the Copyright, Designs and Patents Act 1988
to be identified as the author of this work.

ISBN 978-1-78590-662-6

10 9 8 7 6 5 4 3 2 1

A CIP catalogue record for this book is available from the British Library.

Set in Bulmer

Printed and bound in Great Britain by
CPI Group (UK) Ltd, Croydon CR0 4YY

MIX
Paper from
responsible sources
FSC
www.fsc.org   FSC® C171272

In memory of Richard Daniel Bing

1946–2005

Contents

Introduction

This is a book about how judges have fashioned law to keep pace with modern times. Judge-made law, usually called the common law, has put a tight rein on the use of power by government, benefited the individual by protecting aspects of personal autonomy, free speech and privacy and has identified gaps where old law had failed minorities and the disadvantaged. It is often forgotten that judges in the higher courts, mostly the House of Lords or the Supreme Court, have played their part in moulding modern Britain. In his recent book *Elizabethans: How Modern Britain Was Forged*, the historian and commentator Andrew Marr covers the period 1952, when the Queen ascended the throne, until the present day. He credits many people with having forged modern Britain, but he mentions only one judge, Lord Denning. Even then, Denning appears only because he chaired an inquiry into the scandal that had forced John Profumo to resign in 1963. Denning's considerable judicial innovations, which feature in this book, are ignored. This is not to criticise Marr's choice of the many politicians, trade unionists, entertainers, campaigners, feminists, writers, fashion icons and soldiers who did forge modern Britain. It is to make the point that judges are often overlooked for the part they have played.[1]

Judges play their part by making common law, which is a body of law derived from judicial decisions, not from legislation. It is called common as it is common to all Her Majesty's courts. It evolves through the process of judicial decision-making in a multitude of cases and becomes known through law reporting, an essential feature of common law.

A precedent is a judicial decision which contains within itself a principle which is the abstract legal reasoning giving rise to the judgment. This principle has the force of law as judge-made law, common law, requires consistency. When judges decide cases, they interpret the current position at law, but at the same time their judgment contains a precedent which assists in the determination of future cases. The American scholar Ronald Dworkin has likened precedent to a 'gravitational force' which compels judges to treat like cases alike.[2] The reasoning of the superior courts must be followed and applied by lower courts providing the facts of the dispute engage the same legal reasoning that was applied earlier. Matters settled by past judges should not be disturbed by judges later on. This confers on the discipline of law a certain innate conservatism which may be avoided when creative and imaginative judges distinguish past legal reasoning from the issues that new cases throw up. In this way common law develops and expands to keep pace with modern times. In the higher appellate courts, the need for stability in law must be balanced against the demand for progress. Law can never stand still. As the Canadian scholar Allan C. Hutchinson has put it, judge-made law is not so much a fixed body of rules but 'a living tradition of dispute resolution ... Great cases are only as authoritative as the political and moral values they represent and by whose forbearance they are held in place.'[3] Society shapes law just as, in rare cases, law shapes society. A. W. Brian Simpson has said that legal cases are fragments of antiquity which exist in their own historical period. They should be seen as both events in history and incidents in the evolution of the law.[4]

Nearly all the cases I have chosen either heralded a change in legal outlook or articulated in a single case the smouldering embers of change that were about to catch fire. There is always a complex interplay between the organic changes in society and the legal reasoning of successive generations of judges who have themselves grown up in that society. Judges, unlike politicians, are not in thrall to public opinion, but neither are they cocooned in their courtrooms, oblivious to a changing world around them. In the first category, the cases that hastened change, are the chapters on Race, Power, Privacy and Free Speech. In the second, those that reflected change taking place in society, are chapters on Life, Death, Protest, Democracy and Sovereignty. Not one of them is the final judicial word on the subject, as the future can never be predicted and common law is constantly evolving. All the cases had an impact on the cultural, political and moral values of Britain in the period 1941 until the present day.

Of course, identifying trends in our own time can be difficult. Looking back at the Victorian times, we can now see clearly how legal cases shaped that era of peace and profit, iron and steel, sewers, reservoirs and factories. Business was expanding, railway lines were cutting swathes through Britain's countryside and the courts were full of landowners seeking compensation. Mine shafts, factories making explosives and the pungent smell of gas were disturbing the peace in England's green and pleasant land. Compensation was the name of the legal game and countless cases in the nineteenth century shaped a nation that became able to live with industrial and commercial change. Even the greed and financial chicanery of the times, immortalised in Anthony Trollope's *The Way We Live Now*, led to a legal case that made that era. Influenza was spreading through Britain after an outbreak in Russia in 1889. Quack cures in the form of 'Parr's Life Pills' or 'Cockle's Antibilious Pills' were presented as the way to stop one catching the virus. The Carbolic Smoke Ball Company was set up to patent a smoke ball which was advertised as having the miraculous ability to cure influenza, catarrh, whooping cough and 'other ailments caused by taking cold'. A reward could be claimed if anybody succumbed to flu after inhaling the 'ball' three times daily for two weeks. A Mrs Carlill claimed her reward after falling ill. *Carlill v Carbolic Smoke Ball Company* (1893) set the law of contract off on a new course. Other famous Victorian cases kept the law abreast of new industrial practices and the need to establish a clear legal relationship between master and servant. Judge-made common law was trying to keep pace with Victorian manufacturing and commercial expansion while keeping a watchful eye on the unscrupulous few who wanted their share of wealth that was swirling around Britain.

The legal challenges in modern Britain are different. The Victorians gave us our infrastructure. The challenge now is how we make our lives in the country the Victorians built. Today, personal space, autonomy and privacy assume an importance the Victorians never considered. Racial and sexual equality are goals that must be achieved if society is to prosper and there is now legislation to promote these aims. For the Victorians such equality was to be resisted at all costs. Racial equality was unthinkable, as fashionable social Darwinism espoused doctrines of natural selection. Women could not vote and privacy was near impossible in the housing conditions endured by most of the population. The Victorian constitution, with a supreme Parliament consisting of Lords and Commons, occupied by independently minded men with private means (Members of Parliament were not paid), is now shabby, careworn and completely out of date. Modern medical techniques and discoveries which can preserve life and postpone death put the ethics of life and death into the public realm for discussion and debate and, sometimes, into the hands of judges for a ruling. Technology in the form of CCTV, long-lens cameras and phone-tapping techniques have enhanced the power of the press but have also ushered in an awareness of the need for privacy.

This book tells the story of ten legal cases that shaped the society we now live in. It is not about legislative change, nor is it about politics. It is about the influence judges in Britain's higher courts have had on the lives we lead. Scotland and Northern Ireland have their own legal systems and the book concentrates on the judiciary of England and Wales, although decisions of the Supreme Court, formerly the appellate committee of the House of Lords, also have effect in Scotland and Northern Ireland.

Legal cases that genuinely have a lasting impact on the way we live our lives are few and far between. Judges spend most of their time deciding facts and then applying the law, made by their predecessors, to the facts they find to be true. Their decisions affect only the parties in the case. In the higher appellate courts, the need for stability in law must be balanced against the demand for progress. Law can never stand still. As the Canadian scholar Allan C. Hutchinson has put it, judge-made law is not so much a fixed body of rules but 'a living tradition of dispute resolution'.[5] Great cases have to earn their authority in the salons and chatrooms of legal and popular opinion as a microcosm of social life. Society shapes law just as, in rare cases, law shapes society.

Writing about modern Britain inevitably involves a decision about the period in our history which can be called 'modern'. I have chosen the Second World War as the event when modern Britain becomes recognisable and perceptions of modernity began to emerge. Franklin

D. Roosevelt made his famous 'four freedoms' declaration in 1941. The Dumbarton Oaks Conference, the forerunner of the United Nations, took place in 1944, the same year that the Education Act for England and Wales, which laid down principles for a child's secondary education that lasted a quarter of a century, was passed by the United Kingdom Parliament. The Beveridge Report, the foundation of modern social security in Britain, was published in 1942 and proposals for a National Health Service were published in an official White Paper by the United Kingdom government in 1944. Having decided that Nazism and fascism must be defeated in 1939, the Allies put an end to an era which had allowed the *Kristallnacht* massacres to take place in Germany, a nation supposedly at peace. In November 1938, hundreds of synagogues and countless shops and homes of Jewish people were trashed, looted and burned in Nazi Germany and 30,000 Jews were deported to concentration camps. Though it was described at the time by responsible British newspapers as a 'medieval pogrom', the British government did nothing, except offer 'sympathy' for the German Jews. There were not even economic sanctions imposed on Germany. In modern times such outrages are usually, though not invariably, regarded as international crimes.

The Second World War was as much about the need to stop the inhumanity of man towards his fellow human beings as it was about territorial aggrandisement. As Kenan Malik has said, 'Modernity brought about a new way of thinking about morality.'[6] He argues that social change comes about when humanity starts to think anew about our moral lives. In wartime Britain, senior judges were beginning to react to the social changes that were ushering in modernity. Learie Constantine was a world-famous West Indian cricketer, but he was turned away from a London hotel in 1943 on grounds of his colour. This blatant racial prejudice ended in court when Constantine sued the hotel. It was the first time that an individual who had been discriminated against took legal action against the wrongdoers. The case is described fully in Chapter 3, Race. In 1940, a Jewish man, Robert Liversidge, who had volunteered to fight Hitler by joining the RAF Volunteer Reserve, was interned under wartime emergency regulations. He sued the Home Secretary, who had signed his internment papers, for false imprisonment. Unfortunately, the tides of modernity had not seeped into the land of Britain's senior judiciary and his claim failed on a technical legal point. However, one of Britain's most distinguished judges at the time, Lord Atkin, disagreed with his colleagues in the House of Lords. He delivered a stinging rebuke to those who wanted Liversidge's claim halted before it even started, proclaiming, 'In this country, amid the clash of arms, the laws are not silent. They may be changed, but they speak the same language in war as in peace.' The story of Robert Liversidge's failed legal action is told in Chapter 4, Power. Lord Atkin was in the minority in believing modern Britain needed a judiciary to stand up to the executive when justice demanded it, not be compliant with it just because there was a war going on. But it is his perception about the proper role of judges when unbridled power is seized by the executive that prevails today.

There are four distinct themes running through the ten cases I have chosen. First, power and the source of power in modern Britain. What is the proper balance in the relationship between the power of Parliament and the power of the executive? Do judges have a constitutional role to arbitrate on that relationship? The story of the huge changes in the balance of power between those three separate constituent elements are told in Chapter 4, Power, Chapter 8, Democracy, and Chapter 9, Sovereignty.

The second theme is the broad topic of autonomy and choice as society emerged from the war and developed new views about family values and relationships, public morals and the value of personal space that must exist as the individual struggles with change going on around them. This theme arises in Chapter 2, Sex, Chapter 5, Free Speech, and Chapter 7, Privacy.

While economic progress after the Second World War brought new wealth and new security to many, the period after 1944 was also accompanied by discrimination towards minorities and a society divided by opinions on nuclear weapons, the use of war and the manufacture of arms. Is law relevant in pronouncing on such topics of controversy? This is the third theme that runs through the cases chosen for this book. In Chapter 3, Race, I have attempted to tell the story of how judges contributed to moves towards achieving equality and dignity for racial minorities. In Chapter 6, Protest, I have described how judges played their part in protecting dissent and the use of peaceful protest as a necessary feature of modern democracy.

The fourth theme is the accommodation the law must make in recognising the huge advances in medical science and, with it, medical ethics since 1944. Babies who are born prematurely and are likely to die can be saved. Modern surgery can mend the most catastrophic of conditions. Life can be preserved and death can be postponed. The ethical and legal issues surrounding magnificent medical discoveries are immense. Sometimes judges have been asked, literally, to rule on life and death. Two legal cases which raise questions of morality on the right to live and the right to die are described in Chapter 1, Life, and Chapter 10, Death.

Also looming over much of the book is Britain's relationship with Europe. It has been a pressing issue which has often dominated political debate during the past sixty years. Britain was rebuffed from entering the European Community when Harold Macmillan wanted to join it and then, once in Europe under Edward Heath's premiership, the Labour Party in opposition was against it. After an apparently conclusive referendum confirming membership in 1975, anti-European sentiment started to stir again, this time among Conservatives and, later, a new political arrival, UKIP. At heart, many in Britain could not come to terms with the loss of sovereignty that membership of the European Union appeared to entail. The whole question revolved around ideas about how the supremacy of a United Kingdom Parliament could be reconciled with membership of a European body that appeared to be above our own Parliament. It was inevitable that at some point the courts would be involved. The catalyst, when it came, was a small group of Spanish fishermen who challenged the legality of Parliament's ability to keep Spanish fleets away from Britain's traditional fishing territory. The story of these remarkable events is told in Chapter 9, Sovereignty.

The second aspect of the controversies about Britain's relationship with Europe is human rights. The Convention for the Protection of Human Rights and Fundamental Freedoms (usually called the European Convention) was drawn up by members of the Council of Europe in 1950 and ratified by the UK Parliament in 1951. It has nothing to do with the European Union and is a treaty which Britain has signed. The principles of the Convention are applied and interpreted by the European Court of Human Rights (ECHR), which sits in Strasbourg. Until 2000, a British citizen who was aggrieved that his or her Convention right had not been recognised or applied by domestic courts could petition the Strasbourg court for a ruling. In 1998, the UK Parliament passed the Human Rights Act 1998, which came into force in October 2000. The purpose of this legislation was to require British judges to take account of Convention principles in their decisions, as far as it was relevant to the proceedings, and to interpret domestic legislation in a way that was compatible with Convention rights as far as it was possible to do so.

These seemingly mild changes to the way judges should approach their task in deciding cases and applying the will of Parliament proved controversial from the start. Parliament was divided on party lines about the merits of the Human Rights Act in 1998 and elements of the British press have not been slow to condemn some Strasbourg decisions as crazy or farcical. Prominent politicians have mocked human rights as providing unmeritorious protections for rapists, murderers and illegal immigrants. When she was Home Secretary, Theresa May even claimed that owning a pet could trigger a human rights claim by a person who was appealing against deportation.[7]

Fortunately, two senior judges have provided more thoughtful observations about the place of human rights principles in English law. Lord Sumption and Lady Hale are two of Britain's best-known and most cerebral judges of modern times. Both were formerly academics and both achieved appointment to the Supreme Court by unusual routes. Brenda Hale taught law at Manchester University before becoming a Law Commissioner. When she was appointed a justice of the Supreme Court, having first sat in the High Court and the Court of Appeal, she had hardly ever done any cases as a barrister. Lord Sumption, on the other hand, was a leading QC who appeared in a host of important cases before being appointed as a justice of the Supreme Court straight from the Bar, without ever having sat as a full-time judge. Luckily for the general public, both Lady Hale and Lord Sumption have written and lectured about law and society outside the courtroom setting. Their views are valuable in understanding how judges make and interpret law and occupy an important place in the fabric of modern society. They disagree with each other about human rights.

Jonathan Sumption first made his views known in his Reith Lectures, later printed, with some changes, in his book *Trials of the State: Law and the Decline of Politics* (2019) and his opinions were further developed in *Law in a Time of Crisis* (2021). He had retired as a judge before going into print. In relation to human rights as a component of law, Sumption poses a fundamental question: what does modern democracy consist of? Is it a constitutional mechanism for arriving at collective decisions and accommodating dissent or is it a system of values? Sumption prefers the first, but Strasbourg, he maintains, are trying to convert it into the second. In his opinion we should value democracy even if it occasionally espouses illiberal policies. Liberal values should be argued for in the political arena and ought not to be given a privileged constitutional status, as the Strasbourg court is trying to do. He is afraid that if human rights law continues to be developed, enlarged and interpreted in the way Strasbourg judges are doing then the truly fundamental rights in a democracy become blurred. He has singled out freedom from arbitrary arrest and detention, equality before the law, freedom of thought and expression, assembly and association and regular and free elections as being the bedrock, non-negotiable foundations of democracy which should be protected. His complaint is that Strasbourg is attempting to impose international uniformity on a whole range of issues which are not fundamental and as such should be decided in a domestic context by elected politicians. Once a political decision has been taken in Parliament, the role of judges is to uphold that decision.

He makes a powerful case, but Lady Hale has put forward a different argument. She favours human rights becoming a real and tangible part of our law which judges have the responsibility of applying. She has written about the place of law in our society in her book *Spider Woman: A Life* (2021) and also in lectures, notably in her Warwick Law Lecture, 'What's the point of human rights?' (2013). Lady Hale maintains that the broad principles laid down by Strasbourg have provided a new freedom for English judges to decide what human rights actually mean in the facts of the cases they have to decide. Human rights law gives judges a freedom to apply basic rights principles to their decisions unless Parliament has given a good reason for restricting them in legislation. She offers as an example the interpretation given to the Rent Act 1977, which provided that if a couple were living together as 'husband and wife', the survivor could succeed to the tenancy on the death of the other. The House of Lords had to decide whether the words in Parliament's Rent Act could be read in a way which did not discriminate against a same-sex couple who lived in a long, monogamous and stable relationship before one sadly died. Article 14 of the Convention forbids discrimination on the grounds of sexual orientation. Lady Hale said the Human Rights Act had given a green light to judges to give a purposeful interpretation of statute law to achieve the objective of equal treatment which was essential for democracy. If any individual is treated less equally than any other, the dignity of the individual is violated and this is damaging to society as a whole.[8]

Lady Hale has welcomed the Human Rights Act as giving practical effect to theoretical principles, giving the state a positive obligation to protect rights, rather than simply a negative duty to stop interfering with them. Without human rights forming a central part of modern law, minorities would not be properly protected, as democracy often allows majority opinion to drown out the unpopular rights of minorities. She disagrees that the Strasbourg court has become too powerful, imposing uniformity in states who are parties to the Convention. Instead she praises Strasbourg for the clarity and care in which broad general principles are enunciated.

Tensions over the proper regard that should be paid to the European Convention on Human Rights were brought to the fore in a case about assisted dying in 2014. The case concerned the request by a man, Tony Nicklinson, who was completely paralysed but who had a settled and determined wish to die. He wanted the court to rule that he could be helped to do so at a time of his own choosing. On the face of it, the law was clear. The Suicide Act 1961 forbade assisted suicide and made assisting or encouraging it a crime. The case was of such importance that nine justices of the Supreme Court convened to hear his application. Normally, only five justices would sit on a case to be argued before them. Both Lady Hale and Lord Sumption were members of the court who heard Nicklinson's plea. Perhaps not surprisingly, Lady Hale and Lord Sumption took entirely different approaches to the ethical, moral and human rights issues the case raised. There was, in fact, little unanimity among the nine justices. Both Lady Hale and Lord Sumption were in the minority, but for completely different reasons. The full story of this fascinating but heartbreaking case, which received widespread publicity at the time, is told in Chapter 10, Death. Like free speech, protest and privacy, the right to die case engaged a consideration of human rights principles. Judges were beginning to grapple with the fact that they might need to depart from earlier case law to give decisions which represented modern public opinion. Whether one agrees or disagrees with the part Strasbourg has played and is playing, it is an undoubted fact that European Convention principles have had a major impact on judicial law-making in modern Britain.

During the past sixty years there has been a remarkable change in judicial perception brought about by the Convention. In the 1960s and

1970s, Harold Evans, the editor of the *Sunday Times*, fought a long legal battle to publish the truth about the behaviour of a large international drugs company, Distillers, which had manufactured thalidomide in Britain. Hundreds of malformed children had been born after their mothers had taken the drug, which was advertised as a completely safe antidote to morning sickness in pregnant women. The *Sunday Times* wanted to tell the public about information in their possession which showed Distillers had failed to test the drug properly before putting it on the market. A number of families were in the process of taking legal action against Distillers and this legal action was being prepared laboriously but had not reached any conclusion. As soon as Distillers learned of the intentions of the *Sunday Times* to publish, they sought a gagging order to stop the story. They placed reliance on Britain's vague and opaque contempt of court laws. Judges who heard Distillers' objections upheld them, including the House of Lords, but Harold Evans took the case to Strasbourg, where he won on freedom of speech principles. The story of this impressive battle to earn a place for freedom of expression being an important public interest is told in Chapter 5, Free Speech. It led to a change in the law and a new Act of Parliament was passed to allow comment about genuine matters of public concern to be aired even if a court case about them was being prepared.

In 1990, a well-known actor, Gorden Kaye, had his privacy in a hospital bed invaded by a photographer and a reporter from a tabloid newspaper. They wanted to report on his medical recovery from a serious head injury after some woodwork had crushed him during a violent storm. The actor, however, was in no fit state to agree to being photographed, let alone competent enough to give an interview. His agent wanted publication stopped. Despite right being on Kaye's side and wrong on the tabloid's side, English judges had to wring their hands and confess that English law did not have a privacy law. The events of the following two decades when English law gradually invented legal ways for privacy to be protected is told in Chapter 7, Privacy. English judges were able to learn from Strasbourg human rights principles in their quest to carve out a law of privacy fit for modern times.

Similar developments were taking place in the law of protest. In 1975, a peaceful picket was organised on Saturday mornings outside a firm of Islington estate agents who were, according to the protesters, complicit in the behaviour of certain landlords who were using heavy-handed methods to evict tenants and gentrify the neighbourhood through house sales. Despite the facts that the police did not object to the picket and it was entirely peaceful and did not physically prevent anybody entering the estate agents' offices, English judges ruled they were unlawfully 'besetting' the premises, a concept so ancient that its modern meaning had been entirely forgotten until this case. Only Lord Denning sided with the rights of pickets to protest, but he was overruled by his two colleagues in the Court of Appeal. Then, over time, English judges began to realise they ought to recognise that protest was important to a democratic society. Eventually, in 2021, the Supreme Court established new law on the subject, greatly influenced by Strasbourg thinking. The story of how judge-made protest law came about is told in Chapter 6, Protest. It is another example of the part European Convention law has played in the evolution of common law in modern Britain.

Another theme running through this book is the role of judges in relation to Britain's fraught relationship with Europe which reached new heights when the United Kingdom decided to leave the European Union. The process had begun with a constitutional novelty, a referendum, and it ended in a constitutional furore which involved the Queen, a novel exercise of power by the Prime Minister and a judgment in the

Supreme Court. It was all about the power of Parliament. Every branch of Britain's unwritten and fragile constitution became engaged, sometimes at the same time, in implementing the legal way Britain could leave the EU. The story is told in Chapter 8, Democracy, and it is the story of one remarkable woman's fight to keep Britain's constitutional arrangements intact while politicians frantically thrashed around to find a way to disengage from Europe. Her name was Gina Miller. Miller wanted a decision to leave European institutions to be made democratically.

One simple point was overlooked by politicians when the government began to interpret the referendum result. It was forgotten that leaving the EU would inevitably involve substituting something else for forty-three years of membership. Gina Miller maintained that Britain's future relationship with Europe could only be decided by our parliamentary representatives as a whole. The referendum result could not, in itself, decide Britain's future relationship, as that question was not on the ballot paper. Leaving the EU was therefore an activity of democracy. The constitutional and legal issues raised by Gina Miller are discussed in Chapter 8.

The end of the gruelling and exhausting process of disengaging with Europe threw up a different legal issue. For political reasons the Prime Minister, Boris Johnson, decided to prorogue Parliament at an important time when MPs were trying to avert a crisis if the government became committed to leaving the EU without a deal having been agreed on the terms for leaving. The decision to prorogue was a political one, but was this prorogation lawful and did judges even have a part to play in the business of Parliament? Once again Gina Miller was in court to argue her points about the nature of our democracy.

The judges hearing Gina Miller's arguments had the difficult task of ruling on the legality of the advice Boris Johnson had tendered to the Queen. The Supreme Court delivered its unanimous judgment in September 2019. All eleven justices decided that proroguing Parliament could only lawfully be done in keeping with constitutional democratic practice and the Prime Minister's attempt to prorogue Parliament was a misuse of his powers.

Judges are now shaping our unwritten, flexible and sometimes inchoate constitution. As the political scientist Anthony King has put it, 'Parliament, in the persons of successive governments, has chosen to outsource to the courts a good deal of its power.'[9] But this is a relatively recent decision by modern British governments. In the mid-1950s, the Master of the Rolls Lord Evershed stated that he was proud of the fact that the judiciary had kept out of politics between 1945 and 1950. When Anthony Sampson wrote the first edition of his famous *Anatomy of Britain*, published in 1962, he identified the principal sources of power in Britain as being the Palace, Parliament and the Cabinet. The law, he observed, was 'trapped in conservatism and mystique' and the protected world of lawyers had become increasingly irrelevant to the great corporate world outside.[10]

Then, gradually, change began to emerge when government decisions became more intrusive into the lives of citizens. Over time, the exercise of public power became a feature of public life, and a system of tribunals was created to arbitrate when an individual was affected by a public policy decision in planning, housing, tax and a host of other activities. Judges oversaw the tribunals that arbitrated on the decisions which intruded into the lives of citizens. As time went by, judges became more confident about their review of the use of power exercised by officials acting on behalf of ministers. Public opinion was generally on the side of the judges as more and more people became aware that an arbitrary exercise of power was not necessarily the last word on the subject. The courts provided a pathway to challenge decisions which had apparently been taken by some remote, anonymous official but which had huge consequences for the individuals affected by them.

The growth of judicial review of the use of executive power is now a significant feature of the legal and political landscape of modern Britain. Anthony Sampson's opinion in 1962 that judges were almost irrelevant to any consideration about the distribution of power in Britain was already beginning to be questioned. Forty-two years later, when he updated his *Anatomy of Britain* in 2004, he concluded that the public now looked to judges as the ultimate safeguard of their liberties and they looked to the law to protect them from the overbearing actions of governments.[11]

The final theme of the book is the judicial involvement in cases about sex and morality. At a time when homosexuality was illegal, judges almost relished in the task of sending men to prison when their activities in cubicles of public lavatories had been spied on by prurient undercover policemen. Sex was troublesome for judges. In the 1950s there was an unspoken presumption that explicit descriptions of sex were bound to corrupt the young and the easily led working classes, and censorship of erotic literature was the way to keep youngsters pure.

It was also the era when judges began to think deeply about the relationship between law and morality. Lord Devlin was one of Britain's greatest judges. He was also a Roman Catholic and in 1959 he published a book entitled *The Enforcement of Morals* in which he argued that morality was not always a matter for private judgement. He maintained that it was society in general who had a responsibility for making moral judgements and this necessarily meant that law could and should represent society by enforcing moral standards. The opposite view was propounded by an equally eminent lawyer. Herbert Hart was a professor of jurisprudence at Oxford and a formidable scholar of legal philosophy.

He published *Law, Liberty and Morality* in 1963 and argued that even if some members of society were to regard a particular sexual practice as immoral, this was not enough to justify the law making that conduct punishable. He maintained that sexual morality was not a seamless web so that deviation in one respect inevitably impacts on others, justifying the law's involvement in prohibiting it. He went further and insisted that the intervention of law in morals could have devastating consequences both in suppressing private impulses and in shaming publicly any individual who did not always conform to society's expectations.

This difference of view became known as the Hart–Devlin debate and it took place in the wake of a three-year inquiry chaired by Lord Wolfenden into homosexual offences and prostitution which reported in 1957. The key philosophical conclusion of the report was that 'unless a deliberate attempt is to be made by society, acting through the agency of the law, to equate the sphere of crime with that of sin, there must remain a realm of private morality and immorality which is, in brief and crude terms, not the law's business'. The function of the criminal law, the committee of inquiry concluded, 'is not ... to intervene in the private lives of citizens'. It recommended decriminalising homosexuality in private.

Nowadays, this sensible and necessary change seems obvious, but on the cusp of two eras, the 1950s and the 1960s, nothing was obvious where sex was concerned. On one side head teachers, senior police officers and church leaders were preaching morality from the position of authority society had bestowed upon them and on the other some progressive politicians were trying to reform homosexual laws and update Victorian obscenity laws. There was little consensus on what to do. Parliament had voted in 1960 not to implement the Wolfenden recommendations, and it was not until 1967, a decade after the Wolfenden Report, that male homosexuality was partially decriminalised.

Two years after the Wolfenden Inquiry concluded, however, the obscenity laws were changed, and it was the arrival of the Obscene Publications Act 1959 that provided the launching ground for contemporary confusions and disagreements about sexual morality to be tested. Penguin Books decided to publish the unexpurgated text of D. H. Lawrence's novel *Lady Chatterley's Lover*. The new law allowed the public interest in publication and the literary merit of the work in general to be judged alongside content that might, in isolation, appear obscene. The stage was set for a criminal trial against Penguin Books. The story of this trial is told in Chapter 2, Sex, which sets the case within the social and cultural scene of morality at the time. The trial took place in October 1960, when the morality of the 1960s had hardly arrived and the morality of the 1950s was being questioned, sometimes mocked and almost certainly not observed by the private behaviour of many. Would the verdict of the jury point the way forward to a new morality or would the jury confirm the attitudes many in authority wanted to preserve? I have endeavoured to describe the trial with these questions in the forefront of the chapter. The verdict signalled a change of attitude which began in the mid-1960s and has continued, despite efforts to halt it from figures like Mary Whitehouse and Lord Longford, until the present day. The culmination of steady progress towards tolerance on matters of sex occurred when David Cameron, as Prime Minister, lent his support for gay marriage. When he said, in 2011, 'I don't support gay marriage in spite of being a Conservative; I support gay marriage because I am a Conservative', he closed down a controversy. In those few words, a debate which a great judge, Lord Devlin, had initiated suddenly seemed entirely irrelevant.

Since the 1950s and 1960s, when sexual morality divided opinion, the debate has moved on. Ethical considerations now weigh more heavily on the modern mind than morals. Much of this debate centres on commercial ethics, decisions about placing investments, or the ethical reasons for continuing to mine coal, for example. Environmental concerns or the need for global taxation of multinational companies now engage attention in the way that private morality did in the 1950s. Sometimes judges become involved when a decision like the development of Heathrow Airport or the construction of the HS2 rail line has been placed before the courts. Mostly, those seeking judicial review do not meet with success. Generally speaking, a judicial decision does not engage ethics, as the ethics in a legal judgment are contained in the law, which is applied to the facts of the case. Ethics is about what we think *ought* to happen in a set of circumstances. A judgment is about what the law says should happen.

In one recent case, however, a decision could not be reached *unless* the judges applied ethics to their decision. It concerned the agonising choice judges were required to make when two twins, known in court as Jodie and Mary, were born conjoined at the abdomen and the spinal cords were linked. Doctors in Manchester wanted to perform separation surgery which would give Jodie a good chance of an independent life, but her twin sister would certainly die during the surgery. The reality was that Mary was killing Jodie, but Mary did not have an independent capacity to live.

An instinctive answer to this heartbreaking problem would seem to be to take the least worst option and permit the surgery to proceed in order to save Jodie. However, there an ethical difficulty confronted the judges. The parents were devout Catholics and they opposed the separation surgery on religious grounds. When doctors and parents disagree in this way, the Family Division of the High Court becomes involved. Then, in this public legal arena, the Cardinal Archbishop of

Westminster, the head of the Catholic Church in England, intervened. He submitted cogent Catholic arguments that a good end cannot justify the means to that end.

There was, in addition, a further argument, based on law not ethics. The barrister representing Mary's interests argued that if the surgery went ahead, it would entail Mary's murder, and no court of law could permit murder. The judges were faced with an ethical choice that could preserve or curtail life. They had to make an ethical decision which was also one that the law allowed to be made. Not only did the judges have to make the decision; they had to provide cogent reasons for it which could be understood by the many observing members of the public and the Catholic Church, which took a prominent interest in the case.

The last chapter in the book, Death, involves even more difficult choices. Nine justices of the Supreme Court convened to hear the plea of Tony Nicklinson, who was almost completely paralysed and whose life was, in his own words, dull, miserable, demeaning, undignified and intolerable. He wanted to be helped to die, but the Suicide Act 1961 did not allow this. Assisting or encouraging another to take his or her own life was forbidden. It was a criminal offence. How, then, could judges help him? Two justices thought the law could help him if they used a rare legal power under the Human Rights Act to declare the Suicide Act incompatible with Mr Nicklinson's right of autonomy to make for himself an end-of-life decision. Strasbourg had hinted that the Convention was sufficiently broad for a domestic court to interpret Article 8 of the Convention, the right to respect for a private and family life, in this way. However, this power to declare an Act of Parliament incompatible with the Convention is used rarely and had not previously been used when controversial ethical considerations were in play. Some members of the Supreme Court thought that to make a declaration that the Suicide Act 1961 was incompatible with a Convention right was not an appropriate use of the judicial role. They thought that if a declaration of incompatibility were made, the Supreme Court would be making a moral judgment and judges should *not* become embroiled in the morality of assisted death. These justices thought that judges were not equipped to make judgments about morality when there is no general consensus on the rights and wrongs of the issue at hand. Being a judge does not allow that office to be used in order to impose personal opinions into their judgments. If such opinions were imposed, they would lack all constitutional legitimacy. The resolution of this vexed question as well as the conclusion which the majority of the Supreme Court came to in the Nicklinson case is told in Chapter 10.

The cases chosen for this book are my personal choices. Plainly, there are other important judgments which played their part in making modern Britain. For example, the Crossman diaries case involved an attempt by the Attorney General to stop publication of the diaries of Richard Crossman, who served in Cabinet under Harold Wilson for six years between 1964 and 1970, on the grounds that Cabinet discussions are confidential. The action failed, but the judgment of the Lord Chief Justice avoided a legal ruling of substance and allowed publication to go ahead due to the lapse of time between the confidential events and time of publication.[12] Similarly, the *Spycatcher* litigation involving the memoirs of Peter Wright, a former MI5 officer, was an important case turning on the publication of confidential material, but the decision was based largely on the fact that 'the cat was out of the bag' by the time the book would appear.[13] In the area of sex and morality, the Victoria Gillick case, about whether contraceptive advice could be given legally to children under the age of sixteen, was clearly a notable decision which has had repercussions recently when children with gender dysphoria were judged competent to consent to puberty blockers. Alas, for reasons of space and presentation a book containing eleven or more legal cases is less accessible than one containing ten. My own competence to write about them would be stretched to the limit if I tackled any more. I considered it essential not to ignore Britain's relationship with Europe, as it involved no fewer than three topics, sovereignty, democracy and human rights. Race, privacy and protest are subjects which assumed their present significance in the national consciousness after the Second World War, and the thalidomide scandal is a more vivid example of the public's right to know than *Spycatcher* or Richard Crossman.

Taking the book as a whole, three judges stand out as having made an outstanding contribution to the evolution of law by their unusual ability to understand how the law should move forward. Lord Atkin was born in 1867 and died in 1944, the year Lord Denning was appointed to the bench. Lady Hale was born within a year of Denning's appointment. He retired in 1982 when Lady Hale was a legal academic in Manchester, a post that later led to her appointment as a Law Commissioner and then as a High Court judge in 1994. Their lives almost overlapped. Lord Atkin was a colossus of the legal world whose dissenting speech in the case of *Liversidge v Anderson* (1941), described in Chapter 4, set the law on a new course and heralded a new era of judicial oversight on the legality of executive decisions. Lord Denning was an innovator who initiated a culture of a purposeful interpretation of parliamentary statutes. His wisdom crops up in the chapters on Power, Privacy, Free Speech and Protest. Often his judgments were years ahead of their times. He was regularly overruled by colleagues sitting alongside him in the Court of Appeal or by the House of Lords, but many of Lord Denning's judgments have stood the test of time, although he was not a consistent progressive. In the case of the 'Birmingham Six', he tried to block any legal challenge to the veracity of the West Midlands police. This aberration should not for ever cast doubt on his wisdom in the legal cases in which he forged a new path for the law. Lady Hale served as justice of Britain's highest court, the appellate committee of the House of Lords, later the Supreme Court, for a period of sixteen years, three of them as president. Her judgments, especially those focusing on human dignity, sexual equality and fundamental rights, have made an invaluable contribution to the development of law, as has her judgment in the prorogation case. Her influence on modern law is found in the chapters on Power, Democracy and Sovereignty.

The final tribute must go to those brave and determined litigants who initiated their legal claims in the first place. It can be a daunting ordeal and some of Britain's best lawyers spend most of their time keeping their clients out of court. Starting a case does not provide certainty of success, and it definitely does not when the claim is novel, controversial or unpopular. Without litigants prepared to take these risks, often at a huge personal and financial cost, judges would never have the opportunity to make rulings which have the effect of shaping the lives of all of us. The names of these brave people appear in the Acknowledgements. We owe them all a debt of gratitude.

Chapter 1

Life – Jodie and Mary, the Conjoined Twins

In modern Britain the sanctity of human life has gradually and imperceptibly acquired a new meaning. During the first twenty years after the end of the Second World War, if you intentionally took the life of another, you forfeited your own as the penalty under the regime of capital punishment. If you decided to bring your own life to an end voluntarily, you committed the crime of suicide, so a failed suicide attempt could put you in prison. Until 1967 abortion in any circumstances was forbidden unless it was medically necessary to save the life of the mother. Gradually, over time, this absolutist interpretation of the sanctity of life and the imperative of upholding it in almost any circumstances began to change. Capital punishment was abolished, suicide was decriminalised (unless it was aided by another) and abortion, in defined circumstances, was legalised. The ability of medical science to keep patients alive in circumstances which were not possible in earlier times was advancing rapidly. These advances were keeping pace with changing social attitudes and a decline in strict religious observance within the population of Britain. But what were the ethical consequences of these gradual processes of change? Was the preservation of life no longer regarded as an absolute imperative, or was the sanctity of life a value that was qualified

1

in certain circumstances? Could there ever be a situation when a human being was alive and yet not have a life? Is life something that has a comparative value, making some lives more worth living than others? These ethical considerations did not always feature in the process of change which advances in medical science were forcing upon society. The common law could only confront them if judges were presented with a case when a disagreement among the parties about such ethical dilemmas required a judicial decision.

Such cases have arisen from time to time when the ability of doctors to preserve life has clashed with their duty to relieve suffering and judges and juries in criminal cases have become involved in drawing the fine line between the duty to preserve life and the duty to relieve suffering. If the patient is a child and too young to give informed consent, devoted parents may disagree with the clinical assessment of the child's best interests. Here, the judge's task is difficult, emotional and often heartbreaking. These cases are invariably decided by applying the clear legal principle that the paramount judicial consideration is the welfare of the child first, taking into account the medical condition of the child if the doctors seek advance consent to withdraw life-saving procedures. Such cases do not always engage ethics in its purest form. They are decided on a medical assessment.

In one case, however, judges had to confront ethical values in a most acute way in order to reach their decision. It was the case of Jodie and Mary (not their real names), who were born in August 2000. They were conjoined in the mother's womb at the lower abdomen and the spinal cords of each twin were joined and the spines fused. At birth they had a combined weight of six kilograms. This conjoin produced a grossly abnormal vulval configuration and a single orifice for each vulva. Each twin had her own brain, heart, lungs and kidneys, but the bladder was shared and this emptied spontaneously through two separate urethras. Jodie was the stronger twin. The crucial medical fact was that Jodie's aorta fed Mary's. In order to survive, Mary had to rely on Jodie's heart and lungs providing her with oxygenated blood. Jodie was keeping her twin alive, but this was debilitating for her as Jodie's intake of calories was insufficient to allow them both to grow normally. Mary was obviously the weaker twin, with a severely abnormal brain and a dilated and poorly functioning heart, and without Jodie providing circulation she would not be alive as a separate human being. Although Jodie was capable of living in a conjoined condition and was taking food normally, she was likely to live for only three to six months, as the strain of providing blood for herself and her sister was likely to cause heart failure. At some point this would inevitably cause her death. But Jodie had a good chance of survival if she was surgically separated from her sister and this procedure was a low risk for her. On the other hand, if the twins remained fused, Mary was highly likely to develop hydrocephalus (fluid on the brain), which would be very difficult to treat as the insertion of a shunt would be difficult if not impossible in her condition. The reality was that Mary was killing Jodie, but Mary did not have an independent capacity to live. If she remained joined, she was likely to die, but if surgically separated she was bound to die as the separation surgery would involve severing the aorta which sustained her life. If Jodie was to live, she needed to be separated. Her twin was, in law, alive as a distinct personality but was not viable as a separate human being. The clinical team were united in their belief that their professional duty obliged them to do everything in their power to save Jodie, even if the necessary surgery inevitably brought about Mary's death.

Jodie and Mary's parents emphatically rejected this advice. They were sincere and devout Roman Catholics who lived on Gozo, an island off the coast of the main part of Malta. When the abnormal pregnancy was picked up by Maltese doctors, the parents took advantage of arrangements already in place enabling some Maltese patients to come to England to be treated in English National Health Service hospitals. The twins were admitted to St Mary's Hospital, Manchester, a centre of excellence in this field, and the lead consultant responsible for her case there was also Maltese. They were born at St Mary's.

The parents opposed the proposed separation surgery for a number of reasons which were put forward in court. First, they could not contemplate a course of action which involved one of their children dying to enable the other to survive. As devout Catholics, they believed it was God's will that the mother had borne conjoined twins in her womb, but having given life to them they did not understand why they could not make the decision about their daughters themselves. They argued that if the decision to embark on separation surgery was taken out of their hands, it could entail a life for Jodie with a serious disability. They lived in a remote place with limited facilities to cope with a disabled child. There was only a small hospital without staff to care for Jodie in the future. Their wishes were unequivocal. They wanted neither of the children to receive any medical treatment. They would not be able to cope financially and they could not offer the surviving daughter the care she may need. They had considered leaving Jodie in England, but they did not know whether this was possible.

It is perhaps understandable why parents from a small island in Malta should not be acquainted with the responsibilities of the Family Court in England to ensure the welfare of children is observed under English law. In the eighteenth century, English law started to recognise that children had a right to be protected from harm and abuse and that they had rights independently of their parents. In the late nineteenth century, the 'welfare of the child' was given statutory recognition as having a relevant consideration in parental custody disputes. In the twentieth century, the welfare of the child became *the* paramount consideration when any question relating to a child's upbringing was brought to the attention of the courts. For the medical profession there is also a duty for doctors to act in the best interests of a child under their care. But doctors are not infallible; they do not possess unique knowledge about what constitutes a child's best interests and the child's parents may disagree with the doctors on the desirability of the recommended medical treatment. In these circumstances the Family Court has jurisdiction to hear the competing arguments, including those of the child, who is represented by a court-appointed guardian to give voice to the opinion the child might, objectively, wish to be heard.

This is the background to *Re A (conjoined twins)*,[1] a case that made modern Britain. It was heard in emergency circumstances in the summer of 2000 within a few weeks of the twins' birth. The doctors issued a summons under the Family Court's inherent jurisdiction and under the Children Act 1989 seeking a declaration that as the children could not consent and the parents withheld consent it was in the twins' best interests for separation procedures to be carried out. In purely medical terms there was a strong case for the hospital. In Jodie's case, elective separation was a low-risk procedure as her condition was a functional disability not a life-threatening one. She was unlikely to endure psychological consequences of the operation and there was a negligible risk of death or permanent brain damage. There was a good prospect that if separated she could enjoy a good quality of life. Prolonging her life was plainly in her best interests. In Mary's case, however, her prospects of life were bleak. She was bound to die within a short time if she remained conjoined to Jodie, but if Jodie was separated from her, death

5

was inevitable as she lived only through oxygen provided by her sister. The choice was agonising, but the hospital thought their duty was to seek the permission of the Family Court to override the views of the parents.

The plight of Jodie and Mary was a case that went beyond a factual inquiry. It had engaged Catholic theology as the parents were devout Roman Catholics. It was not simply a case of putting the welfare of a child first and reaching a decision which honoured this principle, having balanced the arguments of the doctors against those of the parents. The Cardinal Archbishop of Westminster, Cardinal Cormac Murphy-O'Connor, head of the Roman Catholic Church in England, and the ProLife Alliance (a single-issue political party at the time) submitted written representations in support of the parents' position. The archbishop's arguments, founded in Catholic doctrine, were spelt out for the judges' consideration as follows: God has given humankind the gift of life, which must be revered and cherished; this Christian belief lies at the root of the western humanist tradition and underpins our legal system; human life is sacred and inviolable so there must be a benefit to the person whose life is sacred for the integrity of that person's body to be invaded. This belief, ingrained within a humanist tradition that values human life, forbids an assault on one person in order to preserve the life of another. It is forbidden because it is wrong to invade the sacred integrity of one person if the invasion results in no benefit to that person. In Mary's case, the separation procedure would be an invasion of her integrity which was calculated to cause her death. Any argument that Mary has no life worth living and that a painless death would be to her benefit is misconceived. Finally, the duty to preserve life does not exist if the only available means of preserving life involves a grave injustice. Killing Mary to save Jodie does involve a grave injustice to Mary.

A good end cannot justify the means. English law should not recognise a principle that to kill or commit a lethal assault on one person can result in some good coming of it, even if that good is the preservation of life of another. The archbishop maintained that these ethical considerations are so important that the wishes of the parents should not be overridden.

The archbishop's intervention immediately made Jodie and Mary's case one of seemingly insoluble difficulty. The Family Court was familiar with balancing the recommendations of the doctors against the paramount consideration of a single child's best interest when deciding whether the proposed medical intervention would be approved. Here, there were two children whose best interests were in direct conflict. Saving Jodie involved killing Mary, but unless Jodie was separated both would die. How could the court conscientiously approach its task by giving the best interests of both twins the same consideration?

There were no previous cases presenting the same agonising choice that the court was required to take for Jodie and Mary. One reason that the judges had to make a decision starting from scratch, relying on ethical first principles, was that a live birth of conjoined twins is very rare. It is the rarity of the condition that in earlier times condemned conjoined twins who survived (and surviving was even more rare) into freaks or circus performers. Eng and Chang Bunker were born in what was then known as Siam in 1811 and lived as twins, paraded as circus freaks in P. T. Barnum's circus. They were called Siamese twins or 'double-headed monsters' well into the twentieth century. Surgical operations to separate conjoined twins was considered too dangerous until 1955, when the first attempts were made. Since then, only about 200 operations have been successful worldwide and some points of conjuncture are more easily separated than others. Jodie and Mary were ischiopagus conjoined twins – joined at the pelvis – with four legs. This is very rare; the great majority of twins are joined at the thorax or the navel. Ischio-pagus conjuncture is complicated by the incidence of shared or divided organs in the genito-urinary and gastro-intestinal regions. By the year 2000, when Jodie and Mary were born, medical science was sufficiently advanced for surgeons to be able to preserve the life of one ischiopagus twin. The question for the court was: was this ethical if it entailed short-ening Mary's life?

Once the doctors had applied to the Family Court for a declaration that the proposed separation surgery would be lawful, the parents and each of the twins became entitled to legal representation. On one side were the arguments of the hospital, which were supported by counsel appointed to represent Jodie's interests. On the other side were the argu-ments for the parents, which were supported by counsel for Mary. Once the case had reached the court, however, a new argument was intro-duced by Mary's counsel. He argued that not only would the separation surgery be unethical on sanctity of life principles; it would also be un-lawful. Mary's counsel put forward the following propositions: a surgical operation to separate Mary would involve a deliberate positive act; this act would be an invasion of Mary's body which would cause her death; such a deliberate intentional act would be murder; and the law does not excuse murder if it is committed in order to save the life of another.

These propositions could all be supported by common law and this presented the Family Court with an additional ethical problem. Could the court possibly approve a medical procedure if it was necessary med-ically and was ethically sound but was illegal? Plainly not, but at the same time it would be difficult for the court to rule the operation would be legal if it was ethically wrong. Traditionally, English law and morals have gone hand in hand, but when a unique problem such as Jodie and

Mary's presented itself there was no factual precedent to guide the court towards a decision. There was no case in the annals that was remotely similar to the one staring the Family Court in the face.

The only way the case could be approached sympathetically and intelligently was to think about the problem ethically. If, as the archbishop and the parents maintained, God had provided the conjoined condition in the mother's womb and only God could determine their fate thereafter, what reasons might God have for refusing or permitting the operation? On one view the doctors were helpless to change a situation God had provided for, but an equally tenable religious belief would be that God has endowed upon man an instinct and imperative to preserve the life that God has created. On this view God would expect the doctors at least to weigh up the preservation of life requirement the Almighty had bestowed upon humanity. A religious belief, by itself, did not provide any clear unambiguous signal about how to proceed. An ethical approach would disavow neither religion nor the authority of the archbishop to interpret God's will as he believed it to be but would be an approach providing some objective criteria for evaluating the correctness of the decision. In law this is called the judge's reasons for the decision reached.

The case of the conjoined twins is one of the cases that made modern Britain as the unique facts forced the court to confront the interface between law and ethics in a direct and agonising fashion. The lives of two human beings were at stake. While strict Catholic doctrine is no longer observed officially, and constitutionally Britain is a Protestant country, non-Catholic ethics have not obviously replaced Roman Catholic theology. The failure of Parliament to be willing to confront the ethics of end-of-life decisions, discussed in Chapter 10, is an example of the void in the ethical foundations of modern Britain. In Jodie and Mary's case, one High Court judge and, on appeal, three judges of the Court of Appeal had, at short notice, the task of giving a reasoned judgment which was certain not to satisfy everybody.

The High Court judge who heard the hospital's application for a declaration that the separation surgery was lawful granted the application, but counsel for Mary appealed on the grounds that the declaration involved the unlawful killing of Mary, the ethical point raised by the archbishop. The Court of Appeal rejected the archbishop's absolutist approach. Relying on academic literature, the court said this uncompromising stance was not, in reality, an argument for the importance of the sanctity of life. It was an argument of *vitalism*, the doctrine that holds that human life is an absolute moral value and that it is wrong either to shorten it or to fail to lengthen it. The true *sanctity of life* argument as traditionally upheld by the law, the court decided, does acknowledge that in some circumstances it is legitimate for doctors to decline treatment. It is permitted, for example, when the prospective benefits of the treatment do not warrant the burdensome consequences such as physical pain, psychological stress and social dislocation. Secondly, a cognisant Roman Catholic does not have to embark on procedures to preserve his life in every conceivable circumstance, travelling across the world to receive treatment not available in Britain. A Catholic does not die in sin in these circumstances. There are other pressing social and economic circumstances which would entitle a Catholic not to go to extraordinary lengths to preserve life. This doctrine would enable a Catholic physician to allow the patient to die by declining treatment that, potentially, might be available somewhere else. In analysing the fundamental basis for the absolutist approach, advocated by the archbishop, the court concluded that by accepting that there are some circumstances when a doctor can decline treatment which preserves life, absolutism falls into the trap of approaching the ethical choices from the starting point that some lives have more worth than others. This, the court said, was an argument that engages in discriminatory judgments and arbitrary criteria about which mental or physical disability justifies a doctor in declining treatment.

This, in turn, leads on to considerations of which condition or degree of disability is supposed to make life worth living. However, the court decided that to consider degrees of disability on sanctity of life principles would be a fundamental misconception. The flaw in the reasoning is that it presupposes that one life is more worth living than another. The court refused to accept this proposition as a starting point for an ethical appraisal. Mary's life had its own 'ineliminable value and dignity' as every human life has equal inherent value. Ethically, her life, even if destined for death whether the operation was carried out or not, was equal to Jodie's.

This 'inherent value' principle means human life is possessed of an intrinsic dignity which is entitled to protection from unjust attack. In his judgment, Lord Justice Ward said the right to life was essentially a right not to be intentionally killed. The prohibition of intentional killing is the cornerstone of law and social relationships. The absolutist tenets, on the other hand, would condemn a doctor for killing Mary even if the purpose and intention of the act was to prolong the life of Jodie. This disjunction between the action of separation and the purpose and intention of carrying it out hardly puts the doctor in a superior position of being the arbiter of the value of one life over another, a central plank of the archbishop's claim. The doctor is having to make an agonising decision where his duties and obligations towards Mary clash with those he owes towards Jodie. Where duties and obligations are in conflict, an absolutist position is difficult to sustain intellectually.

The sanctity of life principle, important though it is, is only one of a cluster of ethical principles which we apply in making daily decisions. Another is autonomy and the right of any human being to choose how his or her life is to be led. A third is the respect that should be accorded by one to another about the way a person chooses to live his or her life. These principles are not always compatible with one another. If a person chooses not to embark on potentially life-saving treatment, the decision to exercise autonomy qualifies the principle of the sanctity of life. The judges hearing Jodie and Mary's case endorsed what another senior judge had said in 1993: 'No morally correct solution can be deduced from a single ethical principle ... There must be an accommodation between principles, both of which seem rational ... but which have come into conflict with each other.'[2]

In Jodie and Mary's case, the absolutist position ignores the medical reality that by remaining conjoined the dignity and integrity of both twins is denied. Surgery is plainly and obviously in the best interests of Jodie and it is also in the best interests of Mary. By being conjoined and, in reality, bound to die, she is denied the bodily integrity which is the right of each of them. As Lord Justice Walker put it in his judgment, the separation surgery would give Mary, even in death, bodily integrity as a human being, not because she was intentionally killed but because her own body could not sustain life.

The court went on to disagree with the parents' and the archbishop's argument by focusing on the utterly unique circumstances of the twins' arrival on earth to become part of the community of human life. Jodie and Mary's medical condition was simply not contemplated by Catholic doctrine. By being conjoined in this particular way, with a fusion of spines, Mary had been denied integrity by the cruel circumstances of her birth. Lord Justice Ward put it bluntly: the operation to separate cannot confer any bodily integrity on Mary because she will be dead before she can enjoy any independence, and if she is independent, she will have no capacity for life. There are no best health issues for her.

For Jodie, on the other hand, there was a realistic prospect of life. If the doctors acceded to the archbishop's plea to refuse to commence separation surgery on the grounds that it would kill Mary, where did this leave their duty towards Jodie? If there is an ethical duty to preserve life when it is possible to do so then failing to carry out separation surgery would breach this duty in Jodie's case. The problem seemed ethically insoluble unless the starting point was to consider the best interests of both twins, according them equal dignity and respect, and choosing the lesser of two evils in the final decision. It was not a question of choosing which of the two lives was the more worthwhile; the question was whether the separation surgery was worthwhile. If the question is posed in this way, it is easier to find the way to an ethical answer. For Mary the surgery could not be worthwhile, but neither would it be worthwhile to fail to undertake surgery. For Jodie only surgery could have a hope of saving her from a slow death as her heart grew tired in the process of sustaining her and her sister at the same time. If the doctors did not attempt the surgery, death for Jodie was as inevitable as it was for Mary.

In making this ethical judgment the court thought these considerations carried more weight than those of the parents, who had stressed economic considerations in caring for a possibly disabled Jodie on the island of Gozo. They feared this prospect. While the court sympathised with these practical matters, should they count for more on moral and ethical grounds than the prospect of saving the life of their daughter? The court had a duty to consider the best interests of Jodie, and her best interests were a chance of life. Under English law a doctor is not allowed to treat a patient without the consent of someone authorised to give that consent. In the case of a child this is invariably the parents. If an operation on a child took place in defiance of the parents' refusal, it would be, in law, an unlawful assault on the child. Equally, the law recognises that parental powers exist for the performance of parental duties and responsibilities. The court emphasised that parenthood required consent or refusal for medical intervention to be based on the child's best interests. While parental views should not be disregarded or set aside, the court's duty is to give effect to its own judgment when doctors and parents disagree. A doctor treating a child may seek the court's permission to undertake a procedure for which the parents have refused to give consent. The court has a duty to weigh the competing arguments and make a decision based on the best interests of the child. In Jodie and Mary's case, this meant a decision based on the best interests of both.

The only other known case on very similar facts occurred in Philadelphia in the United States in 1977. A mother who was an orthodox Jew, as was her husband, gave birth to conjoined twins who could be separated but, as with Jodie and Mary, one would surely die in the process. The parents were prepared to agree to separation but only if it had scholarly support from rabbis. Their religious counsellors reported that the operation could be permitted in accordance with Jewish theology on the 'designated for death' argument. The rabbis considered the separation surgery was analogous to the hypothetical situation of two men jumping from a burning plane. The parachute of one does not open as he falls past the man whose parachute will save him if he can attach himself to it. The parachuted man grabs the legs of the falling man but he cannot sustain his grip and he causes his colleague to fall. The action of the man on the parachute has therefore deliberately allowed his colleague to drop to his death even though he might have saved him had he held his legs for longer. Rabbis in Philadelphia advised that if an individual was inevitably 'destined for death' as the parachute did not open in the first place, it is not morally wrong if another fails to stop destiny taking its course. In the Philadelphia cases the judges acceded to the doctors' application for separation surgery without giving their reasons. Commentators have speculated that the judges may, in their haste to give the hospital an answer, have envisaged a 'substituted judgment scenario', which tries to make the decision that the patient would have made if he or she were able to make decisions. By this method of reasoning, it is presumed conjoined twin A would consent to her own death to preserve her identical genes in the body of twin B knowing there was no prospect of her own survival.[3]

Unfortunately, neither the American rabbinical opinion nor a substituted judgment method of reasoning was helpful to the judges agonising over the verdict on Jodie and Mary. Under English law judges are required to decide about medical intervention for children having regard to the best interests of the child. This does not engage speculation about what the child herself might or might not have consented to had she had capacity to consent. Secondly, as a matter of reality the barrister assigned to represent Mary's interests would hardly advance arguments based on a 'substituted judgment' of Mary signalling a contentment that she should sacrifice her life for her sister.

The judges could derive no help from this United States case and they embarked on ethical reasoning of their own which rejected the absolutist position on the sanctity of human life (or vitalism as the court defined it). But having rejected the archbishop's ethical advice the judges were only halfway to being able to uphold the recommendation of the hospital to commence separation surgery. The prospect of illegality and murder had been raised by Mary's counsel, whose simple point was that the surgery would kill Mary and this would be murder because it would be an intentional act. There were really only two previous legal cases that could help the judges: one was about necessity and involved cannibalism on the high seas in the Victorian era; the other was about the tragic consequences that befell a healthy teenager caught up in the Hillsborough football disaster more than a hundred years later. Neither provided a precise precedent for Jodie and Mary.

Tony Bland was a healthy seventeen-year-old when he went to Sheffield to watch his team, Liverpool, play Nottingham Forest in the FA Cup semi-final at the Hillsborough Stadium in April 1989. What happened at the ground was a tragedy of such sadness and anguish that the nation was united in sorrow. A large influx of supporters who had arrived late for kick-off were allowed into the ground and the surge became a bottleneck which crushed many already crammed together on the terraces. Ninety-four fans were killed that day and there were over 700 injured, with three others later dying of injuries sustained at the stadium. Among those who initially survived was Tony Bland, whose crush injury gave rise to hypoxic brain damage. He was unconscious and completely unaware of the world around him. He was dying when he was brought to hospital from the stadium, where he remained for several years. His brain stem remained intact, but there was irreparable damage to the cortex and there was no hope of recovery. He was in a 'persistent vegetative state' (PVS). Skilled doctors, nurses and family members all made repeated efforts to revive him, but scans to the brain revealed he had no appreciation of anything around him. He was fed artificially, and natural bodily functions were attended to by nurses, who devoted four or five hours a day to his care. He had to be constantly moved to avoid bedsores and his bowels were evacuated by enema. He could feel no pain or sensation and was incapable of voluntary limb movement. He was fed with a tube in his nose into which liquified food was pumped mechanically.

The senior doctor concluded there was no prospect of any improvement and his father and other family members agreed with the medical opinion that further care in the hospital would be fruitless. The local coroner, however, warned the hospital that there was a risk that a doctor who withdrew treatment and allowed Tony to die could be charged with murder. The hospital trust took out a summons in the Family Court for a declaration that despite Tony's inability to give consent, the doctors could discontinue life-sustaining treatment if it was for the purpose of enabling him to end his life peacefully. If this was permitted, the doctors and the family agreed he would die with dignity and without pain. The cause of his death would, as a result, be the natural causes of PVS. The trust wanted this court order to be in a form that would not give rise to any future criminal or civil liability. Tony's interests were placed in the hands of the Official Solicitor, an impartial lawyer who has a duty to put forward the interests of those who lack capacity to give instructions. His argument was that withdrawing medical care and allowing Tony to die was no different from killing him and therefore such a decision was forbidden.

In 1993 when the court order was applied for, there had been no previous court case involving a withdrawal of medical treatment without a patient's prior consent. For this reason, the Attorney General instructed a senior barrister to place all relevant ethical considerations before the judges, without necessarily favouring one view over another. As the Tony Bland case was breaking new ground, the final decision was made by the House of Lords, Britain's highest court at that time. The House of Lords resolved the ethical issue by identifying strands in English common law which drew a distinction between cases where a doctor decides *not* to continue treatment which might prolong life and those where active steps, like administering a fatal injection, are taken which will hasten death. The former, according to earlier case law, is lawful, providing the doctor withdraws treatment conscientiously in accordance with a medical duty to relieve suffering, whereas the latter is euthanasia, which the law forbids. Performing an act which crosses the Rubicon between care for the living and actively assisting death would expose a doctor to a charge of murder being laid against him. As Lord Browne-Wilkinson put it in his judgment, it was 'perfectly reasonable for the responsible doctors to conclude that there is no affirmative benefit to Anthony Bland in continuing the invasive medical procedures necessary to sustain his life'. Once that medical conclusion had been conscientiously made, the doctors were no longer under a duty to continue the medical care Tony had been receiving and they would not be guilty of murder if they discontinued the care. The withdrawal of treatment amounted to an *omission* to embark on a positive act towards achieving Tony Bland's death and there was no positive *duty* to continue treatment to keep him alive. In ruling that the doctors could lawfully withdraw treatment, the House of Lords stated that the proposed course of action did not cross the Rubicon.

This ruling did not resolve entirely satisfactorily the ethical issues in the case. As Lord Browne-Wilkinson put it,

How can it be lawful to allow a patient to die slowly, though painlessly, over a period of weeks from lack of food but unlawful to produce his immediate death by a lethal injection, thereby saving his family from yet another ordeal to add to the tragedy that has already struck them? I find it difficult to find a moral answer to that question. But it is undoubtedly the law.

In abstract ethical terms it is difficult to justify the distinction.

In Jodie and Mary's case, where the facts were very different, the judges had reached an *ethical* conclusion that killing Mary was the lesser evil when the alternative meant a slow death for both. The court was looking at Tony Bland's case for guidance on the *legality* of the separation surgery. Again, the Bland case was not helpful. The judges had no hesitation in concluding that the separation surgery bore no resemblance to the discontinuing of artificial feeding which was sanctioned for Tony Bland. The proposed surgery would be an active invasion of Mary's body when doctors needed to examine which organ belonged to each child in addition to the deliberate step of clamping the aorta. Therefore, the Family Court could not give permission for the surgery for the reasons given in the Tony Bland case.

In a search for a sound legal basis for authorising surgery, the court asked itself whether the separation surgery was necessary in order to save Jodie. In other words, did Mary's conjoined attachment to Jodie make it a necessity for Mary to be killed so that Jodie could be saved? The court examined with care the ethical issues surrounding necessity as it applied to murder. The most famous case on the topic concerned cannibalism on the high seas during the reign of Queen Victoria. It was called *R v Dudley and Stephens*[4] and it is one of the most famous legal cases of the nineteenth century.

Captain Tom Dudley was a seafarer with a reputation for undertaking intrepid trips with skill and responsibility. He was engaged to sail a 20-ton yacht, the *Mignonette*, to Australia on behalf of her wealthy owner. The trip would take over 100 days. He recruited Edwin Stephens and Edmund Brooks as mates and Richard (Dick) Parker as cabin boy and the yacht set sail from Southampton in May 1884. As their vessel approached the Cape of Good Hope it was hit by violent storms and the crew had to abandon ship. Grabbing two tins of turnips, the crew made for the lifeboat, a small dinghy. On their first night, they had to fight off a shark with their oars. Thereafter, they drifted in the South Atlantic with only the turnips and a turtle they had miraculously caught to keep them alive. These meagre rations sustained them for twelve days, but there was no fresh water. Dick Parker, the cabin boy, then became delirious and seemed on the point of death. Dudley made the decision to kill him if they were not rescued by the twentieth day at sea. With no prospect of rescue, he cut Parker's throat on the twentieth day and the survivors fed on his body until, by good fortune, the dinghy was spotted by a German steamer. On their return to Falmouth in Cornwall, Dudley relished in telling the tale of their survival, but the Home Secretary, Sir William Harcourt, did not view cannibalism as acceptable behaviour. Eating cabin boys was not entirely to the taste of the Victorian establishment. He initiated a criminal trial for murder.

Once news of the trial became known, popular opinion was firmly on Dudley's side: people thought that their trial for murder was oppressive and unfair. Unusually, the judge did not give the jury the responsibility of finding Dudley and Stephens guilty or not guilty. Instead he asked for a 'special verdict', something which was possible at that time, in which the jury gave their assent to the facts of the case in a draft prepared by the judge. The facts were those described by Brooks, the third survivor, who was a prosecution witness against his other crew members. The facts were then considered by a bench of senior judges, led by Lord Coleridge, Lord Chief Justice, whose task it was to hand down a ruling on necessity as a defence for murder.

Dudley's counsel had pressed upon the Lord Chief Justice the need for the law to recognise necessity as a defence in certain defined circumstance. For example, when men are 'in a state of nature' where ordinary civilised behaviour does not apply, it may be justified to take the life of another if failure to do so would lead to the death of many others. Here, his act could not be said to be truly voluntary and the defence of necessity should be available. Lord Coleridge would have none of it. 'It is enough', he said, 'in a Christian country to remind ourselves of the Great Example whom we profess to follow ... Who is to be the judge of this sort of necessity? By what measure is the comparative value of lives to be measured?' This forthright condemnation of the actions of Dudley and Stephens in killing 'a weak and unoffending boy' was not carried through to its logical conclusion. Having used strong language in refusing to recognise 'a legal cloak for unbridled passion and atrocious crime', Lord Coleridge went on to make a plea that Queen Victoria use her prerogative of mercy to save Tom Dudley and Edwin Stephens from the gallows. The Home Secretary who had insisted the two be prosecuted now had the task of persuading the Queen to commute their death sentence to one of six months' imprisonment, which, with some reluctance, she did.[5] A. W. Brian Simpson has argued that English law was not blind to the perils of the sea but that the establishment wanted to set a limit to cannibalism on the ocean, and that political consideration was the reason Dudley and Stephens were prosecuted. Once the political point had been made, the moral blameworthiness of the action of killing did not merit the ultimate punishment of death by hanging.

The ethics in the Dudley and Stephens case are difficult. The commuting of the death sentence to one of six months' imprisonment simply postponed an acceptable ethical resolution. Were the actions of the accused men wrong but justifiable or wrong but excusable? Was an excuse for doing something simply a factor which made the crime less serious than it might have been, or was it actually a defence to the crime itself? *Dudley and Stephens* did not really provide clear guidance. On the one hand, it was morally wrong for two people to kill one other in order to survive, as it places the sanctity of the cabin boy's life as being less worthy than the physically stronger captain and mate. On the other hand, if the circumstances are such that an agonising choice has to be made, is it not better for two to survive rather than all three to perish? If a ship is sinking and there is an opportunity for escape on a rope ladder to a lifeboat, what should happen if one person blocks the ladder, preventing others from getting to the lifeboat? This, apparently, happened in the *Herald of Free Enterprise* disaster in 1987 when a terrified boy could not remove himself from the ladder to make way for others who were on their way to the lifeboat, near the bottom of the rope and in the water, who were themselves in danger of drowning. The boy was cast aside on the instructions of an army corporal and never seen again, but no criminal proceedings were commenced. The difference between this sea disaster and the *Mignonette* catastrophe was that the terrified young man was unwittingly imperilling the lives of others.[6] It posed a different ethical problem to that in *Dudley and Stephens*.

Since 1884, English common law has developed in a way in which a clear distinction can be made between necessity being excluded as a defence in murder but being recognised as a principle in contract law and the law of restitution. The availability of a necessity defence in virtually all circumstances including criminal acts falling short of murder poses ethical dilemmas in many situations. In essence it is the 'conflicting duties' dilemma which arises in some circumstances when the alleged perpetrator is overborne by the imperative of having to make agonising choices.

One of the judges in Jodie and Mary's case mentioned a real case in Australia in which a very serious fire occurred in the engine room of a navy vessel. The crew could only be saved if the engine room was sealed off and flooded with inert gas, but if there were survivors in the engine room, they would certainly die by gas poisoning. Another dilemma presented to sea captains occurs when an 'abandon ship' order is given. When a ship is sinking the captain has to decide who gets the chance to leave in the lifeboats first. The rule of thumb is that women and children go first, but is the captain complicit in killing those left behind for a watery death?

In medical cases, however, there is a further layer to these ethical dilemmas. Sea captains and rescuers do not have a special professional responsibility to relieve suffering for those under their command. Doctors, by contrast, have a duty to their patients to relieve pain if a patient is in distress. In medical cases, a doctor may foresee death as a side effect of a genuine effort to relieve suffering but not intend death to be the objective of the action. Judges in Jodie and Mary's case were making a decision in a medical case and medical decisions are not obviously taken with only one end purpose in mind. In 1939, when abortion was illegal, an eminent doctor, Mr Aleck Bourne, was on trial for unlawfully using an instrument to procure an abortion on a fourteen-year-old girl who had been violently raped by five soldiers. The doctor would have a defence only if the abortion was done for the purpose of preserving the life of the mother. The mother, however, was not near to death; she had been raped. The judge told the jury the doctor did not have to wait until the unfortunate mother was close to death before removing the foetus; he could do so lawfully if it was done 'with a view to saving her life'. The judge was recognising the defence of necessity in this instance.[7] The jury acquitted the doctor.

In the celebrated 1952 case of Dr Bodkin Adams, an alleged serial killer of elderly women in his care in Eastbourne, the judge gave a similarly generous direction to the jury. Mr Justice Devlin told the jury that if the first purpose of medicine, the restoration of health, can no longer be achieved, there is still much a doctor can do which can incidentally shorten life. Dr Adams's defence was that he was administering diamorphine in increasingly strong doses not to kill his elderly patients but to promote comfort as their lives came to an end. If that incidentally shortened their lives, it was not murder.[8] Dr Adams was acquitted.

More recently, an elderly man was operated on for bowel cancer. Part of his bowel was surgically removed and he was sufficiently recovered to leave hospital to be cared for by his daughter. He suffered excruciating pain at home and became emaciated and his nurses believed he was terminally ill. A transfer to a hospice was recommended. At the hospice, he was prescribed diamorphine by his GP, Dr Moor, which included an additional bolus injection, given a short time later. The patient died soon afterwards and a post-mortem examination revealed a larger presence of diamorphine than Dr Moor had admitted administering.

In the following week's Sunday newspapers a story appeared suggesting Dr Moor had boasted about giving dying patients large doses of diamorphine to bring forward the time of death. Dr Moor gave a television interview stressing that his motives were to relieve pain, but some tabloids labelled him 'Dr Death' and called him Britain's greatest serial killer. It was difficult for the Director of Public Prosecutions not to prosecute him for killing his patient with a lethal dose of heroin, but at his trial in 1999 he was acquitted of murder. The judge directed the jury that they had to be sure not only that the injection contributed significantly to his death but also that Dr Moor's purpose was *not* to relieve pain. If it may have been the case that Dr Moor's purpose was to relieve pain then the jury must acquit. Only if they were sure his purpose was not to relieve pain, and by administering the injection Dr Moor intended to kill his patient, should the jury find him guilty of murder. If Dr Moor thought it was only highly probable that the consequences of the injection would lead to death then he would not have *intended* to kill his patient. If the primary intention is to relieve pain, it is not murder despite the doctor's medical knowledge that his intervention will shorten the patient's life.[9]

In modern times, the Victorian rectitude of Lord Coleridge's 1884 decision to rule out a necessity defence in all cases of murder no longer seems to hold sway. In criminal cases, juries were taking a sympathetic view when a consequence of medication, deliberately given for one purpose, had a consequence the doctor did not desire. These cases where medically prescribed pain relief was a cause, but not a primarily intended cause, of death involve what is called the doctrine of 'double effect'. In medical cases the doctrine prevents the doctor from culpability if he merely foresees, rather than intends, accelerated death as a consequence of treatment.

The judges in Jodie and Mary's case had *Dudley and Stephens*, *Bland*, *Bourne* and *Bodkin Adams* to help them solve the seemingly insoluble, although none of the above provided any direct guidance. The doctrine of 'double effect' had no bearing on conduct directed towards Mary, the judges ruled, unless it could be argued that the mere fact of restoring her bodily integrity, even at the moment of death, could be seen as a good end in itself. In *Dudley and Stephens*, the captain and first mate made a choice to kill the cabin boy, who, if a rescue ship had sailed across the horizon at that moment, might have lived. The judges did not disagree with the philosophical point made by Lord Coleridge that law would become separated from morality if there was a general defence of necessity in murder cases. However, the sad fact in Mary's case was that her condition was such that her life could not be prolonged beyond a very short span.

Despite the dire prognosis for Mary, an ethical and legal justification for separating her from her twin could only be permitted if such treatment was a proportionate one in all the circumstances. The judges found helpful guidance in a Canadian case in which drug smugglers were in a ship caught in a storm and had to seek refuge in a Canadian port, where Canadian patrols found the drugs. Had the smugglers imported the drugs into Canadian territory or was it necessary to bring the drugs to Canada to save the lives of the smugglers? Here, the defence of necessity was based on the choice to enter port rather than to risk weathering the storm at sea. The Canadian court said the captain had no moral authority to flout his legal duties in order to follow his conscience; rather, the court had to take an objective view about whether the decision to make for shelter was a *proportionate* one given the conflicting legal duties which presented themselves.[10]

This test of proportionality was met for Mary as the separation surgery was a matter of life and death. Mary was bound to die anyway if she was not separated, but Jodie had a chance to live. In considering the principle of proportionality, the court was *not* considering the relative worth of two human lives but was considering a decision to permit surgery. Without surgery neither life could have a bodily integrity. The problem was unique. The judges were faced with a factual scenario where the doctors had duties to two patients, Jodie and Mary, and it was medically impossible for them to do their duty towards one without affecting the other. The concept of necessity did arise in the sense that surgical intervention was necessary if either life was to be saved. Mary was incapable of independent existence as she relied on oxygenated blood from her sister for her survival. One judge said if she had been born with that condition without being conjoined, no sensible and conscientious doctor would attempt artificially to prolong her life. The duty to prolong life did not apply, sadly, in her case. Invasive surgery was ethically permitted for Mary as being conjoined to Jodie would deprive them both of the bodily integrity and human dignity which was the right of each of them. Mary would die not because she was intentionally killed but because her own body could not sustain life. There was, in those circumstances, no profound ethical reason preventing the court applying general principles of family law. These pointed irresistibly to the conclusion that the interests of preserving the life of Jodie should prevail over the conflicting interests of Mary.

The decision to permit the doctors to commence separation surgery was not a clear-cut one which separated law from morality. The law's insistence that morality did not allow a defence of necessity in murder existed in order to prevent unscrupulous individuals availing themselves of the defence in immoral circumstances. Such fears did not arise in separating conjoined twins as invariably there will be an opportunity for doctors to obtain the approval of the Family Court before the operation takes place. In a criminal trial where necessity has been raised as a defence, the trial occurs after the act has been committed.

The three judges who agonised over the decision, Lord Justice Ward, Lord Justice Brooke and Lord Justice Walker, had to work under intense pressure. The twins were born in August 2000 and their verdict was delivered towards the end of September the same year. Lord Justice Brooke later reflected that it was the most intellectually challenging case he had ever had the responsibility of deciding. Lord Neuberger, president of the Supreme Court, later commented that the case threw up fundamental moral and religious issues. The three judgments in the Court of Appeal ran to 130 pages of typescript. The case demonstrated the durability of English common law to apply and develop precedent to unusual and apparently insoluble factual situations of anguish.

The extraordinary difficulty of the case, intellectually and ethically, is illustrated by the fact that the four judges who heard the arguments, the High Court judge who permitted surgery to go ahead and three Appeal Court judges who upheld this ruling, all gave different reasons for their decision. The Family Court judge had the unenviable task of reaching a decision under pressure of time with no clear legal precedent to guide him. He concluded that the surgery should be permitted on the grounds that in Mary's case the remaining few months of her life would be worth nothing and to prolong her life would be to her disadvantage. The three judges of the Court of Appeal, who had the advantage of fuller argument from counsel, concluded that this did not honour the principle that each human life has an equal value and they upheld the judges' decision for different reasons. Lord Justice Ward thought that, ethically, doctors were entitled to come to Jodie's defence by removing the threat to her posed by Mary draining her lifeblood. He likened the scenario to a six-year-old child wielding a gun in a playground killing all around him. It would be legitimate to kill him even though he lacked the capacity, on grounds of age, to be criminally responsible. Principles of legitimate self-defence would justify him being killed to stop the further slaughter of others. Lord Justice Brooke thought the real reasons for their decision lay in ancient principles of necessity which had not been overturned in *Dudley and Stephens*. That case was a fact-specific ruling, which did not prevent the court from allowing Mary's death as it was tragically necessary in order to save Jodie. Lord Justice Walker decided separation surgery was lawful and ethical because the purpose and intention of it was not to kill Mary. She was bound to die anyway and the doctors had to reconcile two conflicting duties. It was a proportionate choice, in those circumstances, to separate Jodie from her sister.

The case of Jodie and Mary mercifully had an ending that produced some happiness. The operation was performed in the first week in

November. As predicted, Mary died very quickly and peacefully after the surgeon cut the common aorta. Jodie survived and began to live an independent life. In June 2001, she was well enough to return to Gozo with her parents. Mary's body was taken back to Gozo, where it received a public funeral. She was buried in a corner of the cemetery on a hill overlooking the town. Jodie grew and developed normally and in 2014 she gave an interview under her real name, Gracie, and told a newspaper she was glad to be alive and that she had ambitions to become a doctor.

The parents, who had behaved with bravery and dignity throughout the heartbreaking case, did not bring an appeal to the Supreme Court as many expected them to do. They disagreed with the decision, but they understood why the doctors were urging the course which conflicted with their own wishes. The mother stated in an interview that Gracie had brought much joy to their lives. In 2002, she gave birth to a healthy baby girl, a sister for Gracie. She was named Rosie, after the twin who had died in Manchester.

Chapter 2

Sex – Lady Chatterley Goes on Trial

The trial of *Lady Chatterley's Lover*, D. H. Lawrence's 1928 novel, began in October 1960. It was not, however, so much a trial which took place during the 1960s as a trial which took place at the cusp of two eras. The columnist Bernard Levin said the trial was 'an attempt to stop the decade entirely and replace it with an earlier one'.[1] The 1960s was the era of the neophiliacs, those who were experimenting and searching for change, whereas the 1950s was an era of moralists clinging to conformity. The trial was about whether Lawrence's paean on the joys of sexual intercourse should be condemned on the grounds of obscenity. It took place in one era, but the prosecution tried to pretend it was taking place in another.

The arrival of the 1960s seemed to many a time to put to an end outdated laws relating to obscenity. But when dealing with a subject as difficult and subjective as sex, nothing can be predicted. Sex is one of the most profound and personal forces of nature. For some, it is a drive that binds stable marriages, promotes legitimacy and uncontentious inheritance and is a force which in many respects ensures stability within society. For others, it may be the cause of illegitimacy, unwanted children, botched abortions and failed marriages. It has a potency that can injure, humiliate and demean women in acts of assault and rape. It can fuel violence within the home which forces women into refuges and scars the minds of children for ever. At the same time, sex is one of the least talked about subjects among adults, at least in polite company, so tradition would dictate. Dig below the shyness and hesitation that people take comfort in when sex is spoken about, and important questions are raised. Should sex be separated from reproduction? Can sex be a force for good which should be celebrated unashamedly or is it always to be shrouded in dirt and visualised only as pornography if written about frankly and without inhibition? These were some of the questions the jury in the *Lady Chatterley* case would have to answer. In the event, the verdict was emphatic. The jury rejected the attempt by the Director of Public Prosecutions to stop Penguin Books publishing the unexpurgated edition of *Lady Chatterley's Lover*. This decision made the trial one of the legal cases that made modern Britain. The years that followed the trial, held at the Central Criminal Court, might have been very different had the jury condemned the book. The jury was composed of nine men and three women, whose eligibility to serve as jurors came from their experience of life in the 1950s. The witnesses who gave evidence for Penguin Books were hand-picked progressives who were anticipating the new era of the 1960s. The trial was, in a sense, a battle of cultures.

The differences between the 1950s and the 1960s have been well documented. For much of the fifteen years that followed the end of the Second World War the country still resembled the grey and seedy land of Graham Greene's wartime novels.[2] It was a decade of rigid hierarchies where professionals like doctors and lawyers kept a cold distance between themselves and the ordinary people with whom they came into contact. Rationing of food continued until 1954, parts of London and other major cities in the provinces contained arid empty spaces called 'bombsites' and churchmen, judges, head teachers and police chiefs believed one of their roles was to impose and enforce moral standards on the populace. Homosexuality was illegal, pregnancies could only be terminated by abortionists who worked in the shadows of the back streets and divorce among the upper and middle classes was frowned on. Homosexual couples who lived together, whether male or female, had to do so in secret using euphemisms for their relationship. Heterosexual couples living together were labelled as 'living in sin' in popular parlance. Sir Anthony Eden, the upper-class Prime Minister for a brief period between Churchill and Macmillan, was never completely accepted in aristocratic society on the grounds that he had been divorced, and the Archbishop of Canterbury absolutely forbade the marriage of Princess Margaret to Group Captain Peter Townsend, a divorced man. Harold Macmillan, a man of dignity and graceful manners, never felt able to institute divorce proceedings against his wife, who was conducting a longstanding affair with one of his colleagues, Lord Boothby.

The observance of rules of behaviour which dated from Victorian times was still regarded as important among the population as a whole. The rates of divorce among married couples had increased dramatically during and just after the Second World War but by the 1950s was in decline. The stability of the family resumed the importance it had in the 1930s, before the outbreak of war. As the historian Arthur Marwick has observed, 'Social assumptions, moral attitudes and everyday behaviour were first learned at home.'[3] Church attendances for all denominations rose in the 1950s, as did membership of youth clubs attached to religious institutions. The stability of the period, which was marked by a gentle but uninterrupted rise in living standards, was based on a solid appreciation of the different roles played by men and women within society. There was an ingrained belief that the husband's role was outside the home, following an occupation and earning the family income, while the role of the wife and mother was as homemaker within the home. Divorce and separation would disrupt the equilibrium of this stability and it was actively discouraged by groups and organisations of authority. For example, the Mothers' Union, a Christian organisation which had a large membership among middle-class women, would not admit a divorced mother as a member, even if her husband had deserted her and she was the innocent party to the divorce. Many clergymen in the Church of England would refuse to give communion to a divorced woman.

There was also a public face of prurience about sex in the 1950s. David Maxwell Fyfe, Home Secretary under Churchill, was a campaigner for suppression of anything that had the stamp of sexual frankness about it. In 1954, over 100 individuals were found guilty of publishing an obscene libel and 167,000 books or magazines were destroyed by police in London alone. In the seaside resort of Cleethorpes over 5,000 Donald McGill postcards were seized.

The Home Office kept a secret list of 17,000 paperback novels which chief constables were expected to seize and prosecute. Most were trashy soft-porn novelettes, but the list also included books of obvious literary merit, like *Moll Flanders* by Daniel Defoe and Gustave Flaubert's masterpiece *Madame Bovary*. The application of Victorian obscenity laws in Britain in the mid-1950s was in danger of turning into farce. A bench of magistrates in Swindon condemned Boccaccio's *Decameron* as obscene despite the fact that the book was on open display in the public reference library next door to the courthouse.

When progressive journalists had recovered their sense of composure after reporting the absurdity of the *Decameron* decision, the Home Office conducted its own inquiry. It concluded that the Home Office had been treated most unfairly in the press as it was not a decision of civil servants in London to seek the destruction of the Italian classic and went on to propose that Greek and Roman literature should not be on the list of titles to be destroyed. The chief constables, on the other hand, whose members had not universally been versed in the classics at public schools, as had most senior civil servants, did not agree. The police wanted a free hand in deciding what to ask local magistrates to destroy. Plainly, the law had fallen into disrepute.

In 1956, two volumes of Jean Genet's complete works in French were impounded by HM Customs and Excise before an eager readership in Birmingham could become corrupted by them. In the days when librarians in local authorities had money to spend, the chief librarian in Birmingham had ordered the volumes after reading a favourable review in the *Times Literary Supplement*. The incident produced a national furore, with Members of Parliament taking the side of the librarian. The problem was that as the law then stood, Birmingham City Council had no right to be heard, as only the importer of the books, Blackwell book-sellers, could mount a challenge to the seizure. They did not do so and this enabled Enoch Powell MP, the minister responsible for Customs and Excise, to argue that this amounted to an admission that Genet was an obscene writer. Powell, in truth, had misled the House of Commons as to his knowledge there was a secret list of books which Customs kept as their 'banned book' list. This list dated back to the 1930s and con-sisted of more than fifty titles, including the unexpurgated versions of Pepys's *Diaries* and *Tristram Shandy* by Laurence Sterne.

The mood of sexual prurience and public reticence to engage in any dialogue remotely concerned with sex was evident in the cinema in the 1950s. In Hollywood an unofficial code decreed that nudity and conver-sation about the possible benefits of divorce were banned and scenes in the bedrooms of married couples had to feature two single beds, not a double bed. Expressions of sexual desire between couples had to take place when at least one of the participants, usually the man, had one foot on the ground. This public face of morality was noted by Geoffrey Gorer in his book *Exploring English Character*, published in 1955. He found that two-thirds of the respondents to his survey disapproved of sex before marriage, even though in the privacy of personal relationships many couples indulged in it. There was one publicly proclaimed morality and another which was observed in private. This dichotomy could not survive for very much longer. Obscenity laws and personal morality were out of step with each other.

Obscenity in the 1950s had to be judged on a definition handed down almost 100 years earlier. Parliament decided in 1857 that vice in all its forms should be suppressed, but an Act of Parliament was required to establish a procedure for seizing and destroying obscene literature. The Obscene Publications Act of that year did not contain any definition of what obscenity meant. It was left to the judges to try to fill this gap. In 1868, the Lord Chief Justice of England and Wales, Sir Alexander Cockburn, had handed down a definition which was to give hope to the moralists and despair to writers. *The Well of Loneliness* by Radclyffe Hall, published in 1928, was a courageous and convincing account of love between women. When it was condemned by the chief magistrate at Bow Street as glorifying unnatural tendencies, the magistrate was putting his own interpretation to the nineteenth-century test of obscenity. This was a judgment as to whether the book had the tendency to deprave and corrupt those whose minds are open to such immoral influences, and into whose hands a publication of this sort may fall. The problem with this definition was that it did not require a magistrate, a bench of justices or a jury to consider either the author's intention by including allegedly 'obscene' passages or the book's merits as a whole. It allowed books to be condemned by relying only on the purple passages and placing them, in isolation, before the court.

In the 1950s there was an unspoken presumption that explicit descriptions of sex were bound to corrupt young people and the easily led working classes. In 1955, a senior judge at the Old Bailey solemnly directed a jury that the obscenity laws existed to protect sex and marriage from being dragged into the mud and that if anything was written that might deprave a callow youth or a girl just budding into womanhood it might be obscene. He gave a strong hint to the jury they should follow this homily. After the jury obediently did so, the judge opined that it was comforting the jury had taken a stand so the youth of the country were protected against the fountains of our national blood being polluted.[4] On the other hand, a different judge at the same court had taken a completely different view just a year earlier. He had told the jury that obscenity meant something more than 'shock and disgust'. His view was that if obscenity was to be judged only by the outlook of fourteen-year-old girls then English literature would be confined to nursery rhymes. Writers could not be expected to sweep embarrassing facts under the carpet just to keep on the right side of the laws of obscenity.[5] Judging obscenity had descended into a lottery where the guilt or innocence of a book of literature would be decided on the sympathies or prejudices of the judge allocated to try the case.

The application of nineteenth-century obscenity laws was so confusing and uncertain that after these two contrasting verdicts, two juries were deadlocked in a trial and retrial of another book the Director of Public Prosecutions thought should be banned. The futility of a law framed in Victorian times was now clear for all with an eye to logic to see. In the years that followed, the anomalies of the simple 'deprave and corrupt' definition became difficult of justify. The obvious double standards about moral behaviour in the 1950s spurred a culture of rebellion which, in a short space of time, converted the morality of the 1950s to a new morality that became 'the swinging '60s'. A young breed of writers, artists and, most particularly, playwrights were challenging the repressive conformity that had made the 1950s a dreary place for so many. *Look Back in Anger* by John Osborne, first performed in 1956, is the most famous artistic attack on the mores of the time, but other voices, notably Shelagh Delaney's in *A Taste of Honey* and Arnold Wesker's in *Chicken Soup with Barley* (both of which premiered in 1958), expressed an anger and disillusionment about convention. Novelists from provincial England like John Braine and Alan Sillitoe were exposing many of the hypocrisies of the 1950s. The resentment towards the power of figures of authority was articulated with anger and passion while the real lives of ordinary and powerless working people were depicted with a truth those in authority observed with shock.

Another attack on 1950s conformity was coming from liberally minded politicians. In 1956, when Britain was humiliated internationally in the Suez debacle and the Prime Minister was forced to resign, a young Labour Party politician called Anthony Crosland wrote *The Future of Socialism*. It attempted to forge a new path for his party, which had been defeated in two general elections in the preceding five years. Much of the book is devoted to economic and social policy, but he also dwelt on the need to change 'prehistoric' and unfair divorce laws, abortion laws, licensing laws and the illiterate censorship of books. Crosland had in mind the bizarre and inconsistent ideas about censoring literature that had existed for over half a century.

A change to our obscenity laws was long overdue, but it came about by a lucky chance. In 1959, Roy Jenkins, then a young Labour Party backbench Member of Parliament, won the ballot to decide which backbencher could introduce a new Bill. Jenkins had always taken an interest in the relationship between the state and the individual and he believed the state should draw back from interference in matters which were personal and private to the individual. Sex, or censorship about discussing it, was one such issue. His Bill proposed a change to the law on obscene publications. There had already been some parliamentary agitation to modernise the law, but the initiatives all failed. When R. A. Butler became Home Secretary in 1957, he established a select committee to look at the case for reform. The committee came up with a compromise: to give the police greater powers of seizure of pornography, with a defence of publication for the public good if a book of literary merit was prosecuted on grounds of obscenity. Jenkins was a leading member of the select committee and he had convinced many parliamentary colleagues across party lines of the need for reform.

Jenkins's initiative, which became the Obscene Publications Act 1959, was a huge step forward. Crucially, the definition of obscenity was changed. Under the new Act, the article in question (usually a book) was deemed to be obscene if the effect, taken *as a whole*, was such as to tend to deprave and corrupt persons likely, in all the circumstances, to read, see or hear it. Secondly, obscenity must deprave and corrupt those likely to read it, not just some adolescents who might, by chance, come across it. Thirdly, and importantly, a publisher, bookseller or writer charged with publication of obscenity had a 'public good' defence. This meant that if the jury concluded the article was, in fact, obscene taken as a whole, they could not convict if they were also of the opinion it was for the public good that the book was published. Finally, if the defence raised the 'public good' defence, expert witnesses could be called to testify as to the literary merit of the work.

This is the background to the trial at the Old Bailey when D. H. Lawrence's 1928 novel was in the dock. When the new Obscene Publications Act came into force in August 1959, Penguin Books decided that it was time for the unexpurgated edition of *Lady Chatterley's Lover* finally to be published. The old law had ensured that Lawrence's complete text could never be published in Britain. Ironically, many copies were available covertly. Anybody who really wanted to read it could do so. The book was published and printed in France, and at the time of Lawrence's death in 1930 his earnings from the sale of the book were nearly 90,000 francs. Yet if it was actually on sale in Britain, the full panoply of the law would fall on the unfortunate retailer. In 1955, a bookseller in north London was sent to prison for having the unexpurgated edition of the book on his premises.[6]

In the United States, an attempt to import the unexpurgated edition into the country was blocked by the US Postal Service, but the publishers brought a legal case against the Postal Service. This put the contents of the book on trial. In July 1959, a district judge upheld the publishers' appeal on the grounds that the language used in the book to describe sexual encounters was entirely familiar to citizens of the United States. The US Court of Appeal agreed in a ruling which categorised *Lady Chatterley's Lover* as 'a major and distinguished novel'. In Great Britain, it was time to test in the criminal courts whether D. H. Lawrence's novel would be welcomed or condemned.

In January 1960, Penguin Books announced their intention to publish the full text of *Lady Chatterley* and seven other Lawrence novels to mark the thirtieth anniversary of Lawrence's death and the twenty-fifth of Penguin's birth. There followed a civilised exchange of letters between solicitors for Penguin and the Director of Public Prosecutions, Sir Theobald Mathew. To save time and money and possibly risk to a bookseller, it was arranged that a police officer could call by appointment and collect a copy from Penguin's offices in central London. This was sufficient for 'publication'. The scene was set for an obscenity trial at the Central Criminal Court, Old Bailey, in the City of London.

There seemed to be an agreement that the time had come to test whether a new age of modernity would be ushered in or whether the jury would stick to the comfort of the more censorious mood of the 1950s.

The trial was ostensibly about obscenity, but there was more to the case than Lawrence's unashamed use of Anglo-Saxon vocabulary and his lyrical accounts of the joys of sexual union. The plot involved a titled woman desiring her husband's servant, a desire that was entirely reciprocated by Oliver Mellors, the gamekeeper. Not only was the book about sex across class boundaries; it was about marital betrayal within the aristocracy. The book was, to many, worryingly revolutionary as well as being obscene. The Director of Public Prosecutions wanted it banned. But was that possible under the new law Parliament had introduced a year earlier?

It proved to be, in every sense, a test case for contemporary views of morality and the verdict was by no means a foregone conclusion. For one thing, obscenity trials are different from all other trials in criminal law. Juries exist to try criminal cases because their function is to decide 'facts': who did what and to whom? Who is truthful and who is lying? In obscenity cases, on the other hand, the jury is required to give its *opinion* about facts the prosecution and defence have already agreed. The text of the book is, in a sense, the case for the prosecution and the defence. Those charged with giving this opinion are chosen at random. Their identities are never revealed and their occupations, sexual preferences and home life are irrelevant. They are a body of twelve people who, for the purpose of the case, represent the nation, yet their presence on a particular case happens entirely by chance. The system of trial by jury in England and Wales is to an extent haphazard. When this system requires a random selection of people to give an opinion, which at that time had to be a unanimous one, the result is far from predictable.

The prosecution and defence teams who took their places in No. 1 Court at the Old Bailey on 20 October 1960 could not be more different. The prosecution was led by Mervyn Griffith-Jones, senior prosecuting counsel at the Old Bailey and a veteran of many obscenity cases under the Victorian law which had only just been replaced. He had impeccable upper-class credentials, having been educated at Eton and Trinity Hall, Cambridge, followed by service in the Coldstream Guards during the Second World War. He was one of the best jury advocates at the Bar. His opponent, Gerald Gardiner QC, was also upper-class, as were most of the Bar at the time. But Gardiner had been a rebel at Harrow School and became a pacifist in the Second World War, serving in the 'Friends Ambulance Service' as a volunteer. Gardiner was a member of the Labour Party and a passionate believer in law reform and he set up the Law Commission in 1965 when he was Lord Chancellor in Harold Wilson's first administration. The differences between Griffith-Jones and Gardiner epitomised the differences between the prosecution and the defence in the trial.

Griffith-Jones's opening speech to the jury has entered legal folklore as one of the most ill-judged attempts to persuade a jury of your case in modern times. Yet this verdict, which dogged Griffith-Jones for the remainder of his career, was one made in hindsight, from the standpoint of 1960s culture. At the time, he was only saying what barristers who had an upper-class lifestyle at the time would say. The Bar was an exclusive, clubbable, manly and snobbish profession. Griffith-Jones began rather ponderously giving the jury a law lecture on obscenity law. He had a high-handed, cold and austere manner. At one point he solemnly and incomprehensibly talked about the *locus in quo* when he wanted to emphasise how obscene it was for the protagonist, Connie Chatterley, to have sex out of doors. At another point he patronised the jury by saying, 'For those of you who have forgotten your Greek, phallus means the image of the man's penis.' His disdain and disapproval of the book reached its apogee when he said this to the jury:

A point you will have to consider is how freely the book is going to be distributed. Is it a book published at £5 a copy [£96 in today's money] as a historical volume, or is it a book widely distributed at a price the merest infant can afford? [The cover price was three shillings and sixpence,

fifteen or sixteen pence in today's money.] When you have seen this book
… you may think it sets upon a pedestal promiscuous and adulterous
intercourse. It commends, and indeed it sets out to commend, sensuality
almost as a virtue. It encourages, and indeed even advocates, coarseness
and vulgarity of thought and of language. You may think that it *must* tend
to deprave the minds certainly of some … persons who are likely to buy
it at the price of 3s 6d … Would you approve of your young sons, young
daughters – because girls can read as well as boys – reading this book?
Is it a book that you would have lying around in your own house? Is it a
book that you would even wish your wife or your servants to read?

These remarks have for ever become imprinted in the public mind as
the first nail in the coffin of the prosecution case and have for evermore
labelled his attempt to ban *Lady Chatterley* as the last gasp of the old era
trying to impose its standards on the new. Even Griffith-Jones's clipped
upper-class tones were, according to one observer in the public gallery,
'passionate only in disdain, but barbed with a rabid belief in convention
and discipline'.[7] His rhetorical question (at least he intended it to be
rhetorical), 'would you wish your wife or your servants to read it?' has
found its place in numerous dictionaries of quotations throughout the
English-speaking world.

It is easy nowadays to view the postures of Griffith-Jones as ridiculous
and his skills of persuasion ludicrous, but his opening address to the
jury needs some dissection in order to understand the forces that were
in play. Griffith-Jones was doing his duty in representing contemporary
values, or at least values that had latterly prevailed. But he did not know
what the jury would think of the book. For all he knew, the jury of nine
middle-aged men and three women would be receptive to 1950s values,
an era that had ended only ten months earlier. First, he made the point
about the price of the book. In Victorian culture if a book was beyond

the price of ordinary working-people to buy then there was no obvious reason for the authorities to intervene. People with money had status and power and could enjoy the full fruits of citizenship, including un-bridled sexual pleasure. They were trusted sufficiently not to corrupt or deprave themselves by reading about or indulging in sex. Poor people, on the other hand, had less strength of character and had to be pro-tected from vice and immorality. Vulgarity of thought, as Griffith-Jones quaintly put it, is something it was considered to be the duty of the state to discourage. The potential size of a book's sales was a critical factor in deciding whether to ban it.

The *coup de grâce* of Griffith-Jones's argument, and the one with which his name will for ever be associated, was his question: 'Is it a book you would even wish your wife to read?' The Victorian culture which Griffith-Jones was espousing set strict boundaries for sexual freedom where control and discipline devised and perpetuated by men desexualised women. The culture insisted that sexual ignorance and passivity in women were virtues. Women should not be sensual beings. Sensuality for men, on the other hand, was a different matter entirely. Sex was a recreation which could be enjoyed by taking the initiative and being in control. This outlook permitted prostitution to flourish and refused to countenance the concept of rape within marriage.[8] Victorian morality proclaimed a difference in the sexual appetites and needs of men and women and ordained that this difference should be obeyed and upheld in polite society. Lady Chatterley, who married into the aris-tocracy, broke one of the cardinal rules of civilised behaviour by having a high sexual drive and an uninhibited approach to sexual enjoyment.

The second rule which Lady Chatterley, or Connie as she is called throughout the book, broke is her willingness to have a sexual relation-ship with a person outside her class. Such a liaison tore up the rules in spectacular fashion. The strict demarcations between classes were important features of Victorian society which only began to fall apart in a demonstrable way in the 1960s. Griffith-Jones's appeal to the jury that they might not want 'their servants' to read such a book was both absurd and important. At a time when the middle classes had servants, often living in, there were rules of behaviour which erected barriers between master and servant. The television programmes *Upstairs, Downstairs* and *Downton Abbey* and the novels of Agatha Christie set in the 1920s and 1930s vividly bring to life their separate existences. Unfortunately for the prosecution, this way of life was fast dying out by the time the trial took place in 1960. It is doubtful if a single member of the jury had a servant.

Even before embarking on the 'obscenities' which Griffith-Jones said were to be found everywhere in the book, it is clear that *Lady Chatterley*'s plot was controversial. Connie Chatterley not only had a highly developed sexual nature; she was prepared to have sex with her husband's gamekeeper. Having sex with Mellors was not, in the book, a passing phase, an event to be later regretted. It was a relationship of passion and genuine love. At the end of the novel the couple earnestly hope to marry and start a new life together. It is true Connie committed adultery with Mellors, but adultery was something her husband had positively encouraged in the course of the plot. Lawrence had set the scene for the novel within the milieu of English aristocracy. Connie's husband, Sir Clifford Chatterley, was the son a baronet, Sir Geoffrey Chatterley. The baronetcy would continue only if Clifford had a male heir. He could not accomplish this himself within marriage as he was paralysed from the waist down following catastrophic injuries in the First World War. At one point in the story Clifford actually encouraged Connie to conceive a child secretly with another man so Clifford could bring him up as his own. An open affair with a member of the lower classes, however, was unthinkable as a way of preserving the baronetcy.

Lawrence portrays Connie as the heroine in the novel from the very start. The daughter of a bohemian painter and a Fabian socialist, she was a ruddy, country-looking girl who had travelled in Europe with her sister before her marriage. It was in Germany that they both lost their virginity.

The 'promiscuity' in the book appeared to be this pre-marital relationship and a short affair with a playwright who visits the Chatterley country seat, Wragby, after she marries. It was the description of Connie's sexual encounters with Mellors that Griffith-Jones concentrated on in his opening speech to the jury. Having set out his stall as a latter-day Victorian moralist, Griffith-Jones then lasciviously embarked on the 'obscene' bits of the book. These were the thirteen episodes – he had counted them – of sexual intercourse described in a way which left 'nothing to the imagination'. The prosecutor's numerate abilities were applied to the full when he informed the jury of the number of times 'fuck', 'cunt' or 'cock' appeared in the text. That was the case for the prosecution.

The jury were then given copies of the book to read, which was done in the rather uncomfortable accommodation of the jury retiring rooms at the Old Bailey. The judge had insisted they did their reading there rather than being allowed to take the book home. At the end of each day they were allowed to go home and after four days the trial resumed to hear again from Mr Mervyn Griffith-Jones. He did not trouble the jury for long. Having called a police officer to prove the book had been published, he rested his case. There was an audible gasp from those watching and listening from the public gallery of the courtroom. The journalists and writers present had been glued to their seats in anticipation of who the prosecution would call as 'experts' to tell the jury the book had no merit. The Obscene Publications Act 1959 explicitly permitted the prosecution to call such evidence. Alan Travis, who has examined recently released files held in the National Archives, has found out that the prosecution team were indeed planning to call expert witnesses but no expert was prepared to come forward.[9] Among those whom the prosecution hoped would assist them were Nevill Coghill, Lord David Cecil, David Daiches, F. R. Leavis, Noel Annan and Helen Gardner. Each had impeccable 'establishment' credentials, but none was prepared to go into the witness box to condemn the book and Helen Gardner declined tartly, telling the Director's office she would be a witness for the defence. The hapless Director of Public Prosecutions had to tell Griffith-Jones, 'There is a general feeling in the literary world that this prosecution is in principle repressive and unwarranted and people ... are not prepared to assist.' This left the floor for the defence.

The defence case, presented by the quietly urbane Gerald Gardiner, was of a different quality altogether. With forensic polish, he made an opening speech explaining the difference between pornography and literature. Pornography was 'filth for filth's sake, no thought, no message, no inspiration, just filth'. He could do this as it was a definition used by a judge in an earlier case. Pornography could, Gardiner conceded, have the ability to deprave and corrupt, meaning that the reader might *do* something he might not otherwise have done in a morally bad debasing fashion. Pornography could render the mind of the reader morally unsound and could destroy moral purity in the mind of the reader. That was pornography, but D. H. Lawrence wrote literature, not pornography. To deprave did not mean encouraging an extra-marital relationship and in any case Lawrence was not advocating promiscuity. The book advances Lawrence's view that casual sex was unsatisfying. The book's central message was that the functions of the human body were as important as the functions of the human mind. Modern society, the society of 1928, devoted insufficient attention to the joys of the physicality of love and that was what Lawrence wanted to convey. As the subject of sex is a matter of general concern to society, it was to the public good that a book about the physicalities of sex should be published if it had literary merit. Gardiner then presented the evidence to support this contention.

Thirty-eight witnesses, drawn from a wide spectrum of society, made their way to the witness box in Court No. 1 at the Old Bailey. Eight of them were women who were not in the slightest degree embarrassed to give evidence in support of the book. The English literature academic Helen Gardner, who was publicly known as a broadcaster on literature on the BBC, said Lawrence had succeeded in putting into words experiences that are really very difficult to verbalise. He had also redeemed the word 'fuck' from its low and vulgar connotations into something related to the natural processes of sex. While she conceded that *Lady Chatterley* was not Lawrence's greatest novel, certain passages in it were among the greatest he had ever written. As to the four-letter words, they were not deployed by Lawrence in a brutal and disgusting sense but in the context of the book as a whole. One of the purposes of the book was to make us feel the sexual act was not shameful and he had used the word 'fuck' therefore in its original sense.

Griffith-Jones asked just two questions: 'Is Lawrence a great writer?' 'Yes.' 'Was this one of his greatest books?' 'No, but it contains some of his greatest writing.' This was an astonishing act of surrender on the part of the prosecution. Not only did Griffith-Jones fail to challenge the main planks of the testimony of this distinguished academic, but by asking those questions he enabled Gardiner to ask further questions in re-examination. 'You said that certain passages in the book are among the greatest things that Lawrence wrote. Will you tell us which passages you had in mind?' 'The expurgated passages come into this class,' Ms Gardner replied.

A school teacher at Keighley Girls' Grammar School said that girls in the school knew four-letter words from the age of ten and that the book would be a suitable one for girls over the age of seventeen to read as it deals openly and honestly with the problems of sex, but that the majority of the girls in the school would not want to read it. 'Why?' asked an incredulous Mr Griffith-Jones. 'Girls know what they want to read and they are bored reading what they don't want to read.'

The most dramatic moments of the trial occurred when Richard Hoggart, author of *The Uses of Literacy*, was in the witness box. He was an academic of working-class origins, orphaned at birth, who was an expert on the novels of D. H. Lawrence. He was asked whether he agreed with the prosecution's description of the book as 'little more than a vicious indulgence in sex and sensuality'. Hoggart replied that the book was not in any sense vicious; it was virtuous and, if anything, puritanical. 'Did you say "virtuous" and "puritanical"?' interposed the judge, who had, until then, remained largely silent on the bench. 'I did,' answered Hoggart. He was in the witness box for over an hour, during which he explained that the honesty and depth of the relationship between Connie and Mellors had increased as the number of sexual encounters grew. He read from the end of the book when Mellors writes to Connie: 'I love the chastity now that flows between us. It is like fresh water and rain. How can men want wearisomely to philander.' In cross-examination, Griffith-Jones adopted a high-handed and sarcastic tone. Long answers to short questions provoked the rebuke: 'You are not at Leicester University at the moment' or 'I don't need another lecture' by the increasingly angry and frustrated prosecutor. Hoggart remained calm and when he was challenged forcefully on his use of the word 'puritanical', Hoggart said its original English meaning was intense responsibility for one's own conscience. It was, in that sense, a puritanical book. He did not use the word in the sense of being against everything that was pleasurable.

Hoggart's robust and well-argued defence of the merits of the book was the turning point in the trial. Other witnesses included household names in the field of literature, Dame Rebecca West, E. M. Forster and Cecil Day-Lewis; three Church of England clergymen, Dr John Robinson, Bishop of Woolwich, Prebendary Stephan Hopkinson and the Rev. Donald Tytler; and two well-known female journalists, Anne Scott-James and Dilys Powell. There were academics, educationalists and school teachers. Not one of them yielded to Griffith-Jones's increasingly angry insistence that the book had no merit, was obscene and should be condemned. He was reduced to crass displays of fulmination when witnesses testified that the book was about a love that was natural. 'Perfectly natural!' shouted Mr Griffith-Jones. 'Perfectly natural that Lady Chatterley should run off into the forest to copulate with her husband's gamekeeper?' 'Yes; it is in her nature,' was the calm reply from the Professor of Poetry at Oxford, Cecil Day-Lewis. 'It is in her nature because she is an oversexed and adulterous woman,' rejoined the rattled prosecutor, who was now retreating into his comfort zone of classifying obscenity as a story about adultery and a woman who was prepared to enjoy the experience. As Gerald Gardiner was able to point out in his final speech, if adultery was obscene then much of the world's greatest literature, including Shakespeare's *Antony and Cleopatra*, would fall foul of the country's obscenity laws.

The prosecution was being worn down by the sheer number of distinguished and well-known figures from the world of letters who testified as to the book's worth as literature. All had said sexual intercourse and four-letter words associated with it were central and necessary ingredients. Three full days of the trial were taken up with this evidence; the remaining days were either counsel's speeches or the judge's summing up. If Griffith-Jones could not open cracks in the defence's wall then the case was lost. At times he did not even attempt to do so and asked no questions of many of the literary experts called by the defence.

Counsel's final speeches on the fifth day of the trial were completely different in their approach and reflected the chasm between the prosecution and the defence which the jury had seen opening up before them during the trial. Gerald Gardiner QC spoke first, as was the rule at the time. The first thing he did was to identify the elephant in the room, the fact that nobody had so far mentioned: the Obscene Publications Act 1959 expressly permitted expert evidence to be given by the *prosecution* as well as the defence, yet as Gardiner pointed out, 'when their turn came to call evidence, they called no evidence at all'. Nobody from the literary world was prepared to help them.

Gardiner continued by poking fun at the prosecution by telling the jury that if the book induced thoughts about sexual intercourse then the whole population had obviously been depraved and corrupted from an early age. He emphasised the point that Penguin were responsible publishers who wanted only to publish what Lawrence had actually written, not a version that the censors wanted his public to read. It was in the public interest that thirty years after his death the full text of *Lady Chatterley* should finally see the light of day.

The prosecution speech was entirely different. Griffith-Jones began by telling the jury that there were certain standards of language and morality that were essential for the well-being of society, but those standards were falling. When one looked around, he argued, there was unbridled sex everywhere, there was a lack of discipline among the youth. It was time to restore some restraint in the education of the young. He made a direct appeal to the jury to return a verdict on behalf of what he called 'ordinary people', not a verdict that reflected the view of bishops or lecturers. Griffith-Jones associated himself with the ordinary people,

'people like us who do not have great literary or academic qualifications'. He invited the jury not to look at the book from the 'Olympian
heights' but as representatives of the man in the street. He pleaded with
them to condemn the book as a piece of foul literature having a tendency to promote a 'false conception of what proper thought and conduct
ought to be'.

Mervyn Griffith-Jones knew what he was doing and understood how
best to pitch his case. His method, in the circumstances, was the very
best he could do to suppress publication. He was appealing to what was
undoubtedly a strand within the British character which existed in the
1950s. The historian Dominic Sandbrook has argued that the nation
as a whole was uninterested in censorship or the merits of high literature. The broad populace was content with the prevailing mood, where
Salad Days (1954) and *My Fair Lady* (1956) were far more popular in
the theatre than 'new wave' dramatists. The young were not promiscuous and sexual activity was associated with coupledom and marriage.
In 1969, a survey of people's attitudes to the changes made to Britain
since 1960 found that only 1 per cent identified the *Chatterley* trial as
the most important event of the decade, compared with 39 per cent who
identified man's conquest of space in the moon landings and 14 per
cent who chose the death of Winston Churchill.[10] The progressivism
of Crosland and Jenkins was certainly not reflected in the 1959 general
election result, when the Conservatives won their third general election
in a row. In his autobiography, *Gentle Regrets: Thoughts from a Life*,
the philosopher Roger Scruton, who was born in 1944, wrote that the
English character instinctively knew that sexual puritanism could safeguard something more valuable than pleasure and that the repression
which preceded the changes that came later was valuable as it prevented
people from abandoning values that can easily slip away – chastity, marriage and the family.[11]

The existence of these strands of conformity meant that the acquittal of Penguin Books was by no means inevitable. The verdict of a jury, chosen at random, could not be predicted with any confidence by law reformers. The words 'not guilty', delivered by the jury's foreman, came as a huge relief. It will never be known whether the jury were not persuaded that the book had a tendency to deprave or corrupt or whether despite its obscenity there was a public good achieved in publishing it. A jury is not required to say how or why it reached its verdict; only whether the defendant is guilty or not guilty.

The trial of *Lady Chatterley's Lover* was a legal case that made modern Britain for a whole number of reasons. The year 1960 was one of shifting sands in attitudes to the depiction of sex outside marriage. John Trevelyan had been appointed head of the British Board of Film Censors in 1958. He described himself as a 'censor who did not believe in censorship' and films about sex outside marriage like *Saturday Night and Sunday Morning* (1960) and *A Kind of Loving* (1962) were passed for general consumption. In January 1960, Hugh Carleton Greene had been appointed Director General of the BBC. Like Trevelyan, he had strong liberal inclinations, and he wanted the BBC to take risks, to be unconventional and to nurture youthful talent. Greene wanted the BBC to be ahead of public opinion and he made space for new writers like Alun Owen, whose gritty, realistic plays about working-class life were screened before the *Lady Chatterley* trial took place. On the other side, however, there was a tide of opinion which felt that this new openness about the reality of life and of people's relationships was capable of undermining traditional family values and was a threat to hearth and home. Mary Whitehouse, who was fifty at the time of the *Chatterley* trial, had been involved in evangelical Christianity and the Moral Re-Armament movement since before the Second World War. She founded the National Viewers' and Listeners' Association in 1965 to protest at the direction in which Greene was taking the BBC. Although much mocked for her simplistic solutions to complex problems, she has been described by the historian Paul Addison as 'genuinely representative of a part of the viewing and listening public that was still wedded to Victorian ideals of morality and tone deaf to irony, scepticism, and irreverence'.[12] The pull towards values of the past was as embedded within Britain as the push for a new refreshing modernity.

The verdict in the *Chatterley* case was an important event in tilting the scales towards the forces of modernity. Had the jury condemned the book on the grounds that its depictions of sex were obscene, it is likely that William Burroughs's 1959 novel *Naked Lunch* or Philip Roth's 1969 novel *Portnoy's Complaint* would also have found themselves at the Old Bailey, with Mervyn Griffith-Jones once again on his feet pleading with the jury to condemn them. They were not. Nor were Henry Miller's series of novels *Tropic of Cancer*, *Tropic of Capricorn*, *Sexus*, *Plexus* and *Nexus*, whose amiable adulterous hero found sexual satisfaction among prostitutes and drunks in pre-war Paris. The Director of Public Prosecutions and his staff had learned their lesson. The *Chatterley* verdict marked a new era. It chimed with a general mood in the country that it was time for longstanding laws in relation to sex, pleasure and personal autonomy to be relaxed.

Shortly before the *Chatterley* trial a person could be (and usually was) sent to prison if he or she failed in an attempt to commit suicide. The anguish of failing to end an unhappy life by your own hand was rewarded by being branded a criminal for doing so. This was remedied in the Suicide Act 1961. The strictures on betting and gaming were relaxed in the same year, when betting shops were allowed to open. Women were, for the first time, allowed to become Members of the House of Lords as peeresses of the realm. All these reforms, occurring just before or just after the *Chatterley* trial, were visible examples of changes to behaviour which were happening, some spontaneously, within society. The year 1960 was the beginning of a time of transition in the structure of relationships between the sexes, between classes and between generations. The most significant and important of these changes was the empowerment of women. D. H. Lawrence's novel is written largely through the character of Connie, whose sexual choices and needs were so vehemently condemned by the prosecution in the trial. Lawrence chose to make the main character of the book a woman with a strong sexual drive who had married into the aristocracy. Women were not supposed to flaunt their erotic power if they were respectable, and the suppression of erotic literature was supposed to allow power relations between the sexes to be aligned to a certain way of life. This was the way of life in which men were in charge. Griffith-Jones believed in this unspoken assumption when he asked the jury (which actually contained three women), 'Is it a book you would even wish your wife to read?' Empowerment of women, however, did not provide an open door for pornographic literature that degraded women or depicted them simply and only as people who provide sexual pleasure for men. A jury at the Central Criminal Court found *Last Exit to Brooklyn*, which depicted scenes of gang rape on the streets of New York, obscene (although the conviction was quashed on appeal as the judge had materially misdirected the jury on the law).

During the 1960s there was a rapid change in the power relations between men and women and the most important reason for this was the arrival of the contraceptive pill, which provided the easiest way for sex to be separated from reproduction. The pill, as it came universally to be called, arrived on the scene in 1961 but it was only available to married women whose health would be endangered by a further pregnancy. In 1962 there were only 150,000 women who were prescribed it, but this grew to half a million by 1964. This was due in large part to the decision by the Brook Advisory Clinic to provide contraceptive advice to unmarried women in that year. The historian Hera Cook has described the arrival of the contraceptive pill as a metaphor for the 1960s as a whole in that it shifted the associations of contraception away from the slimes of rubber, the condom and the cap, to the sterilised laboratory of Harold Wilson's technological revolution.[13] Sheila Rowbotham, who was born in 1943, has described her experience of the 1960s as one of a kind of cusp in sexual attitudes: 'Prohibition and permission were shifting but had yet to realign.'[14] There was still confusion and ambivalence about the place of women and their sexuality within the society at the time of the *Chatterley* trial.

The distinction between what was public and what was private was becoming blurred; the jury's verdict was one of the pointers to a pathway out of the confusion. Having sex became a personal choice; it was not the business of your priest, your teacher or your parents, still less the business of the censor. Sex, and the enjoyment of it, was a choice for the individuals involved, not anyone else. Jeffrey Weeks has quoted a chant shouted in early feminist demonstrations: 'Not the church, not the state, women must control their fate.'

The verdict in the *Chatterley* trial dealt a blow to the counter-movement opposed to the new sexual radicalism which was gearing up under the leadership of Mary Whitehouse. By the time the counter-revolution gathered pace in the 1970s and 1980s, the 'fashionable theories and permissive claptrap' which Margaret Thatcher had identified as being the evils of the 1960s had already taken place. She could only look back in anger at an era in which so much change occurred. In the few years that followed the trial there were striking changes in attitudes towards sex. In 1962, Helen Gurley Brown published *Sex and the Single Girl* and Edna O'Brien published *The Lonely Girl*. One was a factual book about female sexual desire; the other, a work of fiction with the same theme. Each was a bestseller. The fearlessness with which women felt able to talk about their experiences of sex would have delighted D. H. Lawrence had he known about it. In his book *The Sixties*, the historian Arthur Marwick notes that emancipation and liberation were movements common to the United States, mainland Europe and the United Kingdom. In all these countries there were political movements critical of establishment attitudes; a new breed of young entrepreneurs; a new celebration of the human body in fashion and art; and a reduced inhibition in the lyrics of popular music. A little-noticed but nonetheless important feature of the period, however, was 'the silencing of the pompous, hidebound male'.[15] Perhaps he had in mind the senior prosecuting counsel in the *Lady Chatterley* trial.

Chapter 3

Race – The Cricketer and the Hotel

The case of *Constantine v Imperial Hotels*, heard in the High Court in London in the summer of 1944, would have been entirely unremarkable were it not for the identity of the claimant. Learie Constantine was a Trinidadian British citizen who was also a world-class cricketer. He was resident in Nelson, Lancashire, where he played as a professional in the town's Lancashire League team in addition to being part of the national West Indies side. When he became a litigant in the Royal Courts of Justice, it was news. Everybody wanted to know why the famous cricketer was suing a London hotel. It was the first publicised legal case about race in the twentieth century. The cricketer had been turned away from the hotel where he had made a reservation in advance on the spurious grounds that American soldiers and airmen who were also staying there might not like a 'negro' and his family being under the same roof. It was as blatant a case of racial prejudice as is possible to imagine, yet no one at the time treated it as a dispute touching on race or discrimination. The lawyers and the judge all regarded it as a case about the obligations of innkeepers to provide shelter for travellers. Only Learie Constantine himself and some of the general public who read about it grasped the full significance of his action against the hotel. It was 1944 and discrimination and prejudice towards black people was prevalent in Britain, but it was hardly ever discussed openly in white society. At best it was treated as a fact of life to be acknowledged but not to be outlawed. It was certainly not something to be confronted in a court of law.

Indeed, discrimination in general was barely understood by people in Britain before and during the Second World War. When a teacher in Bournemouth confronted her employers in 1926 for dismissing her on the grounds that she was married, a senior judge said it was perfectly reasonable for her to be dismissed on these grounds. It was not as if her employers had sacked her for frivolous reasons such as having red hair.[1] English law and English judges could not comprehend that some members of society might be disadvantaged or discriminated against.

Learie Constantine's case against the Imperial Hotel broke new ground. When he won, he gave momentum and inspiration for a fundamentally new approach to tackling racial disadvantage. He became a campaigner, writer and diplomat after his retirement from cricket. Despite his prowess on the field, his later career as a leading figure in the struggle for dignity for black citizens will endure longer than the memories of him as a cricketer. What Constantine started in 1944 remains unfinished business to this day, but his decision to take a stand against discrimination in a court of law was novel and ground-breaking.

When war broke out in 1939, there was hardly any immigration, as we use the term today, from the West Indian colonies. Fewer than 20,000 men and women (they were mostly men) of Caribbean and West African descent were living in the whole of the United Kingdom. Of the 150,000 black people living in the country in 1944, the overwhelming majority – 130,000 – were American servicemen stationed here to prepare for the Allied invasion of Europe. They were not, however, immigrants, and everybody understood that the GIs would depart when the war was over. Immigration, in the sense of arrivals from overseas who intended to settle permanently in Britain, was very small and they were mainly based in the port cities of London, Liverpool and Cardiff. In Britain as a whole, the general opinion about black people was unfavourable.

The much larger contingent of American servicemen, meanwhile, were white, and they brought with them the bigotries and prejudices of their mandatory segregated existence in the United States to British shores, living and working as separate 'races'. Black and white service personnel were billeted in separate camps, had meals in separate canteens and spent their free time in separate service clubs. This was the toxic backdrop to the case of *Constantine v Imperial Hotels*.

During the slave trade in the eighteenth and early nineteenth centuries, it was possible to perceive the black man as a faithful servant and a symbol of a servile gratitude owed to the kindly slave owner. There was little idea that the citizenship of the black man or woman corresponded in any way to that of the white slave owner. The slave trade inculcated a disposition of 'natural' racial superiority over anybody who was of a different colour. This extended to a widely held belief, fostered by the social Darwinists of the late nineteenth century, that there was savagery and ignorance within the minds of black people while the white man possessed natural intelligence, wisdom and qualities of leadership. Colonial rulers believed in their inherent superiority to be able to govern large colonial territories with only a small number of white administrators. A similar view was held by missionaries who believed that God had endowed them a superiority and intelligence that could be put to good work by converting the 'heathen' African. These attitudes filtered back to families and friends at home and into schools, where teachers had no general knowledge about the realities of colonialism or the history of slavery.

With the exception of those who had been involved in colonial administration or expeditions with a missionary purpose, virtually nobody in Britain had any first-hand knowledge of Caribbean African people in the years before the Second World War. Attitudes towards race were based almost entirely on stereotyped ideas which were taught in schools by teachers speaking in front of maps with large sections of the world shaded pink, the colour of colonial occupation. At the Empire Exhibition held in Wembley in 1924, the population of Africa was depicted by images of Africans sitting in mud huts threading beads. It is hardly surprising, therefore, that the very few Caribbean and African sailors who chose to stay in Britain before and during the war to fill urgent vacancies in munition factories were to face a hard time.

For the most part, the early arrivals slept in YMCA hostels where the corridors were segregated and the dormitories were not heated. It was difficult, if not impossible, for black factory workers to find lodgings outside the hostels. Rooms for rent were invariably refused to applicants when the colour of their skin became apparent and even in the rare cases when Caribbean men clubbed together to buy a house, the deal would fall through on grounds of their colour. Overt discrimination applied equally to women. Before the outbreak of the war, a young black woman applied to twenty-eight London hospitals for a position as a nurse. She was refused employment by each one. A young black volunteer for the Women's Land Army experienced similar rejection.

In all these cases, the grounds were familiar. As Peter Fryer has made clear in his book *Staying Power: The history of black people in Britain*, landlords, estate agents, sellers of houses or employers never admitted their own prejudices.[2] The reason they invariably gave was that *other* people would be offended. A landlady would give an excuse such as 'the neighbours wouldn't like it' or 'my husband wouldn't approve'. One of the hospitals that refused to employ the nurse told her, 'We don't apply a colour bar, but people in the East End have very strong colour prejudices.' The Land Army volunteer was rejected not on her abilities but because 'the farmers would not like it'.

These prejudices existed before the arrival of the American servicemen, but their presence in Britain during the war brought jaundiced American views into public spaces. During the summer of 1942 there were well-documented occasions of the sheer vindictiveness of American racial prejudice. On their nights off duty, many GIs, black and white, would flock to the bars and dance halls of Britain's towns and cities. They had money to spend and publicans welcomed them with open arms. Unfortunately, there was a ceaseless stream of incidents in which white American servicemen attacked, assaulted or abused black GIs.[3] The ingrained hostility of white American soldiers and airmen towards their black comrades in arms was both shocking to the English and disagreeable to the young black West Indians who encountered American boorishness on the dance floor. On the whole, black American servicemen were popular with girls. They were considered good dancers and had a reputation for being polite. By contrast, the white GIs were often ostentatious and arrogant and believed they had a right to impose their power over 'anybody who was black, regardless of nationality. A black West Indian RAF gunner was attacked at a dance hall by white American GIs when he asked a white girl for a dance. Caribbean and African factory workers were routinely humiliated and verbally insulted by white GIs. Learie Constantine later recounted an experience of his own. He visited a dance hall in Liverpool and was chatting with some white men and women when an American Air Force officer aggressively shouldered his way through the crowd standing around and shouted at Constantine, 'Get out, we don't allow n**s to mix with white people from where we are.' Constantine was so shocked that his immediate reaction was to challenge the officer to a fight outside. After a moment's reflection he reported the officer to a steward instead, who then asked the officer to leave and barred him from returning.[4]

By the time Constantine brought his case against Imperial Hotels, he was a cricketer who was admired across the world for his skill as an all-rounder for the West Indies side. His origins and background, however, were no different from the West Indian factory workers in Liverpool, Cardiff and London. The only difference was that as an international cricketer people would take notice if he became involved in a legal case, especially if it involved a sensitive but important subject like discrimination. Discriminatory behaviour towards people with different racial characteristics from the majority population was a shameful but commonplace occurrence in English society. But it did not engage the law at all. Those who suffered discrimination could not afford to go to court, and even if they did the prospect of success was poor. English judges barely recognised the existence of the word 'discrimination', let alone gave it a legal meaning.

Learie Constantine was about to change all that. As a litigant, he had a backstory which was, to say the least, impressive. Born in 1901 in a small settlement in north-west Trinidad, he was the great-grandson of a slave. The island of Trinidad had been ruled as a Crown Colony since 1797 and when Constantine was growing up, Creoles (white people whose ancestors were born in Trinidad) shaped the fortunes of the descendants of slaves. The island's most prestigious cricket club, Queen's Park, operated a colour bar and Constantine played in a black club, the Shannon. The racial divide in cricket was startling. There would be no black captain of the West Indian Test side until 1960 even though the captain was the only white player in the side. Constantine had displayed precocious talent in his youth and having progressed through black club cricket in Trinidad was selected to tour with a West Indian team to England in 1923 and 1928.

He was familiar with England when he accepted a contract to become a professional for Nelson, a town in the Lancashire League, in April 1929. The team consisted of amateurs, but the club had accumulated enough cash reserves to engage a professional. When Constantine accepted the town's offer, there were no black residents in Nelson, but he and his wife settled easily into local life. He had fame and status and his income as a cricketer enabled him and his wife to live a comfortable existence. They enjoyed the affection and respect of the town's inhabitants. He had encountered prejudice from American GIs, not his neighbours in Nelson.

As a UK resident he was available for recruitment to help the war effort and, in an inspired move, the Ministry of Labour in London offered Constantine the position of welfare officer to the black community in Liverpool in 1942. There were certain tensions between the West Indians who were in the city as volunteer workers in the munition's factories and the West Africans who worked mostly in the docks and in shipping. Constantine had skills as a conciliator and, as a Trinidadian based in Britain for many years, his views commanded respect from both the host community and new arrivals.

Constantine's work as a welfare officer provided him with first-hand experience of the discrimination on open display in housing provision, something he had not encountered himself as a member of the only black family in Nelson. It was a profound shock to him to learn about the exclusion many of his West Indian compatriots experienced in finding lodgings. By the time of the legal case he brought against Imperial Hotels, Constantine was well versed in the two glaring pieces of racial prejudice in wartime Britain: discrimination over accommodation and abuse and racial insult in public places. These two ingredients were to come to a head in the shameful behaviour that took place in the Imperial Hotel in the heart of London in July 1943.

A cricket match had been arranged to take place at Lord's cricket ground between a Dominions XI and an England XI as a morale-booster for war-weary Londoners. Constantine had been appointed captain of the scratch West Indian side to play a team from England consisting of cricketers who were not on war service. He had arranged in advance to stay with his wife and daughter at the Imperial Hotel in Russell Square for the duration of the match. The Imperial was a large, imposing Edwardian hotel with more than 600 rooms. When he made his booking, he had asked whether there would be any difficulty about it, a reference to his racial origins. He did this from an abundance of caution following his own experiences as a welfare officer. He was told there was none and he paid a deposit. He booked two rooms for four nights. When he arrived to check in with his wife and young daughter, some truly shocking events occurred. He was told by the manager, a Mrs O'Sullivan, 'You can stay for one night but not any longer.' When Constantine asked why, the response from the manager was: 'I can turn you out when I like.'

Constantine's reaction was to stand his ground and he made contact with a colleague at the Ministry of Labour, who hastened to the hotel from Whitehall. In the presence of the civil servant, Mrs O'Sullivan elaborated: 'We are not going to have these n*****s in our hotel. He can stop the night, but if he does not go tomorrow morning his luggage will be put outside his room and his door will be locked.' As a witness to these odious statements, the civil servant was able to tell the judge at the trial how disconsolate and unhappy Constantine and his family had been when spoken to in this way. By this time a more senior hotel manager had arrived and the civil servant pressed him for a reason for their refusal to honour their contractual obligations to the Constantine family. It was only then that the senior manager at the hotel gave a reason; it was, he said, 'Because of the Americans.'

It turned out, unknown to Constantine and his family, that a very large group of nearly 300 white American GIs were staying at the hotel. In these circumstances the management persuaded Constantine that it might be more 'convenient' for him and his family to stay at the Bedford, an adjoining hotel. This was coded language for the well-known fact that many, if not most, white American GIs were unashamedly racist and were not shy about saying so. The hotel management seemed prepared to be complicit in any bad behaviour, because by their attitude they were acknowledging that American GIs could be racists. The hotel was happy to accommodate them and to exclude the Constantine family. As Constantine pointed out at the time, they were aliens but he was a British subject. The Constantine family did, in the end, accept the offer of alternative accommodation. Constantine's reasons for doing so were not relevant to the court case, but it may have been his natural inclination to reach conciliation rather than confrontation and his wish not to expose his wife and daughter to experiences he had endured in earlier encounters with racists. He had been humiliated on racial grounds many times in the past, including in a London bar and in a dining car on a train. He had been abused by a white American Air Force officer in Liverpool and he had knowledge of numerous incidents when West Indian factory workers had been denied lodgings on the grounds of their colour. What had happened in the lobby of the Imperial Hotel was the last straw. He decided it was time to take a stand.

At that time there were no laws against racial discrimination, nor were there any laws against racist language which could alarm or distress the victim. Unless somebody was prepared to take a stand, nothing would change. Learie Constantine therefore broke new ground in deciding to take on the Imperial Hotel in a legal case. Success was not guaranteed. Apart from the absence of any concrete law of racial discrimination, there was the fact that he had accepted the alternative accommodation the Imperial had offered him. It was a similar hotel and was nearby. He had therefore suffered no quantifiable loss and was in no worse position than he would have been in had the Imperial provided the rooms. The Imperial were confident enough about this to defend the case and risk any adverse publicity that would follow. Constantine's legal team relied on an old common law principle that an innkeeper could not unreasonably refuse accommodation to a traveller who was in need of food and shelter. They argued this right was absolute and could not be violated simply because the claimant had suffered no loss. Neither side were able to argue the case on the territory of discrimination as there was no legal basis for so doing, but everybody knew it was a case about race. It was the reason Constantine was so determined to go to court.

The trial, when it came, attracted wide interest. Nowadays, Learie Constantine would be called a celebrity. He was one of the best-known cricketers in England. He also had an equable temperament and never put a foot wrong in public. He was a respected welfare officer in Liverpool and an author of a book on cricket, *Cricket and I*. As Constantine was a well-liked and well-known personality, it was perhaps surprising that the Imperial did not seek to settle the case out of court. They could have paid the Constantine family damages for the hurt caused to them. The hotel's decision to fight was probably because the manager, Mrs O'Sullivan, and the senior manager denied they had used any racially insulting language. In any event, *Constantine v Imperial Hotels* was set down for hearing in the King's Bench Division of the High Court in the Royal Courts of Justice for June 1944.

It was not just a run-of-the-mill case. The treatment accorded to Constantine was becoming common knowledge and the behaviour of the hotel was raised in the House of Commons. Eight Members of Parliament put questions to the Secretary of State for the Colonies. Members pointed out to the minister that the hotel had successfully imposed a colour bar on guests and he was asked what steps the government would take to prevent innkeepers from doing so in the future. The minister stonewalled, refusing to give any commitments or undertakings.

The importance of Constantine's legal case was demonstrated by the expense he was prepared to lay out in his choice of counsel: his legal team was probably the best it was possible to find in wartime. His leading counsel was Sir Patrick Hastings KC, perhaps the most accomplished advocate at the English Bar, and his junior was Rose Heilbron, who went on to become one of the country's two first female King's Counsel (now Queen's Counsel) in 1949 and the second female High Court judge in 1974. The Imperial had an equally impressive legal team. The judge was Mr Justice Birkett, who, as Norman Birkett KC, had achieved legendary fame as a lawyer and advocate of outstanding merit. There was a factual dispute between the parties. The Imperial's managers claimed they had neither used racially insulting words nor threatened to lock the Constantine family out of their rooms if they refused to leave after one night. The judge had no difficulty in finding that Constantine and his witness were truthful about both the language used and the threat to lock them out. This left only one point calling for a decision. Had the Constantines suffered a loss? Mr Justice Birkett affirmed the ancient principle that an innkeeper could not under common law unreasonably refuse shelter to a traveller and this law held good even if the traveller had suffered no loss. The judge awarded nominal damages to Constantine as his right to be lodged had been violated. He did, of course, recover his costs.

It is possible to argue, as some historians have done, that the case achieved very little other than to provide bad publicity for the hotel. No new legal principle had been established to change behaviour in cheap boarding houses or pubs. All Constantine had done was to illustrate that the common law was a redress available to all, providing they had the means and the resources to go to court.[5] But there are stronger arguments the other way. Firstly, it was the beginning of Constantine's own work and achievements in race relations, which were enormously influential in setting Britain on the path towards legislation on race discrimination. Secondly, the case reaffirmed an important legal principle that every human being is of equal worth, irrespective of race, and thirdly the case brought racial prejudice out of the shadows and into the limelight, where it could be seen. While the judgment was dressed up as a case about hotel law, it was in reality a judgment that an individual has a *right* not to be discriminated against. Learie Constantine and his family had been humiliated by the language and behaviour of the hotel staff and the judgment affirmed their rights to have their dignity respected. The wide publicity the case generated helped create an environment within society in which each individual should be able to make their own choices. It was Constantine's choice to spend four nights at the Imperial Hotel, a choice that had been denied him while the hotel was content to accede to the choice of a large number of white American GIs to stay there.

Learie Constantine, by temperament a modest man, explained in his book *Colour Bar*, published in 1954, why he took on the hotel: 'I was content to have drawn the particular nature of the affront before the wider judgment of the British public in the hope that its sense of fair play might help to protect people of my colour in England in the future.'[6] In hindsight, this is rather coy. Black people in wartime were on the whole poor and too busy surviving privations to be able to pursue legal cases. In the unlikely event of them doing so, their attempts at litigation in the High Court would be unlikely to receive publicity even if they succeeded. Constantine had the resources and the fame to take on the hurt and affront caused to him, to bring to public notice the daily degradations that were commonplace in English society.

When the war had ended and the doctrines of racial superiority in Nazism had been defeated, racism in Britain became less acceptable. In addition, the post-war era was able to draw a line under the thinly disguised racism of the eugenics movement of the 1930s. There was a lot to be said for Constantine's appeal to a British sense of fair play in actually asking them to confront the obvious unfairness of racial prejudice. It was the first time this had been done in the forum of the courtroom, where the press eagerly followed the trial. Each day *The Times* covered the proceedings in some detail.

The timing was also important. Until the late 1950s there was no large-scale immigration from the colonies to Britain. Constantine's court case of 1944 provided a shot in the arm to all who believed there should be civilised standards applied to all who lived on British soil. As David Olusoga has observed, the case was a national embarrassment.[7] No longer could a blind eye be cast on the presence of prejudice and discrimination in Britain. Having won a victory in the Imperial Hotels case, Constantine went on to record his own experiences of discrimination and prejudice in excruciating detail in his book *Colour Bar*. In many respects it was hard-hitting, pointing out that in large parts of the United Kingdom black people were expected to live in segregated communities. In other respects he was rather too idealistic in supposing that problems of integration and assimilation could be solved if only there was greater civility and warmth and an observance of the principles of universal citizenship proclaimed in the Universal Declaration of Human Rights of 1948. Nowadays, Constantine is regarded as being too unambitious in his wish to achieve racial equality by accepting that the route to progress lay in the black man aspiring to be the same as the white man. These views now seem quaintly old-fashioned in all respects; women barely featured in Constantine's writings. In addition, he wrote nothing about the merits of black identity. His work, however, must be understood in the context of the times, 1950s Britain.

English judges were content to believe in the principle that, in English law, every citizen is of equal worth in the courtroom, and race, wealth and status should never determine the result of a case. But as the Irish judge Sir James Mathew had quipped, 'English law is open to all, just like the Ritz Hotel.' He was stating the obvious. In an environment of privilege by social class and power through economic wealth, the principle that justice was open to all existed in theory, not in practice. Constantine's contribution was to demonstrate that when it came to racial equality the theory had to be put to the test. As his biographer Jeffrey Hill has concluded, Constantine's outstanding achievement was in transmitting to the public at large the fact that racial oppression was something many people had to put up with in their daily lives and therefore race relations was a problem in need of a solution. But who was to provide the solution? Was it for Parliament or would the judges play a role?

In the 1940s and 1950s, there was a general wish to improve race relations, but nobody knew how to do it. The Labour government of Clement Attlee introduced the British Nationality Act 1948 in order to create the status of Commonwealth citizen. This remarkably liberal measure granted a legal right to all those living in the colonies and dominions to come to the United Kingdom to settle permanently. Potentially, millions of black and Asian people could come to Britain if they chose to do so, but it was simply not envisaged that black citizens would take advantage of this right. It was assumed that only the white settlers in southern Africa, Australia, Canada and New Zealand would need a right to return to Britain when the time came for a decision to leave the colonies. But reality was staring the government in the face. The *Empire Windrush* had already set sail, with eager workers from Jamaica determined to fill the vacancies in the job market colonial administrators had told them were there for the taking. The ship docked at Tilbury in June 1948 just as the British Nationality Bill was due to be passed in Parliament. The *Windrush* was only the beginning.

In the 1950s, the National Health Service and the London Transport Executive had recruiters stationed in the West Indies to encourage emigration to Britain. The problem for governments of all hues after 1945 was keeping a balance between upholding the ideal of the Commonwealth and the notion of free movement within it on the one hand and the social consequences of black immigration on a large scale from the Commonwealth to Britain on the other. When incidents of violence by youths directed towards immigrants in 1948 and 1949 turned into more organised hostility by 'Teddy Boys' in the 1950s and the Notting Hill race riots of 1958, the government decided to act. The Institute of Race Relations was established in 1958 with the object of studying race relations and rather lamely concluded that relations were worse in neighbourhoods where a concentration of new arrivals occurred too quickly. The solution was to encourage Commonwealth countries to put up hurdles to emigration from their territories to Britain.

The rather uninspired recipe from the institute involved promoting a narrative that immigration created social problems, so it was necessary to limit the influx. The approach involved legislation to limit immigrant numbers but without any legislation to curb discrimination and prejudice.[8] The Commonwealth Immigrants Act 1962 only addressed numbers of entrants, not their treatment once they had arrived and settled. Judges remained on the sidelines. Twenty-two years after the Imperial Hotels case, a judge was perfectly happy to rule that a trust fund created for the benefit of 'British-born students' who were not Jews or Roman Catholics complied with English law.[9]

It was not until 1965 that any legislation outlawing discrimination and prejudice appeared in the statute book with measures for integration as the stated aim. The Race Relations Act 1965 prohibited discrimination on grounds of 'colour, race or ethnic or national origins', but the prohibition applied only to 'places of public resort' like hotels, pubs, libraries, public transport and so on and not to housing and employment, where discrimination really mattered. The purpose of the legislation was to enshrine into law the principle that equality of opportunity could be available to citizens within ethnic minorities only if there was a recognition of diversity through the prism of tolerance.

The good intentions behind the 1965 Race Relations Act were admirably summarised later by Roy Jenkins MP when he defined racial integration as 'not a flattening process of assimilation but as equal opportunity, accompanied by cultural diversity in an atmosphere of mutual tolerance'.[10] But even this eloquent statement reveals both the modesty of the measure and the optimism of the intention. He assumed that mutual tolerance between the host community and new arrivals could be achieved if only the right laws were on the statute book and he underestimated the aspirations of new arrivals who brought with them their own identity from their countries of origin. This assessment of the improvements legislation might make was probably satisfactory to the Windrush generation who had arrived more than fifteen years earlier, but it was utterly unsatisfactory to their children, growing up in Britain during the 1960s, who were legally and socially British, and it was of limited value to the new arrivals from India and East Africa.

When Jenkins spoke of 'assimilation', he meant it exactly as Constantine had meant it: 'coloured people' progressing upwards towards 'the pinnacle of Europeanism, adopting the habits and thoughts of those who were not coloured'.[11] There was not much new thinking from the approach Constantine had advocated in 1954 in his book *Colour Bar*, in which he espoused the notion that integration was an end in itself while failing to see the need for a pride in racial identity.

Jenkins's reasons for legislation were also founded on assumptions which are only now being scrutinised and found to be woefully idealistic. Both Constantine and Jenkins believed that if the host population was tolerant and reasonable and black citizens were sufficiently ambitious to pull themselves out of poverty, natural harmony would result. But it soon became apparent that the 1965 Act was deficient in its scope. It was far too limited and within three years its provisions were enlarged to cover employment, housing and other services in the Race Relations Act 1968. Then came the Race Relations Act 1976. This was a further improvement as it introduced the concept of indirect discrimination. It has been described as one of the strongest pieces of legislation of its kind in Europe.[12] The legislation extended protection against discrimination to goods and services in addition to housing. It was now clear that the part law could play on the vast subject called 'race' was confined to the concept of discrimination and nothing else. Discrimination was capable of a definition and could therefore be enforced and interpreted by judges. The modern meaning of discrimination is either direct discrimination – treating someone less favourably than others because of a protected characteristic – or indirect discrimination – putting rules or arrangements in place to apply to everyone but which put those with a protected characteristic at a disadvantage.

When the history of race relations is looked at in this way, the importance of Learie Constantine and his case against the Imperial Hotel becomes clear. In the 1950s, Constantine used his fame as former world-class cricketer to become a writer and a respected BBC broadcaster who had something unique and important to say. He pointed the way towards a type of society in which discrimination and prejudice should be outlawed. When the 1965 Race Relations Act was passed, he was appointed by Harold Wilson to be a member of the newly created Race Relations Board. This came about as a direct result of his involvement in race relations, beginning with his work as a welfare officer in Liverpool during the war. But it was the Imperial Hotels case which had propelled Constantine into the national consciousness as a recognisable face of anti-racism. When he embarked on the litigation to sue the hotel, Constantine initiated a legal case that helped make modern Britain.

Constantine could claim with some justification that when he took his action he was a spokesman for his community. He could represent many when he was a single target of discrimination and he could make one simple point. He wanted to establish a threshold for what was tolerable in a society that considered itself civilised. He wanted an English judge to mark the behaviour of the hotel in excluding him and he wanted their reasons for doing so to be marked. The amount of damages was irrelevant. He did not pursue the case for money. He wanted the threshold to be established. But in the years following *Constantine v Imperial Hotels* the responsibility for erecting the threshold or the red lines beyond which behaviour will not be tolerated had passed to Parliament. Judges remained on the sidelines.

Discrete, piecemeal bits of legislation were passed to deal with issues when groups within society demanded changes in the law. For example, the exemption accorded to Sikhs who wore a turban from wearing a motorcycle helmet was granted in 1973 and a similar exemption from wearing protective headgear in the workplace was granted in 1976. The statute book is full of ad hoc measures to accommodate different dress codes, time off work for religious observance, language support in schools and recognition of different marriage and divorce traditions within different communities. When the Imperial Hotels case was heard, the small black population of England mostly originated from the West Indies and west Africa. There were very few immigrants from the Indian subcontinent. In 1944, the only organisation campaigning against racial discrimination was the League of Coloured Peoples (LCP), which was almost exclusively a body of men originating from the West Indies. Constantine was a member of this organisation. There were no groups at all representing Muslims, Sikhs, Hindus, Chinese people or indeed women who were black or Asian. The period in which families from India and Pakistan came to Britain was mostly between 1955 and 1964, followed by the bulk of arrivals from Bangladesh in the years 1980 to 1984.[13] Now there are numerous bodies representing, or purporting to represent, not just different ethnicities but different viewpoints within those ethnicities. Asian ethnic groups now comprise 4.2 million people, 7.5 per cent of the UK population. The black population is less than half that, 1.8 million or 3.3 per cent of the population. The issue of race, which was relatively clear-cut to Learie Constantine, has now become much more complicated. In today's Britain, age, disability, gender reassignment, sexual orientation and religious discrimination have engaged policy-makers and provoked public debate in ways that were unthinkable in the 1940s and unrecognised in the 1960s and 1970s.

The Equalities Act was passed in 2010 and it introduced the concept of protected characteristics, which consist of age, disability, gender reassignment, marriage and civil partnership, pregnancy and maternity, race, religion or belief, sex and sexual orientation. Race was now only one of a number of 'characteristics' needing legislation to guard against discrimination. The legislation is very ambitious in scope. Its aim is to reduce socio-economic inequalities and introduce a new duty on public bodies to eliminate discrimination, victimisation and harassment and to advance equality of opportunity. The purpose of the Act is to change an attitude of mind. This is one which consciously or unconsciously places certain groups within society or certain people at a stage or condition of their lives at a disadvantage from others. This is a political, not a legal, project.

Judges continue to play a role in issues relating to race, but few modern cases break new ground in the way Learie Constantine did in his action against the Imperial Hotel. It could be said that nowadays legal rulings about race will identify questions of discrimination only in discrete areas, affecting only certain groups. In 2007, the House of Lords had to decide a sensitive issue about Muslim dress. A fourteen-year-old Muslim girl, Shabina Begum, attended a school in Luton, Bedfordshire, where twenty-one ethnic groups were represented in the school's roll. The head teacher, herself a Bengali Muslim, had, in consultation with mainly Muslim governors, imposed a school uniform policy which permitted girls to wear the shalwar kameez, a loose shirt and trousers, which allowed the school tie to be visible. Shabina was sent home when she arrived at the school wearing a longer garment, the jilbab, which concealed the shape of her body and did not allow the school tie to be visible. She claimed, with the assistance of some older relatives, that she had been unlawfully excluded from school. The question for the courts, ultimately Britain's highest court, the House of Lords, was whether the school had discriminated against her by refusing her the right to express her Muslim identity or whether the purpose of the uniform policy was lawful, having the objective of promoting cohesion in the school and avoiding the creation of sub-groups. The House of Lords sided with the school and ruled Shabina had not been unlawfully excluded.[14] In another case involving Muslim dress, a judge ruled it was not discriminatory to forbid a Muslim teaching assistant from giving language support lessons to pupils while her face was concealed by the niqab on the grounds that her teaching could be effective only if her face were visible to her pupils.[15]

Important though these and other cases are to the parties involved, they do not command the attention and discussion that Learie Constantine's case did in 1944. Judges cannot play a significant role nowadays in making law about race, discrimination, prejudice and disadvantage, as this responsibility has now passed to the legislature. On race, judges interpret and apply Parliament's intentions; they do not make new law. The main reason judges are no longer playing a significant role is that the subject has become too complicated. The government admitted this in their document 'Creating the conditions for integration', published in 2012. The view of the government was that

today, the challenges we face are too complex for laws and powers to provide the sole solution. They cannot be defined simply by race, or faith. Location, socio-economic status, ethnicity, faith, culture and a range of other factors come together to make each neighbourhood what it is. Issues which may affect integration within and between neighbourhoods include cultural attitudes and practices; the ability to participate in society; opportunities for social mobility; and a life free from intolerance and discrimination. Today, integration requires changes to society, not changes to the law.[16]

Nowadays, there is an awareness that demands of racial minorities are not calls to be treated as *part* of white society; they are demands for black identity be recognised for what it is as part of society more broadly.

Law, it seems, has run its course in making any contribution to issues around race in Britain. Learie Constantine helped many politicians in Britain to believe that compassionate and pragmatic liberalism, enshrined in law, could eradicate prejudice and discrimination. To a great extent this approach has been successful, but it also succeeded in empowering communities to seek solidarity in identity. Some contemporary campaigners, the modern-day Learie Constantines, insist that the true picture of race relations can only be found through their own standpoint of a shared experience of oppression. It is only through acknowledging the experience of being marginalised within a privileged society that a solution can be reached. This new 'identity politics' is controversial and the whole subject of race has become highly politicised. Matthew d'Ancona has traced the origin of 'identity politics' to a black feminist collective prominent in the United States during the 1970s which proclaimed that radical politics stemmed directly from their own identity.[17] The politician David Lammy MP has described identity politics as a collaboration between groups to correct a perceived shared injustice on the basis that there is a similarity or continuity between the experiences of different individuals within one oppressed group.[18]

There is a growing understanding among black and minority ethnic commentators that the achievement of white society in outlawing prejudice and discrimination was only work in progress. It is time for a new agenda. Meanwhile, there is a fear among some white people that to move on from treating race as simply an issue about discrimination and prejudice would be a step too far. As one commentator has put it,

> There is an insidious creep of the idea that we are now in a post-racial world. There is a largely unspoken view from politicians and opinion-formers that that *we* have done our bit, in fact we have gone too far in allowing *them* their rights. Now *their* demands risk changing society as *we* want to see it.[19]

Law seemed completely to have disappeared from the debate until an intervention from an unlikely quarter occurred in 2008. The Archbishop of Canterbury was invited to give a talk in the Royal Courts of Justice in the Strand, London, about religious and civil law in England. The Great Hall of the Victorian building, designed by George Edmund Street in the 1860s and used as an ambulatory for barristers on their way to court, was packed with chairs for 800 lawyers and guests. Lord Williams did not disappoint. He made a controversial suggestion that law, in the shape of Muslim sharia law, had a part to play in resolving disputes in Britain. He floated the idea that devout Muslims could choose the jurisdiction under which they could resolve certain tightly defined specified matters. He gave as examples aspects of marital law, the regulation of financial transactions and the structures of mediation and conflict resolution.

These suggestions received some support from the Lord Chief Justice, Lord Phillips, who had chaired the archbishop's lecture. He explained a few days later, after a storm of protest had filled the newspapers, that the archbishop was not proposing a subsidiary jurisdiction for sharia law in Britain. He was only proposing that if two Muslims entered into a contract they could agree between themselves that their agreement be governed on sharia principles. He was also mooting the possibility that marital disputes between Muslim couples could be resolved using sharia principles in mediation meetings. The archbishop's proposals were an attempt to allow Muslim faith to be applied to legal relations in settings outside the courtroom. He was not suggesting a parallel legal system.

Lord Williams's points have now sunk away in current debates about the role, if any, of law in tackling racial disadvantage. The debate has moved on. There has been a huge shift from the consensus view about race that prevailed in the 1960s and 1970s. There is now no agreement about either the cause or the solution to racial disadvantage in Britain.

In the summer of 2020, the Prime Minister asked Dr Tony Sewell to chair a commission to examine disparity and disadvantage in Britain today. The Commission on Race and Ethnic Disparities issued its report in the spring of 2021. The commissioners (all but one from ethnic minority backgrounds) did not accept that the system was deliberately rigged against minorities and they called on those from minority backgrounds to abandon a 'fatalistic narrative that says the deck is permanently stacked against them'. Instead, they concluded the big challenge now was 'building and advancing the progress won by the struggles of the past fifty years'.[20] The report was condemned by a former chair of the Race and Disparities Unit in Downing Street. Lord Woolley accused the commission of failing to acknowledge historical and embedded racism in Britain by retreating into denial and missing an opportunity to propose real change.[21] The historian David Olusoga was equally dismissive, describing the report as historically inaccurate and condescending towards young black activism.[22] The report was certainly controversial in claiming there was no institutional racism in

Britain, and that identity or standpoint politics was in danger of alienating the 'decent centre ground'.

The most eloquent critic of this point of view is Reni Eddo-Lodge, who was born long after the struggle Dr Sewell was alluding to occurred. In 2020, her book *Why I'm No Longer Talking to White People About Race* was the first title by a black British author to reach No. 1 in the *Sunday Times* bestseller list. The problem of race, according to Eddo-Lodge, is structural – by which she means 'the hundreds or thousands of people with the same biases joining together to make up one organisation, and acting accordingly'.[23] This is the raised eyebrow, the snap judgements in tossing away a CV with a foreign-sounding name or the apologetic smile to the unlucky soul who did not get the job. Overt racism, like discrimination and racist language, has been banished, only for covert racism to take its place. Eddo-Lodge argues that we have replaced the odious and obvious racism that Learie Constantine experienced with a denial of racism by the occupants of the many structures within white privileged society. She wants her identity as a black woman to be recognised and her ambition is to 'deconstruct the structural power of a system that marked me out as different. I don't want to be assimilated into the status quo … the onus is not on *me* to change. Instead it's the world around me.' She wants a complete transformation of Britain so that the structures which produced racism are torn down and destroyed, just as statues who commemorate the past should be taken down if the figure depicted was associated in any way with racism in his or her lifetime. But this is only one of many contemporary contributions on race in modern Britain.

Hashi Mohamed is a successful barrister who went from a struggling comprehensive school in north-west London to postgraduate studies at Oxford. He was born into a Muslim family in east Africa who suffered greatly from civil strife in Somalia and had to flee to Kenya. Hashi Mohamed has spent almost the whole of his life in Britain, where he has struggled with the 'tortuous process' of trying to forge an independent identity that bears little resemblance to what his mother expected of him. His father died before Hashi and his siblings arrived as refugees in Britain. Would a permanent settlement in Britain by refugees fleeing conflict be a betrayal of their country of origin, whose ravaged state needs the best and the brightest to return if peace and order are to be restored? These dilemmas cause friction between generations as teenagers try to forge their independent identity in Britain even as their parents insist children born in Britain were not born in their true 'home'. These difficulties are made worse by the 'insistent narrative' from the rest of society that, really, these young teenagers do not belong in Britain.[24] The anguish of this aspect of identity cannot be overstated, as the experience of going 'home' for a visit is often scarred by a feeling that you do not fit in there either. Hashi Mohamed's deeply felt descriptions about the real difficulties of identity are very different from the identity politics of Eddo-Lodge. He does not want to be identified as part of a specific racial group. He has not aspired to change the structures of society; instead he has opted to join them and, emphasising ambition and hard work, to 'integrate' in a way in which he can work and prosper, criticise, agitate for social mobility and campaign to reduce isolation within Muslim communities, as well as fasting at Ramadan and wearing Somali clothing when it suits him. These steps towards integration require a corresponding response from the host community.

Trevor Phillips is a former chairman of the Equality and Human Rights Commission and the Runnymede Trust who chaired the Equalities Review of 2007, which led to the Equality Act 2010. He believes there is now 'superdiversity' in modern Britain and that benevolent liberals have been 'slow to acknowledge the fact that race is no longer a purely black and white issue'. He stresses there are demonstrably different values and behaviours prevalent in many different ethnocultural communities. Unless British society acknowledges this, he says, we will 'sleepwalk to a catastrophe that will set community against community … reverse hard-won civil liberties, and undermine the liberal democracy that has served this country so well for so long'.[25] He believes there is a danger that British cultural institutions, like universities, charities, think tanks and the BBC, could collapse under the wake of 'wokeism' if they continue to pander to demands for gestures of solidarity for fear of being branded racist if they decline.[26]

The views of Trevor Phillips, Hashi Mohamed and Reni Eddo-Lodge are very different and in a mature democracy intelligent people often have very different opinions. It is entirely natural that three writers of colour disagree about race in modern Britain. Eddo-Lodge has a Nigerian mother; Phillips, a mother and father from British Guiana; Hashi Mohamed's Muslim family were raised in east Africa. They all represent a world where discussions about race involve an acceptance or rejection, whether implicitly or explicitly, of 'structural racism', 'intersectionality', 'superdiversity' and 'wokeism', the words that now routinely feature in discussions about race.

The views of Learie Constantine and the intentions of Parliament in 1965 seem a world away from the Britain we now inhabit, where even the existence of racial identity is a topic for debate and disagreement. But in another sense the origins of the individual's place within society are exactly the same. Learie Constantine's birth, upbringing and education took place in a society where the ruling elite in Trinidad was creole (white or mixed-race descendants of Europeans). He did not come to Britain until he was twenty-seven, and he returned to Trinidad twenty-six years later, where he became a Member of Parliament and government minister. He then came back to Britain in 1961 to take up the position of

High Commissioner for the newly independent Commonwealth state of Trinidad and Tobago. He died in London at the age of sixty-nine, two years after being honoured with a life peerage and a seat in the House of Lords. He was black *and* British. Learie Constantine's history was both Trinidadian and British, just as Eddo-Lodge's is both Nigerian and British, Phillips's West Indian and British and Hashi Mohamed's Somalian/Kenyan and British. The presence of all of them in Britain can be traced to the colonial remnants of the British Empire. All are proof of a fact of British history which is seldom appreciated or even admitted. Their Britishness arises from colonial history as well as birth and residence in Britain. As David Olusoga has put it, 'we are here because you were there'.

Black historians have now linked up some facts that white Britons have ignored for too long. Afua Hirsch has put it succinctly:

> British history is the multiracial, interracial story of a nation interdependent on trade, cultural influence and immigration from Africa, India, Central and East Asia, and other regions and continents populated by people who are not white, and before that, invasion by successive waves of European tribes most of whom, had the concept of whiteness existed at the time, would not have fitted into it either.[27]

The historian David Olusoga has made the same point very forcefully. There cannot be some artificial distinction between 'black' history and so-called mainstream history because, for one thing, interracial couples and mixed-race children in Britain have their history which cannot be compartmentalised into 'black' and 'white'. Olusoga fears we may develop a cultural blind spot if we are squeamish about discussing and revealing the truth about British slavery and the darker aspects of British imperialism.[28] What children need is the truth, the whole truth and nothing but the truth about Britain's participation in slavery and

Britain's colonial history. To be British in modern Britain may have involved a journey through parents and grandparents from the Indian subcontinent, Africa or the West Indies, places Britons in the colonial era regarded as British.

Race is history and legal cases about race are important parts of that history. Learie Constantine's legal challenge to the almost nonchalant resort to racism by the management of the Imperial Hotel is a historical event which shaped the course of future race relations in Britain. It helped map the journey towards legislation against discrimination. It is a historical event, not a black historical event. Race, and the place such a word occupies in our history and culture, does not have a single all-pervasive meaning. It conveys something that is elusive and whose meaning changes over time. The 1965 Race Relations Act seems nowadays as old-fashioned and remote as perhaps *Constantine v Imperial Hotels* will seem to the law student of modern times. But there is continuity and connection between Constantine's 1944 legal challenge and the debate and disagreements about race in society today, though the arena for the challenges has moved from the courtroom to the streets and to the libraries and laptops of sociologists and historians. The case of *Constantine v Imperial Hotels* should not be forgotten when the history of race in Britain is written. It was a seminal moment in our legal and political history and for that reason it should be remembered as one of the cases that made modern Britain.

Chapter 4

Power – The Pilot Officer and the Home Secretary

Power is necessary for the functioning of every society, but the instinct of humanity is not to create institutions of power which are absolute, permanent and immune from criticism. When these methods have been tried they have inevitably collapsed under the weight of their own contradictions. People invariably want power diffused. For Aristotle, this meant that power becomes a form of partnership, requiring deliberative, magisterial and judicial elements. In Britain the absolute power of the sovereign was formally curtailed in Magna Carta in 1215. Later, theories about the merits of power being legally separated were advanced by Locke and Montesquieu. But power is rarely equally distributed between the key elements of a modern state, the legislature, the executive and the judiciary. One element usually wields greater power than the other two, and modern Britain, from the 1940s until the present day, has been characterised by struggles over the strength each separate element of power should have over another. For the Victorian political theorist A. V. Dicey, the legislature was supreme, and therefore had greater power than the executive or the judiciary. For Walter Bagehot, another Victorian, power lay within Cabinet, a body which had executive functions but whose membership came from the legislature.

The judiciary has no control over money nor any democratic mandate and nobody suggests judicial power should be equal to either Parliament or the executive. The former has an electoral legitimacy and the latter has the administrative means to carry out the wishes of Parliament. However, without an element of judicial power within the constitution, the distribution of power is demonstrably uneven. Nowadays, we have become used to judges playing a role in defending liberties against an overweening executive and protecting the supremacy of Parliament from being sidelined by the growth of executive power. The evolution of judicial power has been a feature of modern Britain. It has come about gradually, but there is one legal case, in modern times, in which the potential power of the judiciary was pitted against the real power of a minister of the Crown in a stark and simple way. It concerned the liberty of the subject, a topic that historically has thrown up conflicts between the executive and the citizen. Robert Liversidge had been detained without trial under emergency powers introduced in 1940. He took action against the Home Secretary, John Anderson, alleging a civil wrong of false imprisonment. It was a case where the judges could have used their power to make it possible for Liversidge to succeed, depending on the facts, in his action against a government minister. They declined to do so, stopping the case at a preliminary stage before the facts could be ventilated before an impartial judge. Liversidge's case concerned the way in which the minister's decision to imprison a person without trial could be upheld legally. At the time, the early phase of the Second World War, such judicial timidity in the context of the perilous fight against Hitler was not unusual. What was unusual, remarkable and brave was the dissent of Lord Atkin, one of Britain's finest judges of the twentieth century. Lord Atkin described the decision of his brethren in the House of Lords as being 'more executive-minded than the executive'.[1] Lord Atkin's withering attack on his House of Lords colleagues was almost brutal in its dissection and demolition of their arguments, which upheld the Home Secretary's decision not to reveal to Liversidge the reasons he had for detaining him without trial. Nowadays, it is Lord Atkin's approach to judicial oversight over the legality of executive action which is followed by judges.

Robert William Liversidge, born Jacob Perlzweig in London in 1904, was the son of a rabbi who had fled Russia with his wife to make their home in England. Jacob's brother, Maurice, was also a rabbi and when war was declared in September 1939 he was on the executive committee of the World Zionist Federation and a founder member of the World Jewish Congress. It is beyond doubt that 'Jack' Perlzweig (as he was then known) was not a Nazi sympathiser. Having left school at fourteen, he became, in adult life, a successful businessman. By 1938, he was a director of the Allied General Investment Trust, a collecting company for oil royalties. He also had a substantial property portfolio.

In 1926, he was on friendly terms with a man called Dore Baumberg, who was convicted at the Old Bailey of fraudulently obtaining share certificates from a widow called Mrs Brett and sent to prison. It was suspected that this fraud was carried out by Dore and his brother David Baumberg, but David was acquitted. Perlzweig later admitted that he had disposed of the certificates on the open market although he did not know they had been obtained by fraud. The police believed he was involved in the original deception, but he was never put on trial, let alone arrested or questioned about this.

Perlzweig left London in 1927, believing that better business opportunities were available abroad. Among the people he met in America was a man called Schapiro who had apparently committed a share swindle in New York. There was a suggestion that Perlzweig may have been his accomplice, but he was never charged with any offence, nor did the Americans seek his extradition to stand trial once he had returned to

Britain. In California, he helped develop sound recording equipment for the Hollywood studios, which were then in transition from silent movies to the 'talkies'. Robert William Liversidge, as he was now known, made money. He went to Canada and continued to succeed in business, but by 1931 his British passport had expired and he needed a new one if he was to return to Britain.

He then made a serious and costly mistake which involved deceit. He applied for a Canadian passport, using the name by which he was known in the United States and Canada, Robert Liversidge, and falsely stated he had Canadian parentage and had been born in Toronto in 1901. These declarations were, of course, false, but he returned to Britain in 1936 on the Canadian passport. The following year, with the assistance of his solicitor, Lewis Silkin, he formally changed his name by deed poll to Robert William Liversidge. From that moment on, he was legally Robert Liversidge and all his company and personal business was conducted in that name. He was successful and rich. He was also patriotic. At the time of the Munich crisis in 1938, he mentioned at a family gathering that if ever war was to be declared he would be the first to volunteer. He did in fact volunteer for a commission in the RAF a few days after Germany invaded Poland on 1 September 1939. He was, on the face of it, a most unlikely candidate for internment under emergency wartime regulations on the grounds of 'hostile associations'. But this is exactly what happened in May 1940 after he had given eight months of unblemished service to his country as a commissioned officer in Fighter Command of the Royal Air Force. He was arrested, detained and not finally released until December 1941, by which time he had become an embarrassment to the authorities. The story of how Liversidge came to be detained in Brixton Prison for a period of eighteen months is shameful and reveals antisemitic prejudice which infected the view the authorities took of him.[2]

The tale begins in March 1940 when three alien detainees, all German Jews, were apparently planning to offer bribes to secure their release. For some reason Liversidge's business address cropped up in their plot. Liversidge was, in fact, never involved in this enterprise, nor was he ever accused of being part of it, but the alleged plot set in train the events which led to his arrest and detention. He was labelled, in MI5 files, 'an international crook who fled the country in 1927'. This is a reference to the Baumberg and Schapiro swindles for which he was never questioned or charged. However, by early April 1940 his telephone was being tapped on the grounds that he was believed to be 'connected with subversive activities to release aliens in internment camps'. When Special Branch informed MI5 that Liversidge was born Jacob Perlzweig, the authorities thought this was a discovery of great importance as it demonstrated that Robert Liversidge was an imposter. It was perfectly true he had previously been known as Perlzweig, but he was not a crook, nor was it necessarily a deception for Liversidge to use his adopted name, changed by deed poll, to apply to be a volunteer reserve pilot officer. However, for Special Branch and MI5, Liversidge was a suspicious individual who should be watched. His bank accounts were scrutinised, his house was searched, his personal correspondence was intercepted and his safe deposit box was opened, all under wartime warrants which permitted invasions to personal privacy 'for the purposes of defence of the realm and the efficient promotion of the war'. Nothing to Liversidge's detriment was discovered.

It was then, on 25 April, that a plot was hatched to entrap Pilot Officer Liversidge in order to have him detained under RAF disciplinary regulations. It was a cloak-and-dagger operation of the most disreputable kind. The authorities had got it into their heads that as Liversidge was a 'crook' and as he had possible access to sensitive material thanks to his RAF commission, he was a danger to Britain's war effort. A meeting was arranged between MI5 officers and the group captain who was Liversidge's commanding officer at RAF Uxbridge. A memorandum of the meeting states: 'It would be well if Liversidge could be placed under close arrest on a formal charge pending action between MI5 and Sir Norman Kendal [Assistant Commissioner at Scotland Yard] with a view to the internment of this man under the Defence Regulations. The RAF deputation agreed.' But what formal charge could possibly be laid against him justifying detention for breaching RAF rules? Reliance could not be placed on the application form to enlist as a volunteer officer, as he was not subject to service discipline at that time. During his eight months of service in Fighter Command doing sensitive night-time photographic work, his record was unimpeachable. This placed the authorities in a quandary. It is clear from the memorandum of the 25 April meeting that the minds of MI5 had already been made up. They wanted Liversidge interned, but how and on what grounds?

The entrapment operation was cunning and devious. By an oversight, Liversidge had omitted to state his next of kin on his application form to become a commissioned officer. Nobody had noticed this at the time. The ruse involved him being called in routinely to complete the form. As he had applied in the name of Liversidge with a date of birth in 1901 to match his Canadian passport, not 1904, he was obliged to state close relatives as Liversidges, which was naturally untrue as his father and brother were prominent Jews named Perlzweig. No sooner had Liversidge put pen to paper with the names of false relatives than he was put on a charge and detained under RAF regulations. He was subject to instant dismissal as an officer.

Liversidge elected to make a declaration of truth in a written statement even though he was under arrest and not obliged to say anything. He gave details of his movements in and out of the United Kingdom and continued, 'Since 1935 I have moved freely as Robert Liversidge. I changed my name officially by deed poll about five years ago and I had an attestation made by some persons who have known me as Liversidge for about ten years.' He went on to emphasise that he was a Jew, that Jewish people were being persecuted and that his reason for joining the RAF was 'to serve my country'. This clearly rattled the authorities. Sir Norman Kendal wrote to MI5 a few days later to say that 'unless you have enough on him to justify internment there is nothing which can be done by anybody except possibly the Air Force'.

Sir Norman Kendal's observations went unheeded by MI5, who were determined to see Liversidge's internment accomplished. On 4 May, the Director of Public Prosecutions contacted MI5 to say he was impressed by Liversidge's witness statement and on 11 May he gave a written opinion about the case. Sir Tindal Atkinson had been the DPP since 1930 and was a highly experienced lawyer. He pointed out that if the RAF selection board had placed serious reliance on the name Liversidge and were keen to establish his identity, it was surprising the Air Force had not sought police checks on whether the applicant had any other names. He added, 'In law a man's unsavoury past and even his present contacts, if provable, are not relevant to the only available charge.' This would have been a summary matter punishable with a maximum of three months' imprisonment, but the DPP added that with good testimonials Liversidge might only be bound over by the magistrate. Then, in a scribbled note, he gave MI5 this warning: 'Internment would be the only remedy for that and I fear this is a practical impossibility.'

This wise advice fell on deaf ears and an MI5 officer, Captain Stephens, then wrote a memorandum in which he stressed that Liversidge had obtained a commission by fraud and that he had an unsavoury police record. 'As to the DPP's counsel of caution, a principle is at stake and I fail to see why rottenness of procedure, apparently in existence in this country today, should affect the principle in any way.' Intelligence officers at MI5 were much more impressed by a letter written by Sir Archibald Sinclair, the recently promoted Minister for Air. Sinclair had written directly to his political colleague the Home Secretary John Anderson on 15 May asserting that it was 'most undesirable that a man with the unsavoury and indeed dangerous associations of Perlzweig, who has had access to information of a most secret character, should be left at large'. He also set out the options: the first was a prosecution on a 'trivial charge'; the second was surveillance by MI5, ruled out as a bad use of resources; and the third was internment.

Events now had their own momentum, which was pushing the authorities towards internment even though the grounds for doing so were flimsy. The alternatives were a charge, which the DPP had advised against, or release, which MI5 and the Air Ministry did not want. The succinct opinion from the Minister for Air was exactly what the intelligence community wanted to hear. Words of caution, provided by the Assistant Commissioner to the Metropolitan Police and the Director of Public Prosecutions, cut no ice with MI5. Officials at the Home Office had obtained a statement from the RAF group captain heading the interview board which had accepted Liversidge's application to join the RAF. The board had been impressed with Liversidge's business and administrative knowledge, his keenness and sense of drive and his 'social qualities'; however, a superior officer sent a supplementary statement declaring that had they known Liversidge had been born to a Russian rabbi, further enquiries would have been made about his identity. The suggestion that a Jew of Russian parentage might be unsuitable for war service was typical of the innate antisemitism of the time.

The intelligence services were obsessed with the idea that Liversidge had sought entry into the RAF by fraud. This was a complete misconception. He had changed his name from Perlzweig to Liversidge by deed poll in 1937 and this entitled him to use the name Liversidge on

his application to join the Volunteer Reserve. His experience in photographic matters put forward on the application form was perfectly
true, although to hide the fact he had left school at fourteen and to improve his chances of being selected as an officer he claimed to have had
a secondary education. There was nothing in any alleged unsavoury
background to suggest he was a security risk. On the contrary, he was a
principled anti-Nazi.

MI5 were scrabbling around to mount a case against him in the febrile atmosphere that was enveloping the country about a 'fifth column'
in our midst. In April, Germany had invaded Norway and the country
had been taken over by the Nazis without any noticeable resistance. An
American journalist based in Oslo wrote an article for the *Daily Telegraph* on 16 April 1940 claiming the Germans had only succeeded in
their invasion through a 'gigantic conspiracy' involving highly placed
Norwegian civilians who had, in some way, facilitated the German invasion. This claim is now discredited by historians, but at the time it was
taken extremely seriously in Britain. In May 1940, the Joint Intelligence
Committee, reporting to Cabinet, concluded that it was credible there
was a fifth column operating in Britain. This belief was reinforced the
following month when Hitler invaded Holland. Sir Nevile Bland, who
was Special Envoy to the Netherlands, prepared a long memorandum
for Winston Churchill, who had very recently succeeded Chamberlain
as Prime Minister, warning of the 'fifth column menace' in Holland.
There was little cogent evidence to support Bland's theories about
civilian Dutch Nazis helping Hitler's troops enter the Low Countries,
but the narrative was compelling and in Britain all the powers to round
up suspects were ready to be used. It only remained for Churchill and
the Cabinet to make a decision about how to combat the supposed fifth
column menace among the civilian population.

The Emergency Powers (Defence) Act 1939 had been passed in a single day by Parliament on 24 August 1939. The Act gave ministers wide powers to bring in regulations which, in addition to detention without trial, could limit industrial action, curtail freedom of speech and enlarge police powers of search and seizure. The regulation which enabled Liversidge, and many others, to be detained in prison without trial was the notorious Regulation 18B. It stated:

> If the Secretary of State has reasonable cause to believe any person to be of hostile origin or associations [the applicable words in Liversidge's case] ... and that by reason thereof it is necessary to exercise control over him, he may make an order against that person directing that he shall be detained.

By the time Liversidge's case came up for consideration, the Secretary of State was Sir John Anderson. A former colonial civil servant and a naturally cautious man, Anderson had urged restraint in Cabinet on the use of draconian powers. He was concerned that it would be counter-productive to intern every member of Oswald Mosley's organisation, the British Union of Fascists, unless there was good reason to believe specified individuals were assisting the enemy. But the mood in Cabinet and the country was not for restraint. Arrests under emergency powers began on 23 May 1940 and by the end of May over 400 detentions under Regulation 18B had been signed, of which sixty-nine related to native-born citizens of the United Kingdom.

Robert Liversidge fell into this category. On any view he was British and a Jew and most certainly not a supporter of Oswald Mosley. MI5 found themselves clutching at straws to make out a case against him, but they believed they had a new lead. They had discovered that in the 1930s a Dutch citizen by the name of Van Lighten had made an application to join the British security services and had named Liversidge as a referee. Van Lighten was suspected of being a spy and his application was refused. The link between Van Lighten and Liversidge was a business connected with diamonds. Van Lighten dealt in diamonds in Holland and Liversidge knew him in that capacity.

It was perfectly true that Liversidge had an interest in diamonds: in particular, he was interested in the design and manufacture of industrial diamonds. At that time, techniques for making industrial diamonds for use in precision engineering were being developed and it was not unlawful. A business associate of Liversidge called Nussbaum was apparently suspected of exporting industrial diamonds to Germany, which was prohibited under wartime regulations. Liversidge explained later that Nussbaum and a man called Marcus persuaded him to help them set up a company, the Carbonite Diamond Company, whose purpose was to produce industrial diamonds. But Liversidge had fallen out with his co-directors, Nussbaum and Marcus, which ended in litigation. Unfortunately for Liversidge, Marcus was a German national who had been interned as an alien at the outbreak of the war and Nussbaum was a suspected swindler. MI5 grabbed hold of these facts to build a case for Sir John Anderson to sign.

For them, an 'association' with Nussbaum and Marcus was the foundation of the case they were trying to construct. In relation to the diamond business, the Home Secretary was told 'it was highly probable this business was dishonest' even though there was no evidence it was. The 'statement of case' presented to the Home Secretary was, sad to say, a most unpersuasive document. For example, it stated: 'Having obtained a Commission by giving false particulars he is now an Intelligence Officer able to acquire information of a highly secret character.' As the DPP and Sir Norman Kendal had pointed out, it is far from clear that Liversidge gave false particulars *in order* to obtain a commission. He was using the name his deed poll legally gave him. His skills, acquired through business, were truthfully stated on his application form even if his educational qualifications were not. As to secret information, there is absolutely no evidence that he divulged anything sensitive while serving on Fighter Command. The statement of case then comments that Liversidge's record shows him to be 'completely unscrupulous'. This damaging assertion is not backed up by anything other than suspicion founded on the discredited rule of guilt by association. Nonetheless, the Home Secretary signed the following order: 'I have reason to believe Jack Perlzweig/Robert Liversidge to be a person of hostile associations and that by reason thereof it is necessary to exercise control over him … In pursuance of Regulation 18B I direct the above mentioned … be detained.'

With Sir John Anderson's detention order in their hands, Liversidge was taken from his confinement at RAF Uxbridge on 30 May 1940 to Brixton Prison, where he remained for the next eighteen months. He immediately gave notice of his objection to his detention, as he was entitled to do under Regulation 18B. His objections are heart-rending. 'I must personally state', he wrote,

> it is fantastic that a person in my position (a Jew, a serving member of HM Forces and a person controlling some £180,000 of houses in London) should be detained. If (God Forbid) we should lose the war, not only would I lose everything I possess, but my life would most certainly be at an end because of my family, my father and brother both being Jewish Rabbis.

He then requested an early hearing before the advisory committee. This body, created under emergency powers, was informal and inquisitorial, but it enabled detainees to make representations against their detention.

Liversidge's detention was intensely uncomfortable. In August

1940, his solicitor wrote to the Home Office to say that Liversidge was surrounded by Nazi sympathisers in prison, also detained under the emergency regulations, and the experience was making him unwell. Liversidge did, in fact, have to undergo medical treatment during his detention. At this point Norman Birkett KC entered the case; he would go on to play a very important part in the whole Liversidge saga. Birkett was one of the most formidable advocates of his generation and a well-known personality as so many of his cases were reported in the newspapers. He would shortly become a High Court judge and he was highly regarded for his qualities of impartiality and objectivity. He had been appointed to chair the committee and he sat with two colleagues, military men who had served their country in the First World War. Fortunately, a transcript of Liversidge's hearing before the committee in October 1940 survives. The proceedings were entirely inquisitorial and Liversidge was not allowed legal representation, but Birkett, as would be expected, presided with scrupulous fairness.

Liversidge gave full explanations about his associations with the Baumberg brothers, Schapiro, Nussbaum, Van Lighten and Marcus. He submitted a reference from a senior RAF officer who served alongside him, who stated that Liversidge was 'very definitely' opposed to the present German regime, and others from former business associates, including a retired lieutenant colonel, who stated that Liversidge's loyalty was not in doubt.

The secretary to the committee had been warned in advance that Liversidge's case was a sensitive one. The committee's detailed reasons for their decision were sent to the Home Office in November. In essence, the committee had put off a final decision as Birkett felt they did not have sufficient information about Liversidge's past business dealings. He advised that Lewis Silkin be given an opportunity to demonstrate that past business affairs should not be seen 'as a skeleton hanging round his neck', thereby demonstrating there was no 'ulterior motive' in Liversidge's decision to volunteer for military duties. Towards the end of the hearing, Birkett commented, 'You have had a long detention and nobody regrets it more than we do.'

The committee did not recommend his release at this stage, as the RAF had made it abundantly clear that on security grounds he should remain in detention. But the committee were clearly troubled about the reasons why Liversidge was detained. Birkett reported:

> The nature of this case is plainly one of very peculiar character. The grounds upon which the order was made were that Liversidge was a person of hostile associations ... After a full examination of the evidence it appears this ground is really difficult to substantiate. The real ground would appear to be that Liversidge is a rather unscrupulous character who will not hesitate to deceive where his own interests were concerned and as he used a deception to obtain a Commission he is not a man whose loyalty can be trusted ... The Committee has no reason to suppose that whatever information he had as an Officer he would use it in order to injure this country.

The committee recommended continued detention for the time being, with the proviso that they would return to the case at a later date. Liversidge had reason for optimism. Not only might he soon be recommended for release when the committee read the files on his business dealings; he had been advised by solicitors that he might succeed if he took a legal case against the Home Secretary, Sir John Anderson, for false imprisonment. He therefore issued a writ against Anderson in March 1941. By now, Herbert Morrison had succeeded Anderson as Home Secretary, but D. N. Pritt QC, whom Liversidge's solicitors had instructed, had advised that it was the individual who had signed the warrant for detention who should be sued.

For the next nine months there was a flurry of activity involving lawyers as well as senior personnel in the RAF and the intelligence services. While Liversidge's action against the Home Secretary was wending its way through the courts, an intelligence officer noted, in an internal memorandum in April 1941, that evidence of hostile associations was not very strong and that the real reason Liversidge had been detained was that 'the RAF wished to get rid of him and have him detained as he was an untrustworthy person with a very bad character'. This was, of course, the clear view of Sir Archibald Sinclair, but RAF objections, in themselves, would not have been sufficient to make a case for the Home Secretary to order detention without trial. Liversidge had been detained as a result of the MI5 representations, not those only of the RAF. When Norman Birkett began reconsidering the case in July, there was something of a panic within MI5. It was beginning to dawn on them that they really did not have anything very incriminating against Liversidge. Responsibility for his detention, the lawfulness of which Liversidge was challenging, was shifted to the RAF. The Air Ministry were asked by MI5 whether it was really any longer necessary for Liversidge to be detained. Surely any secret information he may have acquired a year earlier would now be stale? Pressure was now mounting within the intelligence services, for whom Liversidge's continued detention had become something of an embarrassment. Unfortunately for MI5, the reply from the Air Ministry could not have been more emphatic. 'Liversidge is, as you know, an international crook and the functioning of the Operations Room, of which he had knowledge, has not changed. His release should be opposed.'

In November, when Liversidge's resumed hearing before the now elevated Mr Justice Birkett was imminent, Captain Watson at MI5 recorded a minute stating that Liversidge was originally detained 'at the instance of the Air Ministry as he succeeded in falsifying his papers and getting a senior position in Fighter Command'. This, of course, was patently untrue. MI5 had themselves wanted Liversidge detained. By this time MI5 were anticipating that Birkett would order his release. Then at last, on 2 December, just two days before the resumed advisory committee hearing, the Air Ministry conceded there was now no objection to Liversidge being released.

The resumed hearing on 4 December was something of a formality. By now, the committee had voluminous material on Liversidge's business dealings. There was nothing to his detriment in any of them. At the end of the hearing, Mr Justice Birkett commented, 'I have assumed you are heart and soul with the British cause? I have never had any reason to doubt it myself.' The report of the committee's conclusions, sent to the Home Office, was even more forthright. It stated:

> They [the committee] always entertained the gravest doubt whether his detention on the grounds of hostile associations could ever be substantiated, but now that the real reason for the detention is removed it is obvious that the only course before the Advisory Committee is to recommend immediate release ... The committee have never entertained any doubt about the essential loyalty of Liversidge.

The report then recommended:

> Full consideration ought to be given to the question of Liversidge's restoration to the Air Force ... If this is not possible the committee would be glad to see him being employed in some capacity that would be suitable

for his abilities and specialised knowledge and where his undoubted desire to help the country might have full scope.

Liversidge remained in prison for another three weeks after this devastating conclusion reached the Home Office. It was on Christmas Eve 1941 that Herbert Morrison, Anderson's successor, revoked Liversidge's detention order. Once released, Liversidge sought meetings with the Home Office to try to ascertain why he had been detained. In February 1942, he was told that such a meeting would serve no useful purpose. The policy of the Home Office had been clear since March 1941, when officials were informed that Sir John Anderson was being sued for false imprisonment. A memorandum in March 1941 noted, 'It was not the custom to add anything to the reasons contained in the order for detention.'

It was this custom that presented the obstacle to Liversidge and his legal team. The warrant Sir John Anderson had signed did not provide any reasons. The reasons, such as they were, had been provided by MI5 and these were flimsy to say the least. Liversidge was obviously not allowed access to security services material. The legal case that Liversidge had started in March 1941 was now stalled in tactical confrontations in the High Court. English law required that Liversidge, as the claimant, should set out in court pleadings (written documents) the substance of his case. This he was unable to do other than to assert that Anderson had 'procured his unlawful detention'. Anderson, for his part, admitted he had ordered Liversidge's detention under Regulation 18B but did not admit anything else. It was stalemate. Neither side put forward any facts to back up their respective cases; Liversidge because he was unable to, and Anderson because he did not want to. There then followed a procedural skirmish which went to the House of Lords as a preliminary point to the real issue in the case, which was *why* Liversidge had been detained. Liversidge wanted to know why Anderson had kept him in Brixton Prison for eighteen months, and Anderson did not want to tell him.

Liversidge's lawyers sought a court order requiring the Home Secretary to provide particulars in writing of the grounds upon which Anderson had reasonable cause to believe Liversidge was a person of hostile associations. The detention was only lawful if Anderson did have a reasonable cause to believe in the state of affairs which justified the use of draconian powers given to him by the Emergency Powers (Defence) Act 1939. The wording was important as the regulation had originally been drafted to allow the Home Secretary to use draconian powers if he was 'satisfied' that detention was required. A group of MPs, led by Dingle Foot, who became Solicitor General some years later, had persuaded the government to amend the regulation so it specified that the Secretary of State had to have 'reasonable cause to believe' detention should be authorised on the grounds specified in Regulation 18B. The amended regulation was in force at the time Liversidge's order was signed.[3]

The preliminary clashes were therefore of great importance. Was it enough that the Secretary of State *thought* he had reasonable cause to believe Liversidge had hostile associations and therefore had to be detained, or was it necessary that the Secretary of State should *actually have* reasonable cause to believe Liversidge had hostile associations? Despite the choice appearing to be obstruse and technical, it was, in fact, of huge significance. It went to the heart of a constitutional question of how power could be used and how an abuse of power could be restrained. The Home Secretary had the power, there was no doubt about that; Parliament had given the power to him – but what if he abused it? Who would and could guard against that? The answer to that question engages acute and vital consideration of constitutional principles. If, in a situation of this sort, a member of the executive could deploy power if he *believed* he had reasonable cause to deploy it then English law could refuse any claimant, Liversidge included, the right to have disclosed to him the grounds giving rise to the belief. If, on the other hand, a member of the executive had actually to *have* reasonable grounds for exercising a power, then it gave power to a court of justice to investigate whether reasonable grounds for belief existed. In a nutshell, Liversidge had initiated a power struggle between the executive and the judges.

Four of the five Law Lords who heard the case in the House of Lords in November 1941 found against Liversidge. They, like the Court of Appeal before them and a High Court judge before them, had the job of deciding what the words 'had reasonable cause to believe' meant in law. Lord Maugham said that if the Home Secretary was required to reasonably believe something which was within the knowledge of that individual then the words 'had reasonable cause to believe' only required that individual to act on what he thought was a reasonable cause. If Anderson possessed information which he thought provided him with a reasonable cause for detaining Liversidge then there was nothing Liversidge could do about it. The only way Liversidge could succeed would be if he could demonstrate Anderson was not acting in good faith. Liversidge did not make this claim. Maugham was supported by three other Law Lords who each reflected a view of judicial respect for executive action that had existed since the 1914–18 war. During that conflict, the Lord Chief Justice, Lord Reading, had said, 'It is of course always to be assumed that the executive will act honourably and that its powers will be reasonably exercised.' A. W. Brian Simpson has called this outlook 'the Reading presumption of executive innocence'.[4] This attitude was expressly adopted in the speech of Lord Wright, who said German methods of poisonous infiltration among British subjects were immensely more subtle and ingenious than in the previous war.

'Even a judge', he said, 'may be allowed to take notice of the words Fifth Columnists and Quislings.' It is not clear whether he meant that Liversidge's mind, as a British subject, had been poisonously infiltrated by German propaganda or whether he was, in Lord Wright's opinion, a fifth columnist.

The only Law Lord who disagreed with the Reading presumption of executive innocence was Lord Atkin. His speech (the word used for judgment if delivered by the judicial committee of the House of Lords) can only be described as a forensic masterpiece. Atkin's central point was that the regulation contained plain words that could only have one meaning. Atkin used logic, legal learning and a highly developed command of language to demolish the arguments of his brethren. He posed this question: If the Secretary of State (A) has reasonable cause to believe (X), what is meant by that statement? He asserted, and this is difficult if not impossible to contradict, that X is the condition of something the existence of which can be ascertained. So, if a man has a broken ankle, the fractured ankle does not exist just because the human brain of the individual believes his ankle is broken. The existence of the broken ankle is the condition giving rise to the reasonable cause for the individual to believe he needs medical attention. Atkin then asserted that, as a matter of logic, 'reasonable cause for an action or belief is just as much a positive fact capable of determination by a third party as is a broken ankle'.

Atkin went on to demonstrate that over many years and in many legal cases judges had adopted this objective meaning to the words 'reasonable cause to believe'. In the law of arrest, for example, a constable has to have reasonable cause to believe the suspect has committed an offence for the arrest to be lawful. If a suspect challenges the lawfulness of his arrest in court, the judge must decide, objectively, whether the condition for the constable's reasonable belief existed. The judge does not necessarily have to have the same reasonable belief as the constable. The judge is concerned about whether the conditions for the constable forming his belief existed. Atkin's unparalleled legal learning alluded to numerous examples over the years in which the courts had given an objective meaning to the words adopted in the regulation.

The conclusion Atkin arrived at is now famous as a *cri de coeur* for judicial oversight over executive action.

> I view with apprehension the attitude of judges who, on a mere question of construction, when face to face with claims involving the liberty of the subject, show themselves more executive-minded than the executive. Their function is to give words their natural meaning ... In this country, amid the clash of arms, the laws are not silent. They may be changed, but they speak the same language in war as in peace ... In this case I have listened to arguments which might have been addressed acceptably to the Court of King's Bench in the time of Charles I.
>
> I protest, even if I do it alone, against a strained construction put on words with the effect of giving uncontrolled power of imprisonment to the minister ... I know of only one authority which might justify the suggested method of construction. 'When I use a word,' Humpty Dumpty said in a rather scornful tone, 'it means just what I choose it to mean, neither more nor less.' 'The question is,' said Alice, 'whether you can make the words mean so many different things.' 'The question is,' said Humpty Dumpty, 'which is to be master – that's all.' After all this long discussion the question is whether the words 'if a man has' can mean 'if a man thinks he has'. I am of the opinion that they cannot, and that the case should be decided accordingly.

This passage is one of the most excoriating attacks by one senior judge on his colleagues that has ever been uttered in English legal history.

It caused a storm that went far beyond the hallowed chamber of the House of Lords. Lord Atkin himself wondered, in a letter to his daughter, whether he would remain on speaking terms with his colleagues afterwards.[5] His speech ruffled the wigs of many senior members of the profession. The Lord Chancellor, who had seen a draft of the speech, tried to prevail upon Atkin to take out the Lewis Carroll bits. Atkin refused. The press had a field day and sides were taken, for or against Atkin, and the correspondence column of *The Times* printed letters in support of or opposition to Atkin's analysis and strongly expressed legal conclusion.

There is little doubt that *Liversidge v Anderson* was one of the legal cases that made modern Britain, not because of the wisdom of four Law Lords, three members of the Court of Appeal and one High Court judge who were all content to draw a veil over judicial control over executive power. The case was important because of the dissenting speech of Lord Atkin, a colossus of the legal world in the 1930s and 1940s, whose dissent could not be shrugged off. Atkin had shone a light into the darker recesses of the British constitution, but it took time for people to recognise what Atkin's beam had exposed. Legal, political and academic opinion were so well versed in the theories of Dicey, Bagehot and Erskine May, Victorian figures each of them, that it was generally accepted that power lay in the Palace of Westminster or around the Cabinet table in Downing Street. Few politicians and civil servants were willing to concede any power to the judges, and the judiciary for their part were willing to abide by this state of affairs. In Liversidge's case, one of the judges, Lord Wright, articulated this attitude of mind succinctly. 'In this country', he said, 'there are no guaranteed or absolute rights. The safeguard of British liberty is in the good sense of the people and in the system of representative and responsible government which has evolved.'

Judicial oversight of executive power granted to ministers or civil servants by Parliament was not considered to be a proper function of the courts. Lord Evershed, appointed Master of the Rolls in 1949, had prepared a memorandum for the Lord Chancellor in 1950 asserting that the protection of the individual *against* the state could easily be overrated.[6] Evershed was particularly proud of the fact that the judiciary had kept out of politics between 1945 and 1950 and had not attempted to sabotage the social welfare legislation of Attlee's Labour government. Anthony King has suggested that this period of judicial restraint lasted from 1945 until 1970, when 'the judiciary was at most a twig of government, never a branch'.[7] When Anthony Sampson wrote the first edition of his famous *Anatomy of Britain* in 1962, he identified the principal sources of power in Britain as being in the Palace, Parliament and the Cabinet. The law, he observed, was 'trapped in conservatism and mystique' and the protected world of lawyers had become increasingly irrelevant to the great corporate world outside.[8]

The irrelevance of judges to the distribution of power in Britain during and after the Second World War was summed up by the great constitutional expert Sir William Wade, who said in the period after the war 'a deep gloom' had settled on administrative law and that judges had little stomach for imposing law on government.[9] Then, gradually, change began to emerge. When government decisions became more intrusive into the lives of citizens and the exercise of public power became a feature of public life, a system of tribunals was created to arbitrate when an individual was affected by a public policy decision in planning, housing, tax or a host of other activities. The question then arose, in the late 1950s, about whether these tribunals were an extension of an administrative function or whether they resembled a judicial role. Sir Oliver Franks, a former diplomat and scholar, was asked to study this question and he concluded, unequivocally, that the creation of tribunals could not oust the jurisdiction of the ordinary courts in overseeing the legality of their work.

At the same time, judges were becoming more creative in their interpretation of statutes and were looking behind the words in an Act of Parliament to divine what Parliament's intention had been in passing a piece of legislation. But progress was in fits and starts. When Lord Justice Denning said, in 1952, that judges should not put an 'ultra-legal interpretation' on words in a statute if the result caused obvious injustice, he was given a stinging rebuke by the Lord Chancellor, Lord Simonds, who said it was not the law of England for courts to try to divine the intention of Parliament. He deplored the notion that judges could usurp the supremacy of Parliament.[10]

It was Denning, however, who was pointing the way forward and Simonds who was the voice of the past. Denning had grasped that judges had a role to play in protecting the rights of individuals against overweening power in the executive. This is exactly what Lord Atkin was saying in his dissenting speech in *Liversidge v Anderson*. It took more than twenty years, however, for Lord Atkin's view that judges must have a role in curbing abuse of power to take hold. Atkin had revealed a void within the constitution which Dicey had overlooked. A. V. Dicey's *An Introduction to the Study of the Law of the Constitution* was first published in 1885 and went into eight editions during his lifetime, the last in 1915. His descriptions of how the British constitution worked assumed a status of infallibility for generations of lawyers and politicians for a period of at least sixty years from the end of the nineteenth century onwards. Dicey's clear view was that citizens themselves did not possess inalienable rights which were beyond the power of Parliament to abrogate. Dicey maintained that Parliament alone could ensure liberty flourished, as everything was permitted unless Parliament prohibited it. Dicey, however, was writing at a time when the House of Lords had equal supremacy with the Commons. When, after 1911, the House of Commons became all-powerful and the complexities of modern life meant ministers had significant discretionary powers, the balance of power in the constitution shifted and it became necessary for the courts to assume a more active role in protecting the individual citizen against the power wielded by the executive. The chamber of the House of Commons was not full of independent-minded people who held the executive to account. The majority of its members were tied to the party line, which itself was defined and controlled by the governing party. Opposition parties in Parliament had no power. It took time for this change in the balance of power to be fully realised, but the role Lord Atkin played in identifying it cannot be overstated.

By the mid-1960s, the changes in power distribution in Britain were explicitly acknowledged in a case about the price of milk.[11] At that time, milk prices were set by the Milk Marketing Board, a body set up by government in 1933 to control the price producers should receive. The board set a price depending on the region in which each individual dairy farmer worked. Every farmer in a designated region received the regional price, but there was a price differential within the United Kingdom as a whole. The differential existed to acknowledge the extra costs involved in distribution and this resulted in a large differential existing between farmers in the far west of England and those in the south-eastern region. Farmers in the south-east could not get the differential changed by a decision of the board because their region never had a majority. However, Parliament had provided in 1958 that if a region had a complaint about the differentials set by the board, the minister could appoint an independent committee to consider the complaint. Farmers in the south-eastern region requested their complaint be referred to the committee, but the minister refused.

The question posed in the case was whether the discretion of a

minister to refer a complaint to a committee could be challenged judicially. The traditional view had always been that if a minister of the
Crown was given a discretion to act in one way or another by Parliament then the courts ought not to become embroiled. The minister had
decided not to set up a committee because the complaint would have
consequences for the entire milk industry. If the differential was altered
for the south-east, there would be a knock-on effect on everybody. The
ultimate decision, therefore, was a political balancing exercise of power
which was not a matter for the courts. The House of Lords, in their judicial capacity, disagreed. Parliament had allowed an appeal to an independent committee if it was not obviously frivolous, and this grievance
was clearly genuine. The fact that the decision of the committee might
have a consequential effect on other regions was irrelevant. The *reasons*
given by the minister for refusing to refer the grievance to the committee
were subject to judicial review. This case was one of the first examples
of the courts examining with care the use of executive power even if it
appeared that the executive had complete discretion about how such
power should be exercised.

As time went by, the judges became more confident about their
review of the use of power held by government ministers, officials acting
on behalf of ministers and local authorities. On this, public opinion was
generally on the side of the judges as more and more people became
aware that an arbitrary exercise of power was not necessarily the last
word on the subject. The courts provided a pathway to challenge decisions which had apparently been taken by some remote, anonymous
official but which had huge consequences for the individuals affected.

By the early 1980s, the power of Lord Atkin's reasoning in *Liversidge
v Anderson* was taking hold among Britain's senior judiciary. In 1980,
the House of Lords explicitly admitted, in a case about the powers of
the Inland Revenue, that 'the time has come to acknowledge openly that

the majority of this House in *Liversidge v Anderson* were expediently and, at that time, perhaps, excusably, wrong and the dissenting speech of Lord Atkin was right'.[12] The influence of Lord Atkin's broad approach to the importance of liberty even at times of national emergency was vividly illustrated in a modern case about the rule of law in the face of terrorism.

Ever since the atrocities of 9/11 in New York and Washington, the world has been living under the shadow of unpredictable and menacing outrages by terrorist warriors. Many governments in the world, the United Kingdom included, introduced emergency legislation to suspend some democratic norms protecting the liberty of citizens in the face of likely terrorist attacks on the fabric of democracy itself. In Britain, one of the responses to the threat posed by terrorists was to introduce legislation to allow power to be used to pre-emptively detain, without trial, suspected foreign terrorist suspects resident in this country. Just as in wartime, judges had to interpret legislation – in this case the Anti-Terrorism Crime and Security Act 2001. The climate for this task was now less frosty than in wartime Britain of 1941. Not only had judicial scrutiny of the use of power developed in ways Lord Atkin probably would not have predicted; Britain now had a Human Rights Act. The House of Lords had to rule on the lawfulness of the detention in Belmarsh Prison of a number of foreign detainees who could not be deported as they would face torture on their return but who could not be put on trial in a criminal court as the evidence against them was of a sensitive national security character. Their fate was to remain in custody indefinitely without being put on trial.

The Belmarsh case had many similarities with Robert Liversidge's, but the reasoning of the House of Lords came straight from Lord Atkin and owed nothing to the judges who had supported Liversidge's detention. The Lords decided that detention without trial was 'the stuff of nightmares' and the legislation that permitted it was incompatible with liberties protected by the European Convention on Human Rights. The use of executive power had gone too far.[13] The government climbed down and replaced detention without trial with a regime of 'control orders' in the Prevention of Terrorism Act 2005. Under this Act, the Home Secretary could impose severe restrictions on the movement and activities of suspected terrorists without confining them to a closed prison. The House of Lords later ruled the use of this power was compatible with the European Convention on Human Rights.

The changes to the balance of power in the constitution of the United Kingdom since Lord Atkin's speech in *Liversidge v Anderson* have been remarkable. When Anthony Sampson first looked for sources of power in Britain in 1962, he paid little attention to judges, who were irrelevant to any consideration of that question. Judges did their own thing in their own courtrooms and were noticed only when one of them said something spectacularly stupid about modern life. Forty-two years later, when he updated his *Anatomy of Britain* in 2004, he concluded that the public now looked to judges as the ultimate safeguard of their liberties and they looked to the law to protect them from the overbearing actions of governments.[14] He had in mind the developments alluded to in this chapter. Anthony King has noted that in contemporary Britain, judges 'have become part of the ongoing cacophony of British public life'.[15] The changes in the distribution of power within Britain has been achieved by judges themselves, to whom the public have turned when faced with unjust and unreasonable use of power by those in authority. It is now an established fact of legal and political life in Britain that judges have a role in providing a check on the power of the state.

The gradual change whereby the senior judiciary became assertive and not quiescent in their attitude towards those wielding power owes much to the forthright speech of Lord Atkin in *Liversidge v Anderson*.

All the judges who heard the case gave their ruling without having any knowledge of the facts that lay behind Liversidge's complaint. Now that the flimsy grounds for the ruthless pursuit of him as a person having 'hostile associations' are known, the speech of Lord Atkin is all the more impressive even though it played no part in achieving his release. Sir Norman Birkett had a more substantial role in that than the judges in the ordinary courts because he had access to some of the facts. We now know from information that has emerged from the archives that even in the exigencies of wartime Liversidge should not have been detained. Writing in 1992, before the release of MI5 files on the case, A. W. Brian Simpson concluded that the detention of Liversidge came close to a decision being made in bad faith.[16] We can now conclude that, regrettably and shamefully, it was most definitely a decision made in bad faith. Had the majority of the House of Lords sided with Lord Atkin, the result of the procedural clash would have been different. They would have ruled that a burden lay on the Home Secretary to reveal the circumstances which gave rise to a reasonable belief on his part that Liversidge should be detained. He would probably not have attempted to do so and Liversidge's civil action would have been settled with damages paid to Liversidge to compensate him for having been falsely imprisoned.

The story did not quite end with his release in December 1941. By March 1942, Liversidge's file was still open and a security officer commented, 'Liversidge is of no great security interest. He was interned largely because after he obtained a Commission in the Air Force by false pretences, he came into possession of secret information and he could not be trusted not to impart it to others.' But, as Sir Norman Birkett had discovered when he scrutinised Liversidge's business affairs, there was nothing remotely untrustworthy about the way Liversidge had conducted himself. Despite complete exoneration before the adjourned hearing of the advisory committee, prejudice against Liversidge persisted. In

January 1943, Liversidge set up a company called Albemarle Productions with the object of providing 'theatrical shows' to the troops, but the War Office were soon to raise objections. In March 1943, a memorandum stated that 'it was undesirable for a company run by a man like Liversidge to exhibit theatrical shows to camps with the blessing of the War Office'. Without War Office support, the project was doomed. Despite this setback Liversidge's business ventures flourished after the war ended in 1945 and he lived for another forty-nine years, becoming extremely wealthy in his life after internment. He continued to maintain his imprisonment had been malicious, but, of course, his ability to argue this in a court of law had been denied to him by the majority in the House of Lords. By taking on the power and authority of the Home Secretary, Robert Liversidge did lasting service to the law of England and Wales. His persistence and courage in pursuing his claim as far as the House of Lords enabled Lord Atkin to deliver one of the most powerful judgments on the potential dangers of unlimited executive power that has ever been delivered by an English judge. Atkin, like Liversidge himself, was a 'loser' in the legal sense that he could not persuade his colleagues in the House of Lords that his judgment was correct, but he made his mark in the development of English law in a way that the other judges who disagreed with him dared not do. Between them, Robert Liversidge and Lord Atkin have left an indelible mark on the progress of English law in curbing the misuse of power.

Chapter 5

Free Speech – The Thalidomide Scandal

Free speech is one of the most precious but also one of the most abused features of modern democracy. Exercising free speech is essential to being a rational agent with the ability to express facts and opinions to others. It is imperative also that those receiving the words of others are able to preserve their dignity and autonomy by not being violated by harmful speech. These tensions thrown up by the exercise of free speech are often highly charged and difficult to reconcile. As Timothy Garton Ash observed in 2016, 'Never in human history was there such a chance for freedom of expression as this. And never in human history have the evils of unlimited free expression – death threats, paedophile images, sewage-tides of abuse – flowed so easily across frontiers.'[1] The internet and social media have torn up old rules and assumptions about how free speech is exercised. In academia, debates about 'no-platforming', 'safe spaces', 'viewpoint diversity' and 'trigger warnings' have become heated and intolerant, to say nothing of the vitriol which accompanies any discussion of transgender rights. A whole new vocabulary encompassing 'cyberbullying', 'trolling' and 'virtual mobbing' has grown up just in order to have a free speech debate. The boundaries of free speech that a regulator, a censor, a vice-chancellor, a prosecutor or a judge might draw up are often difficult to predict.

The backdrop to the intense debate which is now happening began when the *Sunday Times* took on a powerful drugs company to tell the truth about a medical disaster, known as thalidomide, in the 1960s and 1970s. The *Sunday Times* had to shatter a few ingrained assumptions within the British establishment to allow press freedom to flourish in the way it should. In doing so, the newspaper pursued a series of legal challenges through the courts and made the thalidomide case a *cause célèbre*.

In the 1960s, free speech was much easier to understand. It was a right which mainly benefited print or broadcast journalism, the latter then confined to the BBC and a fledgling independent television channel. The law had little part to play except that judges kept a tight rein on discussion about anything that was pending decision in the law courts, lest comment was in contempt of court. Libel laws existed to protect the reputation of the wealthy. The thalidomide scandal forced Parliament to make a change to the law after the *Sunday Times* took their argument about free speech to the European Court of Human Rights. Forty-three years later, the landscape is completely different. Outlets for the exercise of free speech are plentiful. On the one hand, judges have become engaged in upholding the rights of a minority to express views a majority may find wholly unacceptable, while on the other, Parliament is involved in regulating free speech in places of higher education and preventing the dissemination of harmful material on the internet. When the thalidomide scandal unfolded, judges did not consider protecting free speech was part of their job. Now, judges have been drawn into the modern debate about free speech.

Free speech is now a complex subject where duties and responsibilities become intertwined with freedom and rights. The thalidomide scandal, and the truth the *Sunday Times* wanted to tell about it, is the story of many thousands of grossly malformed children who were born in forty-six countries after their pregnant mothers took a drug to help morning sickness. It is a story of cover-up and medical catastrophe. But it is also a story about freedom of speech in which the *Sunday Times* challenged conventional beliefs about laws on contempt of court in Britain to give voice to the parents of thalidomide victims. These parents were toiling entirely alone to obtain compensation for their children. They were up against the might of a giant company, Distillers, who had made and distributed thalidomide in the United Kingdom and who steadfastly refused to accept they were at fault in putting a dangerous drug on the market. The *Sunday Times* fought for the right to use free speech principles to publicise the plight of hundreds of children who were born with huge disabilities because their mothers had taken thalidomide. The *Sunday Times* wanted to get to the truth of how the disaster happened. Harold Evans, the paper's editor, gave advance notice of what his investigative reporters intended to say in criticism of Distillers. This courtesy was used by the company to obtain an injunction to stop the investigations being made public. After Britain's highest court sided with the drug company, the editor took the case to the European Court at Strasbourg, where he won. The result was far-reaching. The *Sunday Times* exposed the dereliction of duty by Distillers in distributing a dangerous drug, succeeded in putting pressure on Distillers to make proper compensation for the children and persuaded Parliament to change English law and establish freedom of speech as a core component of a liberal democracy.

The story begins in the mid-1950s in West Germany. Thalidomide was the chemical invention of a German scientist who was head of research at Grünenthal GmbH, a company based in Aachen, in 1954. In 1957, the drug was marketed as Contergan, suitable for mothers sedating their infants and for pregnant women who suffered from morning sickness. The company ran advertisements in medical journals pronouncing the new drug 'completely safe'.[2] However, no sooner had the drug been available for general use in West Germany and Switzerland than a problem was spotted. A West German doctor had noticed that some elderly patients who had taken Contergan for their conditions experienced giddiness and slight disturbance to their balance. A Swiss doctor had noticed similar effects when his patients' hands trembled after Contergan had been taken. Doctors suspected the drug was a contributory cause of polyneuritis, or peripheral neuritis: damage to the peripheral nervous system. Doctors were now urgently pleading with the authorities in Germany that the apparently 'completely safe' new drug should be available only on prescription.

The Distillers Company in Great Britain had its origins in the Scotch whisky business. It began as a trade association for distillery and became involved in drug production by pure good fortune. Experience of the distillation process enabled the company to manufacture penicillin on behalf of the Ministry of Supply in 1942 at one of the Ministry's factories near Liverpool. Penicillin, then a new drug, was vital in the treatment of injured combatants in the Second World War. The Scotch whisky company was offered the factory cheaply by the government at the end of the war, and a new era for Distillers began. They formed a new company, Distillers Company (Biochemicals) Ltd, known as DCBL, and went into drug production. In this industry it was often cheaper to buy the rights of a drug already developed than to embark on a synthesising process from scratch. On this business model, DCBL became very interested in what Grünenthal GmbH were doing in Germany.

In 1957, after short negotiations, DCBL entered an agreement with Grünenthal to set up a mutual exchange of new drug discoveries by each company free of royalties. In the case of thalidomide, DCBL could begin marketing it in Great Britain within nine months of the agreement. At that time there was no uniform system for the licensing of new drugs in the UK. The Committee on the Safety of Drugs, created to raise the red flag for possibly unsafe drugs, was not in place until 1963. In the 1950s, DCBL saw their chance to apply their own sleek marketing to the hard work of synthesising that had already been done in Germany. DCBL could not believe their luck. They were looking to make millions if their new drug, under the trade name Distaval, could be made available throughout Great Britain as a sedative and sleeping pill, billed as a non-toxic alternative to barbiturates, which had caused deaths among a few users. Around the world, more than thirty other drug companies were doing the same.

Unfortunately, although DCBL intended Distaval to be used by all women, including those who were pregnant, no clinical trials on animals who were pregnant had been carried out either in Germany or by DCBL. Distillers relied on the drug testing Grünenthal had undertaken, which had included tests on nursing mothers but not on mothers-to-be. Distillers did know, or at least should have known as a result of the reports in Germany and Switzerland, that peripheral neuritis was a risk to those who took thalidomide. After putting Distaval on the market in 1958, DCBL were so confident of its miraculous powers that they circulated a leaflet to general practitioners in 1961 recommending the drug to, among others, pregnant mothers, saying, 'It can be given with complete safety to pregnant and nursing mothers without adverse effects on mother or child.' It was a disastrous mistake. The molecular weight of thalidomide was 258, and it had been established that any drug with a molecular weight of less than 1,000 could enter the placenta of a pregnant mother. If the drug was not safe, it then presented a danger to an unborn foetus.

It remains a matter of conjecture to this day whether DCBL were negligent, in the proper legal sense, in their promotion of Distaval as completely safe. A finding of negligence has never been established in a court of law. The legal actions against Distillers were all settled in Britain without any admission of liability, but DCBL were taking a big risk in their marketing strategy. Grünenthal GmbH had been vigorously downplaying the anxieties expressed by the doctors who had identified thalidomide as a cause of peripheral neuritis. These doctors were actively campaigning in Germany to prevent the drug becoming available without a prescription. The aggressive attitude taken by Grünenthal in support of the safety of the drug was supported by Distillers even though trials in Britain had revealed that the thyroid gland could be affected adversely in some patients who had taken thalidomide. The tragedy was that thalidomide was not withdrawn from circulation until late 1961, by which time deformities in newly born infants in Europe and Australia had already happened.

In the years between 1958 and 1961, a large number of cases of phocomelia, where children born with defective or absent limbs, were occurring in many countries and doctors were mystified as to the cause. It is difficult to express adequately the horror, anguish and guilt felt by mothers who appeared to have been chosen at random to give birth to grossly deformed babies. Infants emerged from their mothers' wombs without arms or legs or with hands emerging from shoulders or legs that ended as flippers. Some children had brain damage, genital deformities or with faces without ears. It was ghastly and horrific. Marriages disintegrated, mothers suffered incurable depression in psychiatric hospitals and doctors were unable to identify the underlying cause. A doctor in Hamburg calculated that while deformities at birth usually occurred at a rate of one in 100,000, between 1959 and 1961 there was an increase of two deformed births in every thousand. He examined the medical histories of fourteen mothers who had given birth to deformed children. In every case the mother had taken thalidomide during pregnancy. He wrote to Grünenthal and urged the company to withdraw the drug.

Sadly, by the time thalidomide had been identified as a probable cause of phocomelia in November 1961, the 'completely safe' new drug had done its work. Four hundred and fifty births with hideous deformities had occurred in Britain alone in a period of three years. It was only in February 1962 that DCBL embarked on tests with pregnant rabbits. Thirteen of eighteen rabbits who were given thalidomide produced offspring with defects. The conclusion seemed obvious, but the frightful damage had been done. Even so, DCBL still wanted the drug to remain on the market, albeit with a disclaimer that pregnant women should not take it.

The disaster of thalidomide quickly engaged the processes of law in countries throughout the world. In December 1961, a criminal investigation against Grünenthal began in Aachen, West Germany, and in Sweden a civil action was started against Astra, the Swedish manufacturer of thalidomide, in 1965. In each case, the grindingly slow processes of law began to clog up the path to a conclusion. Astra wanted a settlement behind closed doors, while pressure was applied to the medical authorities in Sweden to state that the deformed births did not have an identifiable cause. In Germany, a Bill of Indictment against Grünenthal was finally drawn up in 1965, with no trial date in sight. Meanwhile, in Britain, a courageous schoolteacher from Bristol who had given birth to a deformed child in November 1961 wrote a letter to the Minister of Health, Enoch Powell MP, in July 1962. Her enquiry was simple: what compensation did Mr Powell's government propose to give her and the many others who were affected by thalidomide? She pointed out that it was the NHS who had prescribed Distaval to her during her pregnancy.

Powell's reply, signed by an official in his department, was, to say the least, complacent. There was not the slightest reason to suspect, he wrote, that the drug could have such disastrous side effects. He insisted that all the proper tests which existed at the time of Distaval's

manufacture had been done. To put it bluntly, the thalidomide consequences were an unfortunate and unforeseeable accident. As to compensation, Mr Powell's National Health Service was available to treat
every baby should their services be required. This refrain – that all the
tests appropriate at the time had been done – was to feature throughout
the long and exhausting processes as DCBL's main defence.

When the history of the thalidomide scandal was written later by
Phillip Knightley and the *Sunday Times* Insight team, they discerned
a pattern emerging whereby the denial of liability by DCBL was being
placed in the public domain before any civil actions were even commenced by the distressed parents. *The Times* newspaper carried a piece
by an anonymous 'special correspondent'. Under the headline 'Thalidomide tests show no sign of danger', this correspondent stated that it
had been established 'beyond doubt' that before the drug had been put
on the market it had been subjected to all the tests which any pharma-
cologist would have applied in the circumstances at that time and the
clinical tests showed no sign of danger. In similar vein, *The Guardian*
was telling its readers that the tragic number of deformed births was
'completely new to therapeutic medicine and could not have been foreseen'. What was abundantly clear was that there was a public interest in
the thalidomide story in 1962.

For the parents of thalidomide children, however, they were inhibited from engaging in too much publicity, as their remedy was a legal one,
and in order to pursue it they required a legal aid certificate. This could
not be issued by the Law Society until an opinion from counsel stated
that there was a prospect of success if public money was to be spent
on the case. Inevitably, the process was moving slowly. In November
1962, Gerald Gardiner QC, the eminent barrister who had represented Penguin Books in the *Lady Chatterley* trial and who would become
Lord Chancellor two years later, advised in writing. He stated there was

a reasonable prospect of success if a test case was taken by one of the mothers who had taken Distaval after 1960, as by this time Distillers were aware of the risk of peripheral neuritis. In the meantime, Distillers, anticipating litigation, had retained an equally eminent barrister, John Wilmers QC.

At the start of 1963, during one of the coldest winters for decades, the lawyers seemed to be ready to join battle. Writs on behalf of some, but not all, of the thalidomide victims were issued when legal aid was granted. While there was general public interest in the thalidomide story, as soon as a writ was issued the whole affair was sealed by the laws of contempt of court as they existed then in Britain. Distillers, on the other hand, had already ensured their defence had been made public. Commencement of legal proceedings by the claimants put the thalidomide tragedy into a sealed legal cocoon from which it did not emerge for fourteen years. During those fourteen years there were court proceedings in the United States, Germany and Sweden which were all reported fully in the press. In Britain, the anguish of the claimant parents continued without a word being written about them lest the editor fell foul of British contempt laws. It was a law the *Sunday Times* led the field in challenging.

Harold Evans, the editor of the *Sunday Times*, came to be interested in the thalidomide case by a stroke of luck. In 1967, the paper was approached by a medical adviser to the families who had in his possession thousands of Distillers documents that had been disclosed during the tortuous pre-trial process. The medical adviser was under a duty to keep the documents confidential, but he offered them to Evans in exchange for journalistic help with a proposed book he was preparing about the case. The following year, a literary agent from Sweden offered Evans Grünenthal documents that had been disclosed in the Swedish case. By this time events were moving forward gradually and Desmond Ackner QC had become leading counsel for the families following

Gerald Gardiner's appointment as Lord Chancellor. His opponent, John Wilmers QC, had offered to settle the case on the basis that Distillers were notionally 40 per cent liable for the disaster, although liability was not admitted. It would be up to a judge to decide what the damages would be if Distillers were 100 per cent liable and then a financial adjustment could be made to reflect the agreed 40 per cent figure. Ackner issued firm advice that the offer should be accepted and, in 1969, sixty-five cases were settled on this basis, with Distillers paying a total of around £1 million. This was a paltry sum considering the distress and disfigurement the children were suffering and would suffer throughout their lives and was tiny compared with what would shortly follow in the United States. In 1971, a jury in California would award $2.5 million to a single child, with $250,000 to the mother. There was an appeal against this sum followed by a settlement on an undisclosed basis, but the eventual award was certainly greatly in excess of anything Distillers had offered in Britain.

The meagre sum awarded as a result of a High Court judge's assessment of damages had received some publicity and this caused a further 200 or so parents of thalidomide children to come forward. In those days, before the internet and social media, it was difficult for people who were isolated in their lives to make contact with others with similar interests and concerns. It was not surprising that thalidomide parents identified themselves sporadically. By 1971, there were nearly 400 claims pending. This did not include those who had accepted the 1969 settlement. Distillers now offered the sum of £3.25 million to be paid over a ten-year period, but it was an all-or-nothing offer. Either every family had to accept the deal or Distillers would pay nothing. Six families refused the Distillers take-it-or-leave it ultimatum, including David Mason, a wealthy London art dealer, who had the means and the determination to fight on for his daughter Louise, a Distillers victim who was born without limbs. He did not need a legal aid certificate to fight the case to the end. He became the leader of the six families who refused to agree to a public guardian called the Official Solicitor taking over the case and representing all the children, an offer the barrister for the other families was pleading with them to accept. If the Official Solicitor were to represent his child, Mason feared, the Distillers offer would be a done deal. Mason pursued this argument in the Court of Appeal, and Lord Denning, who was later to play an important part in the thalidomide story, supported Mason and the six families by declaring their stance was entirely reasonable. He ruled, in April 1972, that the Distillers offer of £3.25 million which was becoming acceptable to many parents was not so clearly beneficial as to make Mason and the others unreasonable in refusing it. Mason and others could fight on, while the remaining families could continue towards a settlement.

David Mason was a determined man. He was also well-connected and through a friend he contacted David English, then editor of the *Daily Mail*. English took a bold decision to publish three pieces under the headline 'My fight for justice, by the father of heartbreak girl Louise'. The tenor of English's approach was that Distillers were behaving like blackmailers in their take-it-or-leave-it settlement offer. The paper was sailing very close to the wind in respect of contempt of court and the Attorney General, the law officer of the Crown who had a responsibility to initiate proceedings for a contempt of court, warned the *Daily Mail* to desist. The paper complied, as did the media generally, who began to lose interest in thalidomide. It was true that legal action which had begun in February 1963 was still not formally concluded, but to all intents and purposes proceedings had ground to a halt. There was deadlock between the Mason group, which now consisted of 389 claimants, thanks to publicity surrounding the Denning judgment and the *Daily Mail* story, and Distillers. All these claims were still pending as a result of Mason's stance. No agreement had been reached, despite the fact that many of the thalidomide victims were growing up and had so far received nothing. Distillers were holding out on making a new offer.

At the editorial offices of the *Sunday Times*, however, there was no mood to desist, despite the Attorney General's warning to the *Daily Mail*. The medical doctor who had visited the paper in 1967 and provided a heap of Distillers documents revisited the offices in exasperation that the paper had done nothing about the material he had handed over. In fact, journalists at the *Sunday Times* had not been idle in the four years since the 1969 settlement. They had been trawling through anything and everything they could find on the case, including obscure medical and legal journals. In one such journal they read an account by an actuary of how English judges did not appreciate, when setting damages in injury cases, certain recognised calculations about mortality, future inflation, future costs of care and the interest that would be earned by investment of lump sums. It was a complicated and technical article, but the author had given evidence in the 1968 thalidomide cases and he had concluded that the judge had made awards that were only half what they should have been. This was devastating and shocking. It showed that in 1969 the parents who had settled had actually received 40 per cent of a sum which was half of what they should, notionally, have got. A huge injustice was looming on the horizon. Lawyers in nearly 400 cases were negotiating in 1972 on the assumption that the 1969 settlement had been fair. A decision was taken by the *Sunday Times* to publish first a piece about the *moral* justice surrounding the case and later a detailed account of how the tragedy had happened. This first step would tread a narrow path between law and justice, according respect for the former while trying to shame Distillers into recognising the latter. It was a decision to avoid being held in contempt of court.

In September 1972, the *Sunday Times* went to press with a story headed 'Our thalidomide children: a cause for national shame' and an editorial headed 'Children on our conscience'. In essence, the *Sunday Times* were pointing out that the pot of £3.25 million for hundreds of children which Distillers were offering was shameful in comparison with the company's assets of £425 million. Readers were promised a follow-up story later about how the tragedy had happened. Everybody on the paper knew this second step would be problematic as the question of how the tragedy happened was something Distillers had never thrown any light on. For this reason, Evans sought legal advice from independent counsel and took the precaution of giving Distillers advance notice of what they proposed to publish. Evans realised the paper might well be in contempt of court if this article went ahead.

The *Sunday Times*' strategy in the second piece was to inform readers of the following matters of interest. First, that Distillers had not done any trial tests of their own and had relied solely on the Grünenthal tests; second, that they had marketed the drug before any animal tests had been done to determine whether thalidomide could damage a foetus; third, that they were not deterred by the fact that thalidomide was a proven threat to the nervous system; and finally, that they had continued to advertise the drug as completely safe for pregnant women up to a month before its eventual withdrawal.

When Sir Alexander McDonald, the Distillers chairman, saw the draft, his immediate reaction was to ask the Attorney General to seek an injunction in the High Court to stop publication. What Distillers wanted to avoid more than anything else was an exposure to the world about how the thalidomide tragedy had happened. For Distillers, this was more important than the money it might be shamed into paying. The Attorney General acceded to the chairman's request and the case was heard by the Lord Chief Justice, Lord Widgery, and two other judges. The key point was whether the High Court should rule on the case as a balancing exercise. The *Sunday Times* wanted the court to approach the case in a way which would involve the court deciding where the balance lay. There were two competing interests: protecting the administration of justice on the one hand and, on the other, the rights of the public to be informed about facts which, in the public interest, they were entitled to know. These were the facts about how the tragedy happened. The *Sunday Times* was confident that if there was a fair consideration of the case in this way, they would win. The Lord Chief Justice and his two brethren had no hesitation in ruling that balance did not come into it. The only question was whether there was a serious risk that the proposed article might interfere with the course of legal proceedings, which, the court said, were still ongoing. An injunction to stop publication should therefore be granted. This was at odds with what was occurring elsewhere.

After the first *Sunday Times* article, which the Attorney General had not objected to, the Speaker of the House of Commons had allowed a debate on the *moral* justice of the Distillers offer on the grounds that it could not be *sub judice* for Parliament to discuss the moral aspects of the thalidomide tragedy. Two hundred and sixty-five members signed a motion that expressed concern over the meanness of the Distillers proposals for a settlement. Parliament was giving voice to a public concern about the way thalidomide victims were being treated, even if the Lord Chief Justice thought otherwise.

There had been smouldering outrage about the plight of the thalidomide victims for a while. Even some of Distillers' own shareholders were in revolt. One shareholder was Tony Lynes, a leader of the Child Poverty Action Group, a charity which campaigned against child poverty. He had inherited shares from a relative. He and others sought to engage with the large institutional shareholders of Distillers to put pressure on the company to offer more money. Many institutional shareholders were sympathetic. In a separate development, a campaign to boycott Distillers products including the highly profitable whisky business was gathering pace. At last, Sir Alexander McDonald came to realise the whole future of Distillers was in jeopardy unless an offer, comparable to what had occurred in the United States, was forthcoming. There was by now a tough informal negotiating body working in the interests of the children, which included a shareholders committee, a leading Member of Parliament, Jack Ashley MP, and the *Sunday Times*, who were talking serious money with Distillers. Finally, in July 1973, a judge at the High Court approved a cash settlement of £6 million for 340 children, topped up with payments of £2 million a year for seven years for all those children, including those who had settled in 1969, and a generous settlement for the operation of the trust set up to administer the payments. There was an inflation clause of up to 10 per cent if prices rose (which they did). In all, Distillers were to pay £28.4 million when all the cases were finally settled four years later.

This settlement, made on condition that the claimants withdrew allegations of negligence, occurred just after Lord Denning and two other Lord Justices heard the appeal from the injunction forbidding public comment on the causes of the thalidomide tragedy imposed by the Lord Chief Justice. The Court of Appeal came to a completely different conclusion about the place of freedom of expression and its relationship to the law of contempt. The law on contempt was as vague as the value of freedom of speech was obscure in the early 1970s. Lord Denning, fortunately, was presiding in the Court of Appeal. He ruled that while the administration of justice had to be upheld and trial by newspaper was forbidden, it was legitimate for a court of law to balance the public interest on a matter of national concern against the potential prejudice that might be caused to a party in litigation. In this instance, the *Sunday Times* were proposing only to make fair comment about a matter of public interest and it could not prejudice pending litigation as the litigation had been dormant for years. Distillers had provided no evidence of their own to show that what the *Sunday Times* were proposing to say amounted to unfair pressure on them to increase their offer.

As the Lord Chief Justice and the Master of the Rolls had used different approaches to reach different conclusions on an area of law that was vague and unprincipled, it was inevitable the case would go to the House of Lords. Their Lordships' ruling was disappointing. Their judgment did nothing to reassure journalists that judges should conduct a balancing exercise when matters of great public concern were in conflict with contempt of court laws. On the contrary, the judgment focused only on whether the purpose of the article was to put pressure of Distillers to settle on better terms than appeared to be the case. They decided that the proposed article was really about a lack of care by Distillers in their decision to market thalidomide and this amounted to a pre-judgement about a matter that was still unresolved by a court. Such a pre-judgement would amount to a disrespect for the processes of law. If litigants in proceedings felt under pressure then the law of contempt of court existed to protect them. The fact that litigation was dormant was irrelevant, as was general public interest in the thalidomide case. The House restored the injunction restraining the *Sunday Times* from publishing anything on the thalidomide case which prejudiced issues of negligence, breach of contract, breach of duty or any matters of evidence arising out of pending litigation against the Distillers Company.

This restraining injunction was somewhat academic, as a few days before the House of Lords decision a settlement for a large majority of cases had been reached. But an important aspect of the *Sunday Times* campaign was still under wraps. How had the thalidomide tragedy been allowed to happen? Who was to blame and what lessons could be learned? Nowadays these seem elementary questions requiring answers when a national disaster like the contaminated blood scandal, the abuse of children in residential care or the Grenfell Tower fire tragedy occurs. Today, full public inquiries inevitably follow, but in the 1970s English law thought otherwise. It seemed the reasons for the tragedy would remain a closely guarded secret for evermore. The Health Secretary, Enoch Powell, had refused a public inquiry in 1962 and this route to finding out how the tragedy happened was blocked off. Efforts to reverse this decision had all failed.

At the time of the thalidomide tragedy, Britain's politicians and judges were still in awe of the constitutional theories of the Victorian constitutional expert A. V. Dicey. He fondly, and naively, believed that 'at no time has there in England been any proclamation of the right to liberty of thought or to freedom of speech'.[3] In Dicey's conception of the British constitution, the focus is always on the prohibition, not the underlying liberty. It was this understanding of our British way of doing things which persuaded the House of Lords, in 1973, to put a stop to the *Sunday Times*' thalidomide exposure. The prohibition loomed larger than the liberty. In recent times, thanks largely to the dogged campaign in the thalidomide case, the focus has shifted. Nowadays, judges are more aware of the importance of underlying rights.

When the House of Lords restored the injunction, the thalidomide litigation was theoretically still moving forward, as not all the cases had been settled. In July 1974, Distillers obtained a ruling from a High Court judge to ban the publication of any documents obtained during the court process. The *Sunday Times* investigation about the cause of the tragedy was now well and truly blocked from every angle.

There was only one option remaining for the *Sunday Times* to overcome the obstacles English law was putting in their way. At the time, prior to the UK's Human Rights Act, the editor could complain to the European Commission of Human Rights. His complaint was that his paper had been denied rights guaranteed by Article 10 of the European Convention, the right to freedom of speech. The United Kingdom was a signatory to the Convention and its citizens had a right of complaint, but it was a long shot. At that time, 95 per cent of complaints to the Commission were refused as groundless if the complainant had already exhausted his remedies at home, and the *Sunday Times* had lost in the House of Lords, Britain's highest court. Nonetheless, in January 1974, Harold Evans decided to give the paper's thalidomide campaign one last heave. The move was resisted by the UK government, who wanted the complaint rejected at a preliminary stage. However, at last the tide was beginning to turn in favour of the *Sunday Times*. In proceedings behind closed doors at the European Court in Strasbourg in December 1975, the Commission agreed to examine the thalidomide case in more detail. The UK government had failed in their attempt to block Evans taking the case forward. A full ruling from the Strasbourg bench of judges would, however, take some time.

This unwelcome development for Distillers and the British government was a spur to some rethinking on behalf of the Attorney General. Although a negligence action against Distillers had never been resolved, it did appear by now that the severe injunction imposed by the House of Lords might be a little unnecessary as so much time had elapsed since its making. The Attorney General finally decided, in May 1976, that as only a handful of cases remained to be settled, the injunction could be lifted. A High Court judge, in a hearing that lasted four minutes, agreed. The *Sunday Times* were now free to reveal their painstaking investigations, which had discovered, contrary to what other newspapers had been saying in 1972, that it was not uncommon to test drugs on pregnant animals in the late 1950s. The paper could not reveal what Distillers knew about this, as this information was restrained by a breach of confidence injunction issued in 1974, but it was a major step forward.

The *Sunday Times* told their readers in June 1976 the important scientific fact that testing on pregnant animals was not uncommon when thalidomide was put on the market. It was in the public interest for this to be known, especially as the government had turned down a request for a public inquiry into the tragedy.

Fifteen years had now elapsed since the scandal of the thalidomide events shocked the world in 1961 when large numbers of malformed births began to occur, apparently for no known reason. Harold Evans, Distillers and the British government now awaited the decision of the European Commission, which was delivered in July 1977. It was a complete vindication of the stance taken by the *Sunday Times*. The Commission referred the case to the full court at Strasbourg on the grounds that if a matter of great public concern is not resolved in a public inquiry, it remains a matter of public interest for matters to be clarified in other ways. It would only be on the most pressing grounds that information about a matter of such public concern should be silenced. As if to make their point abundantly clear, the Commission attached as an addendum to their report a copy of the draft article, the one the House of Lords had banned from publication. This was a game-changer, as anybody could seek out the Commission's report. The *Sunday Times* obtained permission from a judge to print the Commission's report. On 31 July 1977, the *Sunday Times* made full use of the report in a further exposure of the scandal of the thalidomide children. It was an important victory in the pursuit of a right to publish the truth and to exercise a right to free speech in a responsible manner.

The full hearing before the European Court of Human Rights did not take place until the end of 1978 and the reasoned decision was not handed down until April 1979. The focus of the decision was Article 10 of the European Convention on Human Rights. In essence, Article 10 states that freedom of expression is a right but the expression of that right carries with it responsibilities. It is therefore legitimate for government to make the right subject to restrictions that may be necessary in a democratic society. For example, the use of a right to freedom of speech can be restricted if it is necessary to do so in the interests of national security, the protection of the reputation of another or the protection of health or morals. Among the curtailments to unlimited freedom of speech that are permitted is the maintenance of the authority and impartiality of the judiciary if it is necessary to do so. By applying this article to their reasoning, the analysis of the European judges was different from the approach in Britain's highest court.

The starting point for the Strasbourg judges was to recognise that freedom of speech constitutes one of the essential foundations of a democratic society. Providing the media do not overstep the boundaries necessary for the administration of justice, it is *incumbent* on the judiciary to apply the Convention right on freedom of expression as there is a corresponding right on the public to receive the information. The Strasbourg judges were making a vitally important point that English law had for centuries overlooked. The *Sunday Times* case was not about trying to balance two conflicting principles; freedom of speech on the one hand and the administration of justice on the other. The case was about the foundational principle of freedom of speech being the starting point and then considering whether the interference with that principle was *necessary* in the circumstances. The Strasbourg judges' conclusion (albeit by a majority of eleven to nine) was that the thalidomide disaster raised matters of enormous public concern: the legal or moral questions of responsibility for the disaster and the vexing question of how compensation should be calculated from injuries caused by new scientific discoveries. It was a matter of public interest that such questions were addressed and answered. The court concluded that banning the proposed article was not a sufficiently pressing social need to outweigh the public interest in the right of the *Sunday Times* to exercise its right to freedom of expression.[4]

It was a stunning victory for Harold Evans and his team, headed by Phillip Knightley, Elaine Potter and Bruce Page of the Insight team, who investigated the thalidomide events. It led to a change in the law when the Contempt of Court Act 1981 was passed. Parliament bowed to growing pressure to change the law on conduct which tended to interfere with the course of justice, the conduct the *Sunday Times* was guilty of in the thalidomide events. From now on there would have to be a substantial risk that the course of justice would be seriously impeded or prejudiced and then only if the proceedings in question were active. A newspaper would have a defence if, having taken reasonable care to find out, the publisher did not know or reasonably suspect the proceedings were active. At last the law was stated with the precision Strasbourg demanded. Had this clarity in English law been in force at the time the thalidomide events were unfolding, there would have been no problem with the *Sunday Times* bringing the details of the scandal to public attention. The thalidomide case also brought about a big change in judicial thinking about the value of free speech.

In November 2000, Lord Bingham, as Senior Law Lord, said that people cannot participate in the life of their society if they are not alerted or informed about events around them. The proper functioning of a modern participatory democracy requires a free, active, professional and enquiring press. For that reason, the courts have recognised the cardinal importance of press freedom.[5] He could have added, 'but only since the thalidomide case'. His predecessors in the nation's highest court had simply not thought about the central importance of press freedom in contributing to our modern democracy when they handed down their injunction banning the publication of the *Sunday Times* investigation.

The *Sunday Times* crusade in the thalidomide scandal challenged and swept aside old orthodoxies and paved the way for a new emphasis and priority to be given to the value of free speech in Britain's courts. At the same time, the thalidomide decision opened up a new debate about the value of being able to *receive* information. A central feature of the thalidomide affair was the fact that parents and children cruelly affected by it were kept in ignorance about how the unsafe drug came to be manufactured and distributed in the first place. The decision by the European Court that banning publication of the thalidomide story was not a sufficiently pressing social need to outweigh the public interest of the *Sunday Times* publishing it was ground-breaking. It heralded the way for whistle-blowers to be able to expose wrongdoing without victimisation, enshrined in the Public Interest Disclosure Act 1998, and paved the way for English courts to take a sensible and pragmatic approach when asked to restrain the publication of facts which were freely available in other parts of the world, as in the *Spycatcher* case, a cause also taken up by the *Sunday Times*.[6]

Harold Evans's brave campaign to force change in relation to free expression and the right to know, with help from the European Court of Human Rights in Strasbourg, not only altered the law of England; it changed the way the public began to perceive secrecy within the domain of the rich and powerful. The *Sunday Times* took on Distillers at a time when print journalism was in its heyday and long before the internet, chat forums, social media and all the consequences of technological progress on the exercise of free speech. Nowadays free speech controversies take place on new territory. This does not diminish Evans's achievement; rather, it serves to remind us how important legal cases are to all debates about free speech controversies. Harold Evans died in 2020. His obituaries paid tribute to his tenacity, courage, moral passion, hatred of injustice and absolute belief in the power of freedom of expression to be used for the public good. These beliefs are as relevant now as they were when he began his thalidomide campaign more than fifty years ago. The difference is that there is now a greater willingness among judges to allow free speech to flourish.

Chapter 6

Protest – We Shall Overcome Some Day

Protest, the public expression of dissent by individuals coming together to bring their common cause to the attention of the government, has been a feature of British political life for a very long time. The Peterloo massacre and the Chartist marches in the nineteenth century and the suffragettes' civil disobedience in the twentieth are past history, but in modern times the Aldermaston marches of the 1950s, the poll tax protests of the 1980s and demonstrations and direct action against the Iraq War in 2003 have had lasting influence on the politics of modern Britain. Protest gives voice to opinions which others may not share and usually disrupts the ordinary life of others for the time the protest lasts. Protest engages with law, rights, duties and obligations in a very direct way. There is a tension between the democratic obligation to accept protest as a pressure valve to relieve feeling on the one hand and the authority of government to use its legal powers to repress protest on the other.

This tension was being played out in the first half of 2021, when the Supreme Court were crafting their reasons for permitting magistrates to acquit protesters for deliberately causing obstruction to the highway if other factors, important to the purpose and duration of the protest, were present. The case, *Ziegler and Others v DPP*,[1] was the logical conclusion to laws on protest which judges had been developing since the European Convention on Human Rights was incorporated into English law in 2000. On the other side of Parliament Square, the House of Commons was considering the Police, Crime, Sentencing and Courts Bill, which contained clauses that would restrict the established principles of protest law judges had been gradually developing. The measures would enhance state control over demonstrations and assemblies and erode further the ability of protesters to make their voices heard. The Bill, which was enacted into law in April 2022, had a controversial passage through its legislative stages, with the House of Lords disagreeing with the Commons on important clauses.

A main reason for the tension between the legislature and the judiciary in permitting or curtailing protests is a confusion over the exact meaning of public protest. For some, it can mean a manifestation of the right to free speech, which should be carried out with dignity, politeness and calm. For others, it can mean a method of imposing one view onto others, something which involves strength of numbers, noise, banner waving and singing. Protest in this sense is an activity which impinges directly, not marginally, on the lives of others. This type of protest is usually more than a simple extension of free speech, as it comprises an aspect of direct action. It is a participation in politics which goes beyond just voting in elections. Traditionally, legislators have authority through elections not protests, and they tolerate protest with an element of official ill grace. Protests occur when events initiated or permitted by legislators cause outrage among the electorate. They become affronted and give expression to their indignity by taking action. This may embrace a march through a city centre, for which prior permission from the police must be sought, a spontaneous gathering giving out leaflets and displaying banners in a town centre or acts of civil disobedience to draw attention to specific actions by the government. Even protests involving direct action are regarded as essentially peaceful by their participants as they believe, in conscience, they have lawful entitlement to act as they choose. They believe their protest is at least excusable in law, even if it is not explicitly permitted in law. This type of protest is in contrast to those which are deliberately violent, involving missile throwing and assaults on the police or wanton damage. These are not recognised in law as having any legitimacy, although the social causes of violent protests have been the subject of two inquiries, each led by Lord Scarman, a senior judge.[2] It is the peaceful protest that engages the rule of law. Every protest involves some incursion into the ordinary lives of others who are not protesting. Traffic is stopped, route diversions are created and public streets can be occupied by demonstrators for hours on end.

It should be a judicial function to decide exactly what threat to normal public peace the holding of a protest represents. Despite this rather obvious point, English law has, until very recently, been reluctant to develop any legal principles which govern the law of protest and has been content to rely on convention and compromise to set legal limits on it. The law seemed to be saying that ancient rights to protest were lawful so long as the government of the day had not introduced a law to the contrary. It was not until 2021 that this most unsatisfactory state of legal affairs was examined afresh and some principled flesh was put on the dry bones of protest laws that were supposed to have been settled in the nineteenth century. The new principles were applied by the Supreme Court in the case of *Ziegler and Others v DPP*, principles explicitly influenced by the European Convention on Human Rights and the interpretation of those principles by the European Court of Human Rights.

The facts of *Ziegler* were extremely simple. In September 2017, the biennial Defence and Security International Arms Fair was due to take place at the Excel Centre in east London. The fair's organisers claimed the event would be the biggest gathering in the world for buyers and sellers of armaments to meet and do business. Politicians, dignitaries and arms dealers could all meet under one roof. For others, the fair promoted and assisted the aims of dictatorial regimes in defeating their opponents by force of arms. Arms and armament equipment would be delivered to the Excel Centre prior to opening day. On 5 September, just before the opening, Nora Ziegler and three colleagues took part in a day of action outside the centre to proclaim their view there was 'no faith in war' and to attempt to block deliveries or arms and equipment to the centre. Their method was to lock themselves to a bar in the middle of a box by means of a pipe protruding on each side. Each box was decorated with peace slogans and two demonstrators were attached to the bar in the box with a carabiner clip. The group then lay on the road, two protesters locked to each box. When they declined police requests to remove themselves, they were arrested for obstructing the highway. As vehicles wishing to enter the Excel Centre were prevented from doing so by the protesters, it would appear to be a clear case of highway obstruction. However, not all access roads to the centre were blocked and it would have been possible for delivery vehicles to have turned back and used an alternative route.

A district judge found the protesters not guilty of obstructing the highway on the grounds that in the particular circumstances of the case the obstruction was not so unreasonable that their act of protest was no longer protected by the European Convention on Human Rights.

He took account of the fact that the actions were peaceful, did not give rise to disorder and were carefully targeted towards the arms fair. He also considered it was a legitimate matter of public concern to bring to public attention the fact that the international arms trade could be used for torture by certain regimes or as an act of war against their own civilian populations.

This decision was something of a shock to the Director of Public Prosecutions, who thought the district judge had misapplied the law of protest, and she appealed to the High Court to direct the acquittals be overturned. She was successful, but the case was then taken to the Supreme Court by the protesters, who claimed important matters of principle arose. Obstructing the highway is only a criminal offence if done without lawful excuse, but is deliberate obstruction which prevents others from using the highway capable of constituting a lawful excuse as the district judge had found? So far, in January 2021, English law was clear. Actions which were normally tolerated, such as handing out leaflets in the street or stopping on the pavement to chat to friends, were capable of amounting to a reasonable use of the highway, but lying down on the road with the object of stopping traffic was not. This meant a conviction for obstructing the highway would be inevitable for a protester like Nora Ziegler if she lay down on the road and refused to move when instructed to do so by police. Protesters did not have the option of demonstrating their opinions in that way without incurring a criminal conviction.

When the Supreme Court handed down their decision, by a majority of three to two, in June 2021, the law of protest took a new turn. The judgment of the majority was remarkable in many respects. It restored protest as a legitimate human right which should be restricted only when it was necessary in a democratic society. Of equal importance was the majority view that in assessing the proportionality of restricting the right to protest, the whole picture needed to be weighed up. This included the arrest, the trial, the conviction and sentence. This moved the goalposts significantly in the direction of carving out a legal right to protest. By ruling that the lawfulness of a protest should be judged on all the surrounding circumstances, the Supreme Court were elevating protest to the category of a human right. It could not be judged simply from the point of view of the police officer who decided to remove a protester from the street. A police officer who made an arrest for highway obstruction might find, when all the factors were weighed up later by a judge, that his decision would not be supported judicially. The Supreme Court applied a brake to the arrest process while releasing the accelerator a little for the protester.

Ziegler v DPP was the first time the Supreme Court had looked at protest law through the lens that the European Convention had provided. Under the Human Rights Act 1998, Article 11 of the Convention had domestic effect. Article 11 states:

> Everyone has the right to freedom of peaceful assembly and to freedom of association with others ... No restrictions shall be placed on the exercise of these rights other than such as are prescribed by law and are necessary in a democratic society in the interests of national security or public safety, or the prevention of disorder or crime, for the protection of health or morals or for the protection of the rights and freedoms of others.

The way Article 11, and the other articles, are structured meant, as Lady Arden pointed out, that the focus was for the court to ask itself this question: was it necessary in a democratic society that to protect the

rights and freedoms of others, the rights and freedoms of [the protest-
ers] should be restricted by bringing their protest to an end and charg-
ing them with criminal offence? *Ziegler* put the rights and freedoms of
the protesters centre stage. Until this legal ruling, the approach of the
courts had been to assume that using the highway for the purpose of
protest, causing more than minimal and trivial disruption to the rights
and freedoms of others, was not capable of being a lawful excuse if the
activity itself was not inherently lawful. Binding yourself to a box and
lying in the road was not inherently lawful. The old law placed the focus
on the proportionality of the response to the protest, which was invariably a lawful arrest as this was the only means of bringing an unlawful
protest to an end. In *Ziegler*, on the other hand, it was not the proportionality of the response that mattered but the facts and circumstances
of the protest itself. Nora Ziegler had embarked on a peaceful protest.
Indeed, peace was the message conveyed in the protest against arms
and armaments. Protests which are violent or which threaten or provoke violence do not enjoy protection under the Convention.

The Supreme Court ruled that in weighing up all the facts and
circumstances of a peaceful protest, judges should bear in mind that
protest, by its nature, is symbolic and so the location and timing of the
protest is a consideration to be borne in mind. Freedom of assembly
implies a freedom to choose the time and place of a protest. In this case
Nora Ziegler and her colleagues had chosen an approach road to the
Excel Centre shortly before an international arms fair was due to start.
When a right to protest is exercised by some, society as a whole, represented by the police, must show a certain degree of tolerance towards
protest. Disruption to ordinary life, including disruption of traffic, will
usually occur. The nature of the views whose expression the Convention exists to protect are also a relevant matter to take into account, as

are the peaceful intentions of the protesters. In addition, regard must be had to whether any disorder is provoked by the protest. Lastly, the precise consequences of a protest on the rights and freedoms of others should be taken into account. This protest involved a group using boxes and clips to make their removal from the road by police conspicuously difficult. But – and this was important – the protest did not completely block access for vans and lorries delivering supplies to the arms fair. The district judge had taken these factors into account in his decision to acquit the protesters of the offence of highway obstruction without lawful excuse. The Supreme Court upheld his reasoning and restored the dismissal of the charges against Nora Ziegler and her colleagues.

The Supreme Court decision in *Ziegler* is ground-breaking, but it is not without difficulty. The court considered the short duration of the Excel Centre protest was a relevant matter, but it was short only because the police intervened quite quickly. Would a longer delay in the removal of the protesters have converted a protest enjoying a lawful excuse into one which was unlawful? The implications for police operational decision-making are not easy.

The second important step forward in the establishment within English law of a right to protest lay in the new interpretation given to the meaning of 'restrictions' on the right to protest in the European Convention on Human Rights. Arrest, prosecution, conviction and sentence are all 'restrictions' within the meaning of Article 11. The Supreme Court ruled that the word meant the measures taken before or during the gathering as well as those taken afterwards, including punishment. The Supreme Court were making clear that a protest which may have looked one way to a police officer deciding to make an arrest may look differently to the judge when the whole picture is presented. It is the trial judge's assessment of the proportionality of the police response that is relevant. In Ziegler's case, the district judge had decided that to convict and sentence the protesters for highway obstruction would be a disproportionate *restriction* on their right to freedom of assembly. The Supreme Court upheld this verdict of not guilty.

It is clear from the Ziegler case that the big change of focus came about not because of English common law but directly as a result of the incorporation of the European Convention into English law through the Human Rights Act 1998. Before the Human Rights Act, the general idea in English law was that liberty was protected by the ordinary law of the land and liberties were protected by judges. This is the principle of legality that provided a procedural protection against overreaching power. From the eighteenth century onwards, judges have protected *individual* liberty by insisting that powerful state agencies must have legal authority to exercise their powers over citizens and these agencies must be answerable to the judiciary for the way their powers are used. A. V. Dicey, the Victorian constitutional expert, believed there was no real difference between a citizen's individual liberty and the liberties of a group joining up as a collection of individuals. He cited the following 1882 case, *Beatty v Gillbanks*, as an example of this principle.[3]

The Salvation Army in Weston-Super-Mare decided to demonstrate their evangelical Christianity and their opposition to alcohol by marching through the town with their band resounding to the tune of hymns. Unfortunately, this was not to the liking of some, including a motley body who were neither Christian nor vocalists, nor indeed teetotallers; they called themselves the Skeleton Army, a provocation to the Salvationists, and they planned a counter-march. Fearing the two 'armies' would clash, a local bench of magistrates ordered the Salvationists to call off their procession. When they refused, their leaders were bound over to keep the peace. The High Court emphatically quashed the bind-over and rejected the proposition that 'a man may be convicted for doing a lawful act if he knows that his doing it may cause another to do an unlawful act'. It was the Skeletons, the High Court ruled, who had 'no possible right to interfere with or in any way obstruct the Salvation Army in their lawful and peaceable procession'.

Dicey welcomed this ruling as a vindication of his theory that liberties in Britain did not need the protection of a single document or charter as they were protected by the rule of law, enunciated by judges. For Dicey, there were no collective liberties, like an association of workers or a group joining together in a common cause to demonstrate publicly, but only individual liberty, which the common law permitted a single citizen to enjoy. Dicey did not acknowledge the existence of political liberty; he only recognised the right of an individual *not* to be restrained unless he or she has done something unlawful. However, as K. D. Ewing and C. A. Gearty have pointed out, Dicey's conception provides a very insecure base on which to hold a theory of political liberty if there is no fixed definition of what constitutes unlawful action.[4]

The approach of the English common law to freedom of expression and assembly was hesitant and negative, permitting that which was not prohibited. Dicey had stated in his *Introduction to the Study of the Law of the Constitution* that there had never been a time in English law when judges had proclaimed any right to liberty, still less a right to liberty of thought or to freedom of speech. He also stated, quite correctly, that in the British constitution there is no such thing as any specific right to hold a public meeting. Until the Human Rights Act 1998, Dicey's bland assertion that collective rights were, basically, non-existent was one that English judges, with a few notable exceptions, were content to accept. English judges worked on the assumption that collective expressions of opinion in public were only an extension of the individual's choice to exercise freedom of expression. This assumption hindered any cogent development of a law of protest. In reality, there is a big difference between the liberty that is enjoyed by an individual and the collective liberty of those protesting in a march or in a public meeting held out of doors. Assemblies, processions, marches and meetings have an element of democratic participation, communal identity and active engagement with the community that is different from a purely personal liberty to pursue a chosen path in life, unconstrained by state interference. The case of the Salvationists clashing with the Skeleton Army in Weston-Super-Mare was not an example of the authority of the common law using its innate ability to protect liberty, as Dicey claimed; it simply established that a citizen's liberty may not be interfered with if the conduct was not unlawful.

While judges have traditionally been good at preserving an individual's autonomy within his own property, they have been generally reluctant to go further and give procedural protection the status of a guaranteed right. This has left the law of protest in limbo. It is neither in the territory of personal autonomy of conscience, belief and personal choice nor in that of property and land, whose ownership judges have always jealously protected. Protest must take place in public for it to have any purpose and gatherings in public impact on the lives of others directly, whether they are violent or not. Parliament has feared the power of gatherings and collective action from the time of the eighteenth-century Combination Acts onwards, and offences of unlawful assembly, riot, affray appeared on the statute book to ensure public order was never disturbed by a 'mob'. Trade union activity was always strictly controlled by laws made by Parliament.

Dicey's belief that personal and collective liberty were only different expressions of a single principle of legality was not realistic, as the principle of legality cannot guarantee freedom of assembly or freedom to protest. In 1934, a fiery and persuasive speaker from the Scottish

left-wing tradition called Kath Duncan wanted to hold a meeting outside an unemployed training centre to protest about the recently enacted Incitement to Disaffection Act. She also wanted to defend the right to
free speech. Police intervened to order her meeting to take place further
away. When she refused to move it, she was arrested for obstructing a
police officer in the course of his duty. In May 1933, after a similar meeting, there had been a disturbance inside the training centre and when
the 1934 meeting was advertised to take place, the superintendent of the
training centre feared a similar disturbance. There was no law against
holding a public meeting in the street at that time. However, the police
did possess an ancient power to make an arrest and deprive a citizen of
personal liberty if he feared a breach of the peace was likely to occur.
Where did these conflicting principles leave a freedom to protest in the
circumstances of Mrs Duncan's demonstration against the Incitement
to Disaffection Act?

The case was taken to the High Court before the Lord Chief Justice, Lord Hewart, who said the case raised no points of constitutional
importance about alleged rights to hold a meeting in the street. The
sole question was whether the constable was acting in the execution
of his duty, which he was, as there had been a disturbance on a previous occasion when a meeting was addressed by Mrs Duncan. The
High Court did not even examine whether the case raised important
points about the right to protest under English common law.[5] The case
showed the reluctance of English judges to grapple with principles of
law that impacted on protest. Kath Duncan's protest was neither violent
nor forbidden by any law banning public meetings. She had not physically obstructed the arresting officer in any way, yet Lord Hewart had
allowed the law of police obstruction to thwart the holding of a peaceful
assembly solely on the grounds that the police constable attested he had
grounds to fear a breach of the peace. Even this justification was shaky,

as the superintendent at the unemployed training centre seemed determined the meeting should not take place outside his premises come what may.

Judicial recognition of the place of protest within the fabric of English law was nowhere to be seen until, in 1975, Lord Denning said, '[It is] the undoubted right of Englishmen to assemble together for the purpose of deliberating upon public grievances. Such is the right of assembly. So also is the right to meet together, to go in procession, to demonstrate and to protest on matters of public concern.' He insisted a 'reasonable use' of the highway included a right to protest on matters of public concern and that limited picketing of an estate agent's office was neither an unreasonable use of the street nor a common law nuisance. It was time, he argued, that the courts recognised a right to demonstrate. He went on: 'The right to demonstrate and the right to protest on matters of public concern ... are rights which it is in the public interest that individuals should possess; and, indeed, that they should exercise without impediment so long as no wrongful act is done.'[6] Lord Denning was Master of the Rolls and, by common consent, the country's most outstanding judge at the time. Unfortunately, his statement that a right of protest existed in the rich seams of English law was not shared by his colleagues. Denning was in the minority and therefore his dissenting judgment did not form part of the common law to provide authority for future cases. By the time of the mid-1970s, the law had not moved on from the 1930s.

Lord Denning was giving this dissenting judgment in a civil case which involved the request for an injunction by a firm of estate agents in Islington, north London. At that time, 1975, many multi-occupied and tenanted Victorian houses in Islington were being sought by buyers who wanted the tenants out and the flats converted into homes for a single-family household. Prebble & Co. were a firm of estate agents assisting property developers to make these changes. A group called the Islington Tenants Campaign decided to demonstrate outside Prebble's office every Saturday to draw attention to dubious methods of eviction being used by property developers and to point out that the converted houses were beyond the means of most Islington residents to buy. The local police had been made aware of the pickets on Saturdays and raised no objection. The presence of the pickets did not physically prevent anybody from entering or leaving Prebble's premises. The protest was peaceful.

Prebble & Co. took out a civil case and claimed the protesters were 'besetting' their offices and causing a nuisance on the public highway outside. Denning and his colleagues heard Prebble's application for an injunction to stop the protests pending a full hearing. While his colleagues supported the rights of the estate agents not to be 'besetted' in arid and unmemorable language, Denning insisted that there was (at the time) no law against picketing unless it was violent and that these pickets should not be in a worse position than those picketing in a trade dispute, which enjoyed legal protection.

Lord Denning identified a number of strands which contributed to the law of protest being vague and almost invisible. While the English common law seemed capable of recognising a right to protest, judges were reluctant to seize the opportunity to do so. Protest was regulated by Parliament. While trade disputes fell into a category of their own, other types of protest were in a state of legal uncertainty. For example, Parliament could pass public order laws like the Public Order Acts of 1936 and 1986 or the Criminal Justice and Public Order Act 1994, which imposed conditions on demonstrations and processions and provided penalties for disobeying the conditions. Under the Highways Acts, obstructing the highway without lawful excuse became a criminal offence. Protest thus becomes something which is possible if Parliament chooses to permit it. Parliament's main function is to heed the wishes of the electorate, and defending the rights of protesters has never been a priority in the minds of the electorate.

The second legal constraint on protest is a public duty on police officers (and ordinary citizens) to prevent a breach of the peace occurring. This arises under a common law dating back to 1361. Until recently, the concept of an anticipatory breach of the peace was an elastic one, capable of a generous interpretation. It was the concept used by Lord Hewart to provide a legal justification for the police stopping Kath Duncan's peaceful street meeting in the 1930s. But a generous use of 'breach of the peace' still persisted in modern times. During the miners' disputes in the 1980s, a group of striking miners in a convoy of cars were stopped a few miles away from where another group of miners were working in the pits. The police stopped the convoy and told them they feared a breach of the peace if the convoy got near the pits. When some of the striking group objected to being ordered to turn back and pushed past the police, they were arrested, like Kath Duncan, for obstructing an officer in the course of his duty. There was no direct evidence that any of the miners in the convoy were intent on violence, nor that they would breach the peace if they reached the pits. The High Court upheld the convictions for obstructing the police.[7] This meant that the activities of some miners, those working in the pits, provided a brake to the activities of others, the striking miners, to protest. This decision proved once again that Dicey's claim that citizens' liberties were safe in the hands of the common law, exemplified in the case of *Beatty v Gillbanks*, was not true in many circumstances.

Obstruction of the highway has also been something of an elastic concept. Lord Chief Justice Parker ruled in 1966 that any occupation of part of a road, 'thus interfering with people having use of the whole of the road', is an obstruction. Whether this is done without lawful excuse will depend on whether the obstruction was reasonable, having regard to all the facts and circumstances.[8] Once again there was little certainty about what would or would not be a lawful obstruction, which made it difficult for protesters to know in advance whether their planned use of the highway would fall foul of the law or not.

There was a double lock on the ability of demonstrators to get their views across. Parliament held the levers of power in their ability to control the conditions for processions and assemblies, while the law of breach of the peace and highway obstruction remained in a state of vagueness. It was up to judges to show some initiative if the elasticity in the wording 'reasonable' and 'breach of the peace' were to be tightened to provide a semblance of recognition of the right to protest being part of modern life.

The opportunity arose when, in 1985, a group of animal rights activists opposed to the fur trade demonstrated outside a shop selling animal fur products, holding banners and handing out leaflets. They were convicted of highway obstruction, but on appeal the High Court ruled that demonstrators have a lawful excuse for using the highway for the purposes of protest if the protesting activity is itself inherently lawful. The court acknowledged that in modern life roads and pavements are not always used exclusively for the purpose of moving about and that handing out leaflets is a normal modern activity. If a demonstration is inherently lawful, depending on the facts and circumstances, using the highway to make a protest will not amount to an obstruction.[9]

This was something of an advance on earlier judicial decisions, but a decisive change in the law's approach to protest law did not happen until ten years later, when a small group of demonstrators gathered on the roadside verge to mark the tenth anniversary of the 'Battle of the Beanfield'. The battle had been between a group of new-age travellers (or a 'band of medieval brigands', as Home Secretary Douglas Hurd had called them) and the police when a series of road blocks were created around Stonehenge, trapping the travellers in a field. Serious violence broke out. The convoy of travellers were attempting to set up a free festival at Stonehenge, although there was a High Court injunction prohibiting the festival from taking place. The police were entitled to stop the convoy, but the police presence vastly outnumbered the travellers and there was disproportionate violence by the officers involved, using truncheons and shields to injure many who were trying to get away. Over 500 arrests were made, rendering it possibly the largest mass arrest of civilians in Britain in modern times. Twenty-four travellers successfully sued the police for wrongful arrest, false imprisonment and damage to property.[10] In June 1995, about twenty demonstrators gathered on the roadside verge of the A344 adjacent to Stonehenge's perimeter fence bearing banners proclaiming 'Never Again' and 'Ten Years of Criminal Injustice'. Anticipating there might be a protest to mark the Battle of the Beanfield, ten days earlier Salisbury District Council had made an order banning the holding of a 'trespassory assembly' within a four-mile radius of Stonehenge. This was in response to an application by the Chief Constable, who believed that an assembly on the verge was likely to result in serious disruption to the life of the community if the order was not made. The power to do so existed in an Act of Parliament.

When Margaret Jones and two other demonstrators were asked to move on, having been warned of the council's banning order, they refused, whereupon they were arrested for taking part in a 'trespassory assembly', which Parliament had made an offence. They were convicted by the local justices, but on appeal to the Crown Court, the convictions were overturned. The Crown Court judge was satisfied that no members of the public were obstructed by the demonstration taking place and the demonstrators had behaved entirely peaceably. When the case reached the House of Lords, it was an interesting period in the development of the law of protest. The Human Rights Act 1998 had been passed by Parliament, but it was not yet in force. Its provisions could be anticipated, but judges were not yet bound to take account of the European Convention in their judgments.

By a majority, the House of Lords decided the law should now recognise that a public highway is essentially a public *place*. In that place a number of activities may happen, not just the use of the place for passing and repassing, and the modern law of protest should not make unlawful what is commonplace and well accepted. Providing the activity in a public place is not an obstruction unreasonably impeding the rights of others to pass and repass then there is a public *right* to assemble in that place. This right applies whether the protest is premeditated or spontaneous. Anticipating the Human Rights 1998 coming into force, the majority held that the starting point is that assembly on the highway will not necessarily be unlawful.[11] This case was an important step forward in the gradual progress English law was making into establishing a right of protest. It created a presumptive freedom to use a highway for a peaceful assembly and protest but held back from declaring, as a matter of law, that a peaceful, non-obstructive use of the highway was invariably lawful. The case helped create some legal zone of protection for protest which cannot be interfered with unless there is some countervailing public interest.

After the turn of the millennium, two events of great importance moved the law of protest in a new direction: the Iraq War and the Human Rights Act, which came into force in 2000. The Human Rights Act required judges to take into account the European Convention on

Human Rights when making legal rulings. Articles 10 and 11 of the Convention provided that freedom of expression and freedom of peaceful assembly and association were protected rights. Legislation in Parliament or English common law which sought to restrict the exercise of those rights must be necessary in the interests of national security or public safety, the prevention of disorder or crime or the protection of the rights and freedoms of others. When the Iraq War began in March 2003, protests were numerous and determined. An air base in Gloucestershire, RAF Fairford, contained American B52 bombers and these planes were used to bomb Baghdad when hostilities against Iraq began. The base became a focus of protest from many organisations. One group, White Overalls Movement Building Liberation Effective Struggles (Wombles), had a reputation for violence and had damaged parts of the air base on the lead-up to the war between December 2002 and March 2003. Acts of mass trespass took place. A peace camp was established. Trespassers entered a munitions storage area, damaged lights on the runway and caused extensive damage to vehicles. A person was found near the base with ingredients for a suspected incendiary device. During that period around fifty arrests were made.

When the air bombardment of Iraq began, another protest group, Gloucestershire Weapons Inspectors, organised a protest demonstration to take place at RAF Fairford on Saturday 22 March 2003, the day after Baghdad was hit by US air strikes. Their theme was to parade as civilian weapons inspectors and protesters were encouraged to dress up in symbolic white overalls. The Gloucestershire Weapons Inspectors gave the Chief Constable of Gloucestershire written notification of their proposed demonstration starting in Fairford High Street and marching to the main gate of the base to deliver a petition and lay flowers. Numbers attending were estimated at 1,000–5,000. The Chief Constable in response issued a direction under the Public Order Act, prescribing the time, place of assembly and procession route, and drawing protesters' attention to the criminal offence of failing to comply with the conditions laid down. Attention was drawn to the danger of entering military premises. There were to be designated drop-off points, policed by officers, where protesters would get out of their vehicles. The Chief Constable formulated a detailed plan to escort the procession route and to protect the gate to the base with barriers. There was a large police presence.

The Chief Constable had intelligence that the protesters were likely to include some 'Wombles' known to be hard-line activists intent on entering the base with violence. In these circumstances, he used a power under law to issue a stop and search notice, enabling police to stop coaches on their way to the protest and search for weapons and disguises. Jane Laporte was part of a group of Quakers, pacifists and veterans of CND Aldermaston marches who boarded a coach in London to go to Fairford for the protest. Unknown to them, the coach also had some 'Wombles' on board and when it was stopped some way from the base, police discovered crash helmets, hard hats, homemade shields, spray paint and scissors. The Chief Constable ordered the coach to return to London forthwith, fearing a breach of the peace; he took the view that ordering the coach to go back was preferable to allowing it to continue until violence at the base actually broke out. The coaches were driven to the motorway, where police motorcycle outriders prevented them from stopping on the hard shoulder or turning off to motorway services, even to allow passengers to relieve themselves. Some suffered acute physical discomfort and embarrassment as a result.

Jane Laporte sought judicial review of the Chief Constable's decision to prevent her from attending the protest and forcibly return her to London on the grounds that his actions interfered with her Convention rights. When the case reached the House of Lords, the judges approached their decision by placing a clear focus on the Convention right to assemble peacefully. This meant that any prior restraint on the exercise of that right called for careful scrutiny. It was not reasonable for the Chief Constable to turn the coaches back simply because he anticipated that some protesters might cause disorder later during the procession. At that stage the large police presence would be capable of identifying the violent 'Wombles' element and, if necessary, arrests could be made. A breach of the peace was not imminent at the stage the coaches were stopped and Jane Laporte's right to protest was curtailed. Lord Bingham quoted European human rights cases at Strasbourg when judges had said they must be satisfied that a member state had exercised its discretion to restrict a right reasonably, carefully and in good faith. In addition, a member state had to apply standards in conformity with Convention standards.[12]

This case was a big step forward in the gradual process of evolution towards a law of protest that was principled, clear and compliant with an established right to peaceful assembly granted under the Convention. Secondly, the House of Lords tightened up the elasticity of the ancient principle of stopping something if it was likely to cause a breach of the peace. This concept, unless tightly drawn, placed the balance of power in favour of intervention to stop a protest, as had happened during the miners' dispute and in Kath Duncan's case in the 1930s. *Laporte* established that a breach of the peace had to be 'imminent' for the police to intervene in anticipation of an outbreak of violence. On the facts, a breach of the peace was not imminent when the coaches were stopped some distance from the air base. Judges were now giving Kath Duncan's case the scrutiny it deserved but was not given in the 1930s.

In 1997, a couple of Christian fundamentalists were standing on the steps of Wakefield Cathedral preaching loudly about morality, God and the Bible to a crowd who did not necessarily agree with everything they heard. They decided to express themselves in Anglo-Saxon terms, going beyond good-natured heckling. A police officer asked the preachers to desist, but when they carried on he arrested them as he feared a breach of the peace. A Bench of justices and a Crown Court judge thought the arrest was lawful as the policeman believed a future breach of the peace would be a natural consequence of the preachers' insistence on continuing despite the sometimes noisy reception. Two judges of the High Court took a different view and placed emphasis on the free speech principle the facts of the case threw up. Lord Justice Sedley said free speech included speech that could be irritating, contentious, eccentric, heretical, unwelcome or provocative. English law upheld that right providing the use of the right to free speech did not provoke violence. Britain does not recognise 'state control of unofficial ideas'.[13]

The dividing line between speech which is likely to provoke violence and speech which is merely offensive and provocative is not always easy to draw, but it becomes easier if the starting point is to recognise the importance of the principles of protest and free speech before the limitations or constraints on those principles are examined. When a parade in Luton town centre was held in 2009 to celebrate the safe return of the Royal Anglian Regiment from a tour of duty in Afghanistan, many well-wishers and relatives attended, as did a group who shouted at the soldiers 'terrorists', 'murderers', 'baby killers', 'rapists' 'burn in hell'. The High Court said the words went further than opinions vigorously expressed: they were, in the context of the event, inflammatory and potentially defamatory and were likely to provoke a strong reaction from the majority attending the parade.[14]

Recent foreign wars and especially the Iraq War prompted a new style of protest. Now there was a feeling by some that direct action involving damage to property could be justified if such damage was committed in furtherance of a higher good, the prevention of aggression. A week before Jane Laporte's attempted protest at RAF Fairford, a group had broken into the base and damaged fuel tankers and bomb trailers and a few days later another group plotted to damage the runway at the base and one protester attempted to set fire to a US aircraft. These actions were intended to frustrate and perhaps stop bombing raids on Iraq. At another military facility in Southampton, a group chained themselves to railings and to tanks which were about to be loaded for shipment to Iraq for the purposes of war. English law allows a person to use force or to damage property if it is reasonable to do so in the circumstances in the prevention of crime. The protesters claimed they had a duty to prevent 'aggression' by armed forces participating in an illegal war. The House of Lords, hardly surprisingly, rejected this purported justification for criminal acts of damage. Aggression is not a crime in the domestic law of England and Wales.[15]

The rejection by the judges of lawful excuse for damaging property on the grounds that it was done to stop aggression by a nation state did not signal any judicial retreat from the steady advance towards a more sympathetic judicial approach to protest that was taking place in the early 2000s. By now, protests against Trident missiles, export of live animals, fox hunting, climate change and capitalism were becoming features of modern Britain. Protesters were becoming confident and litigious. Most protesters whose activities were stopped or who were arrested for specific offences argued their corner in court. Judges were forced to rule on the legality of police actions when protests were broken up, protesters were moved on or processions were diverted. Protest law now engaged judges in a way that had not happened previously.

Occupy London was a movement for social justice and part of the international Occupy movement, which defined itself as a loose collection of individuals working to create alternatives to an 'unjust and undemocratic' system. It demanded an end to global tax injustice, objected to a form of democracy representing corporations not people and sought structural changes for authentic global equality. The protests began in solidarity with the Occupy Wall Street protests in New York and the London-based contingent of the Spanish 15-M movement. In October 2011, a large encampment was set up outside St Paul's Cathedral in the City of London on land which was partly owned by the Corporation of London and partly by the Church. Initially, the canon of St Paul's, Reverend Giles Fraser, said he was happy for people to exercise their right to protest peacefully outside, but within a week the cathedral was forced to close.

The camp consisted of between 150 and 200 tents, many of them used by protesters, either regularly or from time to time, as overnight accommodation, and several larger tents used for other activities and services including the holding of meetings and the provision of education (called Tent City University), a library, a first aid facility, a place for women and children, a place where food and drink were served, and a welfare facility. The size and extent of the camp varied over time. By the time a judge granted the City of London power to evict the protesters, the camp had become a semi-permanent feature of the landscape of the City of London.

The protest seemed patently unlawful. It consisted of an informal community with its own infrastructure occupying the land of another, which conflicted with the Highways Act, the Town and Country Planning Act and the Ecclesiastical Courts Jurisdiction Act. The camp put considerable strain on the drainage system, reduced available public space for the use of others, caused a nuisance by the generation of noise and interfered with the Article 9 rights in the European Convention (freedom of thought, conscience and religion) of those who wanted to worship in the cathedral.

While at first sight this particular protest seemed an abuse of a Convention right, the Court of Appeal took care when upholding the eviction to stress that the limits on the right to lawful assembly will depend on a number of factors. To what extent would the continuation of the assembly breach domestic law? What was the actual interference to the rights of others caused by the protest? How long did the protest go on? Lastly, the court ruled that it was appropriate to take into account the general character of views whose expression the Convention was designed to protect. Here, the views the protesters were promulgating were of 'very great political importance'.[16] The care with which Lord Neuberger, Master of the Rolls, analysed the legal foundations of protest law would have been unthinkable to the judges who closed down the peaceful picket at an Islington estate agent's offices thirty-five years earlier.

Judges were now scrutinising carefully the legality of stopping protests, using logical reasoning that judges in Strasbourg were adopting in relation to protests in parts of Europe whose governments often wanted to stifle dissent. English judges were examining and applying the Strasbourg interpretation of the right to protest, which was more generous to protesters than English law had been in the years leading up to the Human Rights Act 1998. An example of the modern, Strasbourg-led approach to protest occurred in a case about the legality of a Ministry of Defence bylaw. A new bylaw prohibited camping on a 'controlled area' outside the Atomic Weapons Establishment at Aldermaston. In ruling on the lawfulness of the bylaw, a judge said this:

> Rights worth having are unruly things. Demonstrations and protests are liable to be a nuisance. They are liable to be inconvenient and tiresome, or at least perceived as such by others who are out of sympathy with them. Sometimes they are wrong-headed and misconceived.

Sometimes they betray a kind of arrogance: an arrogance which assumes that spreading the word is always more important than the mess which, often literally, the exercise leaves behind. In that case, firm but balanced regulation may be well justified. In this case there is no substantial factor of that kind.

The judge was commenting on the protest by the Aldermaston Women's Peace Camp which took place on the second weekend of each month on a controlled area outside the Atomic Weapons Establishment which had been open to the public since 1986. On the designated weekend, vigils, meetings and demonstrations were held to protest about the activities inside the establishment and the protesters stayed overnight from Friday to Sunday in tents. The protest had gone on for over twenty years and was consistently peaceful. Then, in 2007, the Ministry of Defence issued a bylaw which prohibited camping in the controlled area, which brought the peace camp to an abrupt end. The judges ruled that the new bylaw was an unlawful and disproportionate curtailment to the right to protest.[17]

By the time of Nora Ziegler's demonstration outside the international arms fair at the Excel Centre in 2017, English judges had become accustomed to pronouncing on the rights and the limitations on the right to protest. The open-ended and vague notion that permitted the police to intervene and stop a protest on the grounds that it would provoke a breach of the peace were reined in and the notion of breach of the peace was defined tightly. Highways were recognised as public spaces where a variety of activities, including peaceful protest, could take place and protest itself was judicially recognised as an important human right. The purpose and intention of the protesters were factors that could legitimately be taken into account in judging whether restrictions on the right to protest were necessary. These were big changes from the 1970s and 1980s, when a right to protest was not recognised and the nod of judicial approval was given to the police to use 'breach of the peace' as a tool to stop protests in their tracks.

The case of *Ziegler v DPP* applied the principles that judges were gradually developing and gave broad scope to magistrates and judges to focus on the nature, duration and purpose of the protest when deciding, in all the circumstances as they appeared to the court, whether the restriction or curtailment of it imposed by the police was justified in law.

Meanwhile, in Parliament, the government had not lost its interest in curtailing and restricting the activities of protesters. It is ironic that at the very time *Ziegler* was being decided in the Supreme Court, the House of Commons was embarking on legislation to erode freedom to protest and to enhance police powers. The Police, Crime, Sentencing and Courts Act 2022 allows the police to impose conditions on processions and assemblies if they reasonably believe the noise generated by the protest will have an impact on persons or organisations in the vicinity. Impact includes 'alarm or distress' to persons in the vicinity of the protest. The government provided no data or concrete evidence that noise causing distress is a problem which requires legislation to fix. On the contrary, the purpose of the legislation appears to be to restrict protests which by their very nature are an expression of collective solidarity and as such can be noisy. The purported justification for this measure that a proper 'balance' must be struck between the rights of the protesters and the rights of the wider community overlooks the fact that protest is a protected right under the European Convention. Rights are only worth having if they are occasionally boisterous, often inconvenient and frequently tiresome. The new Act appears not to recognise this clear legal fact by including a provision empowering the Home Secretary to make regulations defining what 'serious disruption' means in an Act of Parliament, amending the Public Order Act 1986. In addition, the new Act permits the present or any future Home Secretary to give examples of cases in which a public procession 'is or is not to be treated as resulting in serious disruption'.[18] This effectively gives permission to any Home Secretary to decide which sorts of protests are lawful without parliamentary approval of the power used. But protests should not be stopped on a politician's whim. Protests are a part of democracy itself.

The legislative decisions of Boris Johnson's administration since 2019 have sharply divided opinion in the field of civil liberties. While the House of Commons acceded to every demand by the executive to try to stifle the effectiveness of protest, the Police, Crime, Sentencing and Courts Bill had a less compliant reception in the House of Lords. Lord Hain, a veteran of anti-apartheid protests, stated that the Bill represented the biggest threat to dissent and non-violent protest in his lifetime. He was supported by many Conservatives, including Lord Deben, who thought the Bill went too far in seeking to clamp down on protest, an essential element of democracy. The Bishop of Leeds observed that it was ironic that statues celebrating the dissent of Gandhi and Mandela were in Parliament Square while inside the Palace of Westminster Members of Parliament were legislating to clamp down on protest. The Bishop of Bristol reminded the House that the biblical prophet was rarely silent and certainly not popular with those in power. A series of devastating defeats was inflicted on the government. There was a stand-off between Lords and Commons on key features of the Bill, which was only resolved when the Commons used its majority to insist the Lords' objections were defeated. Now, the government is starting again with a Public Order Bill to prevent protests like Nora Ziegler's by making 'locking on' a criminal offence. This is legally so vague it could potentially criminalise a couple walking in the street arm in arm if they were so enamoured of each other they did not realise they might cause significant disruption to another couple walking in the opposite direction.

Democracies are not silent vessels sailing in a calm sea. Democracies exist in turbulent seas where the vessel of state can be rocked to the discomfort of its rulers. Protests are part of modern democratic life. *Ziegler v DPP* is one of the cases that made modern Britain because judges over the past thirty-five years have recognised this and fashioned the common law and the interpretation of statutes to reflect this fact. The present government's purpose in applying new restrictions on the right to protest will only reinvigorate old tensions between the exercise of rights and the desire of the legislature to curtail them. It remains to be seen how the new restrictions will be interpreted by the modern judiciary.

Chapter 7

Privacy – The Actor and the Redtop

In 1990, Gorden Kaye was one of the most recognisable faces on British television. For the previous six years he had been the star of the long-running sitcom *'Allo 'Allo*, playing the clueless French barman, René Artois, during the German occupation of Normandy in the Second World War. In January 1990, Kaye became an unfortunate victim of the Burns Day storm when hurricane-force winds swept across Britain. A piece of wood from an advertisement hoarding became detached and hit the car the actor was driving. It penetrated the windscreen, leaving him with serious head injuries. He was lucky to survive. He suffered brain damage and needed surgery. Afterwards he was nursed in intensive care occupying a single room at a London hospital so that visitors could be limited. Then, without the consent of his doctors or the hospital authorities, a photographer and a reporter from the *Sunday Sport* newspaper burst into the room, spoke to the actor and took a number of photographs of scars to his head. Gorden Kaye had no recollection of this invasion of his seclusion in hospital, but his agent took action against the editor of the newspaper on his behalf as he was too ill to manage his affairs for himself. Kaye's agent wanted the court to stop the photographs and the story being published.

For most people at the time, the behaviour of the newspaper was utterly reprehensible: the unfortunate actor was helpless to stop his private recovery in a hospital being invaded. The judges who heard the case, *Kaye v Robertson*,[1] had the unhappy task of ruling that there was no law that could help him. English law seemed to be trapped by precedent and history, neither of which had kept pace with the public's appetite for sensational journalism. Britain simply did not have a decent privacy law, at least not in March 1990. Twenty-nine years later, when Sir Cliff Richard learned while he was on holiday that cameras from the BBC were broadcasting his house in England being searched by police, the law had been transformed. When Sir Cliff took legal action, the courts not only recognised privacy as a right but awarded him substantial damages from the BBC.

The story of how a privacy law evolved in modern Britain can be traced directly to *Kaye v Robertson* in 1990. The case exposed a gap in the common law which Parliament had been reluctant to close with legislation to make the right to a private life part of English law. In the period following Gorden Kaye's case, public faith in the ethics of the British media went into decline while people's awareness of the importance of a private life advanced. In this sea change in public perception, Parliament stood on the sidelines. The recognition now that people have a legitimate expectation that their privacy will be respected while preserving freedom of expression as a value was brought about entirely by judges. Privacy rights are now a part of modern Britain and Gorden Kaye pointed the way towards this conclusion in 1990.

There had been, quite literally, an invasion of Gorden Kaye's privacy at the Charing Cross Hospital. The editor of the *Sunday Sport* believed his rivals might be prepared to pay money to interview the famous actor, so he decided he would make a direct approach in order to get free access. On 13 February 1990, a reporter and photographer went into the quiet room on the ward, despite notices forbidding access. Once in, they refused to leave when asked to do so by hospital staff. They had to be ejected by security, but not before they had taken flash photographs of the badly injured actor in bed. The editor had no shame in filing an affidavit with the High Court to boast he had achieved a 'great old-fashioned scoop'. Gorden Kaye's agent, on the other hand, had to wrap the claim to privacy under somewhat unrealistic rights of action which the courts would recognise. His options were libel, trespass to the person, malicious falsehood and passing off, a civil tort of misrepresenting the goodwill of the trade of somebody else. Libel was a non-starter, as it was by no means inevitable a jury would conclude Kaye had been defamed in the circumstances of the case. Trespass to the person, on the facts, was equally weak, as the claim rested on the flash photographs not any physical contact with the actor's body. Passing off was also hopeless, as Gorden Kaye could not be classed as a trader in relation to an interest, namely the story about the accident. That left malicious falsehood, which was a possibility, but only because the actor was in no physical or mental state to give consent to the words the *Sunday Sport* wanted to attribute to him. The words, therefore, could be deemed false and it would be malicious to publish them as the story had potential value to Kaye. He would suffer damage if the photographs were published.

The three judges in the Court of Appeal who gave this ruling were embarrassed that English law was so tepid when it came to recognising the importance of privacy. Lord Justice Bingham, who later became Master of the Rolls, Lord Chief Justice and Senior Law Lord and who was undoubtedly one of the greatest judges of the twentieth century, remarked that it was fortunate that Kaye's mental faculties were such that the law could protect him.

Had he failed to establish any cause of action, we should of course have been powerless to act, however great our sympathy for the plaintiff and however strong our distaste for the defendants' conduct ... This case highlights, yet again, the failure of both the common law and statute to protect in an effective way the personal privacy of individual citizens ... If ever a person has a right to be let alone by strangers with no public interest to pursue, it must surely be when he lies in hospital recovering from brain surgery and in no more than partial command of his faculties. It is this invasion of his privacy which underlies the plaintiff's complaint. Yet it alone, however gross, does not entitle him to relief in English law.

Lord Justice Glidewell said the facts of the case provided a graphic illustration of the desirability of Parliament considering whether and in what circumstances a law of privacy should be created in order to protect the private life of individuals. Lord Justice Leggatt despaired of a lack of a privacy right in Britain, especially as a privacy law had been developed in Germany and in the United States: 'It is to be hoped that the making good of this signal shortcoming in our law will not be long delayed.' At the time, few people disagreed with the judges' plea for a privacy law, but the press were in no mood to give away any of their power to satisfy the whims of those who valued privacy. In November 1989, *The Times* had rather pompously declared:

It is the sincere conviction of responsible journalists from every type of newspaper that any law to enforce ethical conduct – by attempting, for instance, to prohibit the invasion of privacy – would seriously harm the public interest. In the name of protecting the innocent, it would shelter the guilty ... The rights of journalists – to ask questions, state facts, express opinions – are in essence no different from the rights of the citizenry at large. They rest on an identical perception of what it means to be free.[2]

Anybody who believed Gorden Kaye had proved the case for a privacy law was in for a disappointment. The press were riding high and seemingly immune from any control or regulation either by Parliament or by the judges. Two years earlier, the chat-show host Russell Harty, like Gorden Kaye a familiar face on television, was harried by the tabloid press as he lay seriously ill with hepatitis in a Leeds hospital. In the same year as Gorden Kaye received unwelcome visitors in hospital, Diana, Princess of Wales, joined a fitness centre in Isleworth. She used a pseudonym to protect her identity. The owner of the gym saw an opportunity to make money and installed a sophisticated Leica camera above a false ceiling. Not only was the camera capable of high-quality pictures of the exercise machine used by the princess immediately below but the camera shutter was inaudible. The gym owner could activate it from his office via pulses of air sent through a tube to the camera, which was out of sight to anybody using the gym. It was a peeping tom exercise of the most disreputable kind.

Three years later, about fifty pin-sharp photographs of the Princess of Wales exercising in what she was given to understand was a private space were offered to the *Sunday Mirror*. The specious reason given by the paper for this gross breach of confidence was that the ability of an unknown person to take the photographs proved the princess's security was at risk. In the event, the *Mirror* paid substantial damages and costs to the princess in a settlement, fearing, no doubt, that unless they did so Parliament would introduce swingeing new privacy laws.

This was exactly what the chairman of the Press Complaints Commission feared when he issued a warning to the industry in 1992 that its behaviour had to improve. Lord McGregor, a former Scottish academic, warned that unless editors collectively put their house in order Parliament would introduce a privacy law, with sanctions if they did not comply. His purpose was to protect the press from regulation and control. His warning went unheeded. Later that year, the *Daily Mirror* splashed a story about the Duchess of York, Sarah Ferguson, under the headline 'Fergie's Stolen Kisses: Truth about duchess and the Texan millionaire' with a picture showing her feet being kissed by a man by the pool in the grounds of a villa in the south of France. The pictures had been taken with a sophisticated telephoto lens from some distance away. The Texan millionaire, John Bryan, got nowhere in an English court in his attempt to stop publication of the photographs. Hard on the heels of this story, the prominent politician Paddy Ashdown was exposed by a newspaper, relying on documents stolen from Mr Ashdown's solicitor, for having had a brief affair with his secretary five years earlier. The story had no relevance to his political life and was wounding and distressing to his wife.

The early 1990s revealed a chasm in perception. On the one hand, judges and a substantial section of public opinion were in favour of a law which protected privacy; on the other, certain sections of the tabloid press seemed determined to print what they liked, when they liked, if it helped circulation figures. On the surface, Gorden Kaye's case did not appear to have changed anything. This assessment is not, in fact, quite correct. Firstly, the case of *Kaye v Robertson* did result in the High Court ordering the paper to make clear that the photographs and the 'interview' with Gorden Kaye were obtained without his consent. This, effectively, killed the story, as it would reveal the methods used by the paper to obtain it. Secondly, the sequel was happier for Kaye than it was for the *Sunday Sport*. Kaye recovered from his ordeal and resumed his role of René for another two years and then toured with a stage version of the show, giving over a thousand performances. The *Sunday Sport*, on the other hand, went into administration in 2011. The paper's reliance on sex and celebrities was not a recipe for success. Thirdly, and most importantly, the case of *Kaye v Robertson* proved to be a turning point in the development of a privacy law in Britain.

If a law on privacy was to become part of the evolving process of English common law, there were considerable hurdles to overcome. The most formidable obstacle was the power of the press, which has been part of the fabric of the nation since the printing press became a means for distributing news and comment to a wide audience. The nineteenth-century press barons thought William Blackstone, the great eighteenth-century English jurist, provided moral and legal authority for unlimited freedom. He had stated:

> The liberty of the press is indeed essential to the nature of a free state ... Every free man has an undoubted right to lay what sentiments he pleases before the public ... but if he publishes what is improper, mischievous, or illegal, he must take the consequences of his own temerity.[3]

Within twenty-five years of these words being written, stamp duty on newspapers had been abolished, printing presses were fast and efficient, the telegraph and the railways ensured news could spread quickly and the newly literate among the population were devouring newspapers. These developments required some ethical consideration about the purpose of a free press. Newspapers can provide a public forum for information, ideas and entertainment to be circulated and held up to scrutiny. A free press is a condition for the attainment of truth. Different news outlets will present different opinions and thus foster understanding and democratic decision-making. A free press acts as a constraint on power and provides a check on the misuse of political authority. The existence of a free press is an essential part of a liberal democracy, as it can serve as a bulwark against duplicity and tyranny.

These familiar arguments for a press free from censorship, regulation or control have bolstered the power of the owners of media outlets. They can claim, with some justification, to play an important role in the affairs of the nation. The power of the press has been harnessed in a way that has direct appeal to a wide readership. When Alfred Harmsworth founded the *Daily Mail* in 1896, he wanted a paper that would be full of 'disasters, murders, gossip, celebrity, sensationalism, sport, crosswords, competitions and scoops – and news told from a human angle'.[4] It was a recipe of genius and has survived to this day.

Harmsworth's inclusion of gossip and sensationalism as two of the essential ingredients of journalism was shrewd. They engage an aspect of human interest which the cultural historian Fred Inglis has called, simply, 'celebrity'.[5] Celebrity, Inglis argues, is the phenomenon when the doubts, aspirations and predicaments of ordinary people are projected into a colossal visible intimacy, made possible when cinema allowed actors to live in the public gaze but in the pretence of privacy. The private lives of film stars were turned into the stuff of fame when their glamour, power, money, holidays and personal relationships could be observed by those who envied and loved them. The flip side was that their privacy could be invaded by those who hated and despised them. They may be adored or denigrated not simply on account of their behaviour as stars and celebrities but on account of how the reader or audience wishes to perceive their behaviour. Celebrity, Inglis explains, combines knowability and distance. 'Political leader and cinema star are intensely familiar (one of the family) by way of the cinema screen and … their voices on the living room radio', creating an 'informal intimacy watched by the envious and their hired eavesdroppers, the gossip columnists and photographers'.[6]

Inglis's point is that there is a strong wish for our chosen celebrities, whether they are actors, models, footballers, singers or entertainers, not to have a private life. If they lived their lives entirely in private, our desire for glamour and gossip could not be fulfilled. Harmsworth and his successors knew exactly how to tap into a readership. They realised the public's cravings for an insight into the lives of the rich and famous had to be satisfied. But this development did not delight everybody. Samuel D. Warren was a prominent lawyer and socialite in Boston, USA, who often appeared in the limelight when his glamorous dinner parties were commented upon in the Boston press in the 1890s. Warren did not object to this, but when the paparazzi descended onto his daughter's wedding, he used his erudition as a lawyer and his responsibilities as a father to compose the most influential essay in defence of privacy that had ever, up to then, been written. He and Louis D. Brandeis, a future Supreme Court justice, had this to say about celebrity culture:

> Gossip is no longer the resource of the idle and of the vicious, but has become a trade, pursued with industry as well as effrontery ... To occupy the indolent, column upon column is filled with idle gossip, which can only be procured by intrusion upon the domestic circle ... When personal gossip attains the dignity of print, and crowds the space available for matters of real interest, what wonder that the ignorant and thoughtless mistake its relative importance.[7]

These comments appear high-handed, elitist and out of touch with the times when both in the USA and in Europe the Harmsworth formula was selling papers, pleasing the public and lining the pockets of newspaper owners. Celebrity sells papers, as *Paris Match* (founded in 1949 and still in print), *Picture Post* (which lasted from 1938 to 1957) and more recent arrivals, *Hello!*, *OK!*, *Heat* and *GQ*, prove. When a primal desire for familiarity with the famous is placed alongside the historical and principled arguments for a free, unregulated press then the counterarguments for privacy start at a disadvantage, despite the erudition and passion of Warren and Brandeis. When the lives of the readers are largely private because they are not celebrities, there is not a huge popular reason for introducing privacy laws.

Part of the reason notions of privacy as a human right are so difficult to establish is the difficulty of defining exactly what privacy means. On a very broad front it means a place where personal autonomy can thrive, an area of defensible space where we do not have to engage with the outside world. This is the rather opaque concept of privacy meaning the place of personal and emotional security, but these meanings are nebulous and are soon vulnerable to the question of where the boundaries lie between the public and the private. Nobody, apart from those in the strictest of monastic orders, leads an entirely private life, as sociability is an instinct of mankind which ensures survival. Raymond Wacks has argued that privacy cannot become a valuable personal right unless it is defined with some precision. He suggests that privacy is essentially about the protection of personal *information*. What is reasonable for an individual to regard as private about himself or herself? We may all have our own ideas, but the boundaries between private and public have to be objectively assessed. It may be unreasonable for our friends to know anything about our financial arrangements or aspects of our health, but it would be entirely reasonable for the Exchequer to know about the former and our doctor about the latter. By the same token, our personal tastes and sexual preferences are no business of the tax authorities, and our friendships are irrelevant to what our doctor should know about us.[8]

If privacy is looked at in this way, it becomes a matter of what is *confidential* in the circumstances and what is not. Something may properly and objectively be confidential to an individual in one context but not in another. This is a persuasive perspective on privacy and is, as a matter of history, the way in which privacy law has evolved in modern Britain.

What has become known as the law of confidence is the brainchild of our modern privacy laws and it was created by two celebrities, Prince Albert of Saxe-Coburg and Gotha and Margaret, Duchess of Argyll.

Queen Victoria's consort, Prince Albert, was a celebrity in his own right. His biographer, Jules Stewart, has stated that it might be more appropriate to call the period of his fame 'the Albertian age' rather than the Victorian one, such was his fame and his influence on British life.[9] He was, of course, devoted to the Queen, and among the couple's treasured possessions were etchings of the family and the dogs. William Strange was a publisher who had offices near Fleet Street. It became common knowledge in London society that Strange had in his possession some works of art which could command a high price. They were copies of the etchings kept in the Queen's private apartments at Windsor Castle. How did a London publisher get hold of them and how could he be prevented from selling them? If Strange had stolen them then he could be arrested for theft, but Strange had not stolen them. The pictures had come into his possession from somebody who had bought them on the open market. It turned out that an employee at a firm of printers in Windsor, who had custody of the pictures in order to make copies of them, had filched a few spare copies which were lying around in the print room and made off with them. The originals remained the property of the Queen and Albert, the Prince Consort.

The Queen was not amused. In truth, she was so angry that copies of private family pictures were being offered for sale that she wanted to pursue Strange in the courts. She could not do so as the sovereign and so Prince Albert brought the case against Strange, which was heard in the High Court in London in 1849.[10] The purpose of the legal case was to obtain a court order stopping Strange from offering the pictures for sale. Hardly surprisingly, given the identity of the claimant, the judge agreed and Strange was restrained by a High Court injunction from any further dealings with the pictures. Strange appealed, arguing that he would voluntarily abandon plans to market the pictures as he now understood the hurt the Queen had suffered by her private pictures being made available for general public view. His point, in appealing against the injunction, was that the principle of freedom to publish was under attack unless the injunction was lifted.

The Court of Appeal were forced to make a judgment based on sound legal principles and to give a ruling for the future on how, in situations like this, others could be protected. The problem was there was no such thing as any common law of privacy that the vice-chancellor, the senior Chancery judge, could turn to in order to protect the Queen and Prince Albert. Nor was there a breach of contract involved, as Strange did not have any contractual relationship with the royal couple. The ingenious solution devised by the court was to rule that Strange had obtained the pictures in breach of trust owed to Prince Albert. The trust had been betrayed by the worker in the Windsor print shop, a man named Middleton, and he should not be allowed to benefit from this wrongdoing. The royal family were entitled to decide who should have access to their own state of privacy. They had not given permission for the distribution of the pictures and therefore any person who flouted the family decision had *breached the confidence* of the claimant, Prince Albert. This included the defendant, William Strange, who had benefited from Middleton's actions. The court ordered the copies to be destroyed and prohibited any further publication.

It was an ingenious and, for the royal family, an entirely welcome legal development. The basic point the Victorian (or perhaps Albertian) judges established was to rule that the direct or indirect recipients of confidential information may be restrained by the courts from using or disclosing it. Prince Albert had an exclusive interest in the etching and was therefore entitled to a protection from the law to preserve that interest. The prince did not contemplate copies of his private material being distributed. The point established in the case was the *confidentiality* of personal information, not that the information itself was entitled to protection. Prince Albert won because a remedy in equity looks at the conscience of one party (Strange) to stand by his duties, which arise out of his relationship with the other (Prince Albert). This was still something a court of equity would recognise even though Strange had no contractual or personal relationship with the prince. Strange should, in conscience, have known that the prince had a confidential relationship with his printer in Windsor. It was not essential that the etchings were, for the Queen and her family, private for Prince Albert to win on confidentiality grounds.

This set the law of England and Wales moving in the direction of confidentiality rather than privacy, even if, in reality, a future case would be commenced only if private information had been misused. Prince Albert's case did not directly engage the boundary between privacy and press freedom, as no newspaper was involved in the case. The same cannot be said of the complicated, expensive and long-running legal dispute between the Duke and Duchess of Argyll a little more than a hundred years later. The couple exposed their disastrous marriage and bitter enmity to an awestruck public in a series of battles in the courts. The litigation that each seemed to relish in pursuing had just the right mix for popular newspapers: sex and the private lives of the upper classes.

Margaret Whigham, the future duchess, was first married to Charles Sweeny at the Brompton Oratory in 1933 and it made the front page of the *Daily Mirror*. The story was '2,000 gate-crash wedding'. Whether this account was true or false hardly mattered. Margaret was a 'debutante and a socialite' and her marriage to the catch of the London season was news. In 1951, Mr and Mrs Sweeny divorced after each had extra-marital affairs, and Margaret married Ian Campbell, the Duke of Argyll, who had been interned in a prisoner-of-war camp in Germany and had been twice previously married. Margaret's new husband had inherited a home at Inveraray Castle on the shores of Loch Fyne in Scotland and 150,000 acres of land. This was not entirely to the liking of the duchess, who preferred the life of London society in Mayfair, even though she had set her sights on becoming the Duchess of Argyll.

Perhaps inevitably, after living apart for much of the time, the couple lost interest in one another and sought solace elsewhere. Each was to accuse the other of infidelity in a bitterly fought divorce in Edinburgh. The duke had entered his wife's Mayfair flat in search of evidence of Margaret's adultery, which he needed to prove if the marriage was to be dissolved. Margaret admitted nothing and she resisted her husband's petition for divorce. She wanted the marriage to end on the grounds of the duke's behaviour, including, for good measure, adultery. She cross-petitioned. While lawyers occupied their time preparing for a battle royal in the Scottish divorce courts, Margaret sold her memoirs to *The People* newspaper. She also unwisely embroiled herself in a libel action which she lost, costing her thousands. The only winners were the press, who had much to report about the extraordinary goings-on in this most aristocratic of marriages. Eventually, Margaret dropped her cross-petition and asked her lawyers to concentrate instead on preventing the duke from using her incriminating diary entries and – most salaciously – a photograph of fellatio being performed by a naked woman on an unknown man. The picture was kept in the duchess's writing desk. Unfortunately for the duchess, the naked woman in question was wearing a ring which bore an Argyll heirloom, a ring only the duchess had worn. Her explanation that the unknown man was, in fact, her husband cut no ice with the judge.

When the divorce case commenced at the Court of Session in

Edinburgh in February 1963, there was not a seat to be had in the tiny courtroom. It was the case of the decade. The judge, Lord Wheatley, was a sardonic individual who was also a Roman Catholic. He took pains to go through all the evidence in detail when giving his decision. He concluded that not only had Margaret committed adultery but, worse still, she was a highly sexed woman who had ceased to be satisfied with normal relations and had started to indulge in what he could only describe as 'disgusting sexual activities to gratify a basic sexual appetite'. The newspapers could hardly have asked for more. The 'headless man', as the figure in the photograph was modestly called, remained anonymous, but the duchess had been vilified. *The People* published the duchess's memoirs the same year.

The contested divorce in Edinburgh was far from the end of court battles between the Argylls. The duke, no doubt chagrined by his former wife's memoirs in *The People*, wanted to give his account of the marriage. He wanted to rely on all the material he had seized from the duchess's flat, including her diaries. When the duchess learned of her husband's intentions, she took action in the English court of equity, the Chancery Division of the High Court in London. The notion of equity has a long history, and the word connotes fairness and justice. Equitable remedies, like injunctions, were traditionally associated with a court of equity. The duchess took her case before Mr Justice Ungoed-Thomas to restrain her former husband from communicating to the press anything about her former married life, including her personal affairs and private conduct. Her action succeeded and what the judge said about the law of confidence proved to be of great importance in the story of how a privacy law evolved.

The judge ruled that a court of equity could restrain a breach of confidence independently from any right at law. Marriage was, in essence, a confidential relationship and just because a subsequent act of adultery by one party or the other had brought the marriage to an end did not relieve either party from the obligation of confidence that being married had entailed. The nature of marital confidence meant it had to be honoured by all those who got their hands on material about a marriage, including the newspapers who wanted to promote the duke's side. Confidential material was different from that used specifically for the purpose of proof of a marriage breakdown. Here the duke wanted the public to know everything that went on behind the closed doors of Inveraray Castle. As the judge put it, the wife's adultery, 'repugnant though it be, should not license the husband to broadcast unchecked the most intimate confidences of earlier and happier days'.[11]

It was a ground-breaking judgment, but it took many years for its implications to make their mark in the common law. Twelve years after the Argyll case, another equity judge, the vice-chancellor of the Chancery Court, refused to recognise the existence of a law of privacy in England when an antiques dealer with a criminal record complained his privacy had been infringed by the police, who were tapping his telephone under a warrant permitting them to do so.[12] Meanwhile, newspapers continued to behave as if privacy did not exist, and Parliament offloaded responsibility to 'the great and the good' to come up with solutions. In the period 1947–1977 there were no fewer than three Royal Commissions appointed to make proposals for reforming the behaviour of the press. They achieved very little, and Parliament did not want to take on responsibility for legislating to protect privacy. There may have been good reasons for this reluctance, as privacy is notoriously difficult to define in precise legislative language and Parliament did not want to play the role of censor. But so long as tabloid editors refused to restrain themselves, the courts refused to recognise privacy and Parliament refused to legislate, privacy would exist only theoretically, not in reality.

The law of confidence, which the Argyll case had established as a means of protecting privacy, was not much help for most cases. Gorden Kaye could not rely on breach of confidence in his complaint against a gross invasion of privacy as no relationship of confidence existed on the facts of his case. There seemed to be an impasse. Then, quite suddenly, a celebrity couple went to the High Court to complain about press intrusion into their wedding. Privacy was back on the agenda.

The film stars Michael Douglas and Catherine Zeta-Jones got married at the Plaza Hotel in New York in November 2000, just a month after the Human Rights Act 1998 became incorporated into English law. It was a lavish affair. Hundreds of guests attended, but each guest had been told that photography was strictly forbidden. The couple had signed a contract with *OK!* magazine giving it exclusive rights to photographs of the wedding and reception. Unknown to the newlyweds, a paparazzo had infiltrated the wedding and taken photographs and then sold them to *OK!*'s arch-rival, *Hello!*; six of them were published in *Hello!* as exclusives. The case was complicated. Was it a photographic representation of the event which was important, so that anybody who published photographs of the event interfered with *OK!*'s duty of confidence to the Douglases, or had *Hello!* simply replicated in its magazine a representation of an event which *OK!* had already put in the public domain by publishing its own exclusive? And did anybody really care? Privacy is about a private hurt, not a commercial squabble.

The case was argued during many excursions to the Chancery Division of the High Court, the Court of Appeal and the House of Lords in relation to an injunction restraining publication and in substantive breach of confidence proceedings.[13] The Douglases took their case to an English court in the hope that the recently enacted Human Rights Act 1998 would help their claim. In one of the hearings, involving an injunction that a High Court judge had imposed on *Hello!*, Lord Justice Sedley thought that English law had reached a point where it would recognise and protect privacy and that the couple's privacy had been infringed. Lord Justice Keene thought the law had moved on sufficiently so that Gorden Kaye would now obtain a favourable outcome to the gross invasion of privacy he had suffered. Unfortunately, the Douglas case about wedding photographs turned into a commercial dispute between *Hello!* and O*K!* when the case reached the House of Lords. The opportunity to move the law on and to recognise privacy dissolved. When the dispute got to the House of Lords, the majority ruled the case was about the protection of *commercially* confidential information and nothing more. The House seemed determined not to use the facts of the Douglas case to make progress in creating a privacy law. What was important, according to the House of Lords, was the fact that *OK!* had paid handsomely for a confidence imposed on all guests not to take their own pictures and to permit *OK!* to have the rights to the wedding pictures. *Hello!* had not published authorised pictures. The law of confidence was there to protect *OK!*'s authorised images and *Hello!*'s surreptitiously obtained ones were not, in reality, in the public domain.

Those who wanted a celebrity to come forward with a case that really would force judges to come off the fence did not have long to wait. Within a few weeks of the Douglases' wedding, one of Britain's most glamorous models, Naomi Campbell, was spotted attending Narcotics Anonymous for drug counselling in February 2001. This was newsworthy as Ms Campbell had previously stated publicly that she did not take drugs even though the modelling industry was rife with substance abuse. The *Daily Mirror*, acting no doubt on a tip-off, photographed Ms Campbell leaving a counselling session dressed in a windcheater and a baseball cap. The front-page headline was 'Naomi: I am a drug addict'. The caption to the photograph read: 'Naomi emerges from a gruelling two-hour session.' The picture could also provide a strong clue about where the session had taken place. Piers Morgan, then the editor of the *Mirror*, claimed there was a legitimate public interest in the story as the model had misled the public about her addiction.

The case was not complicated by commercial interests like the Douglas case, but the question of Ms Campbell's privacy was not straightforward. It was not a simple case of 'snooping' or eavesdropping on her privacy, as the photographs were of Ms Campbell in a public place and she was no stranger to being photographed. Nor was it a simple case of divulging private information, as the model had spoken publicly about the fact that she did *not* take drugs. Surely it was in the public interest for a newspaper to correct a false impression given by a public figure? Despite the fact that the existence of privacy was finely balanced, on this occasion the House of Lords did decide to look again at privacy as a value of importance.

English law had recognised freedom of expression as an underlying value of law for some time. It was now the turn of privacy. Britain's highest court simply could not ignore for much longer the obvious point that privacy was a fast-developing concept, lying, as Lord Nicholls put it, 'at the heart of liberty in a modern state'. How could this have been overlooked for so long? By a majority, the House of Lords found that the photographs and the accompanying text amounted to sensitive health information and the protection of this outweighed the right of freedom to publish the information.[14]

Ever since Gorden Kaye had exposed a gaping hole in the law to recognise the importance of privacy, essential to civilised behaviour, judges had kept one eye open to seeing the problem by reviving the law of confidence. Now, the House of Lords was no longer myopic about privacy and the House decided it should be looked at again with care. The judges concluded that the law of confidence was no longer dependent on a relationship of confidence; the doctrine had grown and expanded to the extent that it was now capable of protecting Ms Campbell. She was claiming a wrongful publication of her private information. This new thinking, spurred on by the Human Rights Act 1998, enabled English law to recognise that the principles underlying privacy and freedom of expression in the European Convention on Human Rights existed as a relationship between the individual and the press. The Law Lords admitted there had been a shift in the centre of gravity of breach of confidence actions. From now on, English law would focus on the underlying meaning and purpose of breach of confidence, the right that law gave to control the dissemination of information about one's private life and the right to the esteem and respect of other people.

Now, unshackled by years of precedent which had forbidden judges to think about privacy as a legal right, the House of Lords could examine Ms Campbell's claim carefully and logically. First, irrespective of any privacy law, what is private? The House of Lords thought something is private if the person in question had a 'reasonable expectation of privacy' in the circumstances of the case. Their Lordships and Lady Hale concluded that the old law of confidence, first established in Prince Albert's case, has an extended meaning: confidence means private. In considering whether something is private, the law should focus on how an ordinary person placed in the position of Ms Campbell would feel if faced with the same publicity. Ms Campbell said she felt shocked and betrayed by the way the *Mirror* had covered the story. The wrongful disclosure of private information arises if the person making the disclosure knows or ought to know that the information is private.

Fortunately for Ms Campbell, the Human Rights Act 1998 obliged English judges to have regard to the European Convention on Human Rights (which was not in force at the time of Gorden Kaye's case). Article 8 of the Convention provides that everyone has the right to respect for his or her private and family life, but the right is qualified to the extent that an interference with that right may be justified if it is necessary and legitimate to do so on the grounds of some pressing social need or if it is necessary in order to protect the rights of others. There is, however, another human right, the right to freedom of expression, which is set down in Article 10. This right is similarly qualified and therefore Ms Campbell's Article 8 right may legitimately be interfered with if it is outweighed by the *Mirror's* Article 10 right. A balancing exercise is called for in weighing the two competing rights. This exercise arose when Piers Morgan knew or ought to have known that Ms Campbell had a reasonable expectation that her visits to Narcotics Anonymous would be kept private. The essence of the privacy was that Ms Campbell was receiving treatment akin to medical treatment, an aspect of life which is private, and by exposing it there was a risk the private treatment would be jeopardised.

Once the threshold of a reasonable expectation of privacy is passed, the role of the judge is to balance the competing rights: the right to privacy on the one hand and the right to freedom of expression on the other. Neither has priority over the other. An interference with a privacy right may be justified if it is outweighed by the right to freedom of expression. Conversely, an interference with freedom of expression may be justified by the claim of privacy. The decisive factor in balancing the protection of private life against the freedom of the press to publish should be the contribution that the combined material makes to a debate of general interest.

In Naomi Campbell's case, the balance was very fine indeed. The High Court judge who first heard the case and three members of the House of Lords found for Ms Campbell, but three judges in the Court of Appeal and two in the House of Lords found for the *Daily Mirror*. For Piers Morgan, the decision was a bitter blow: 'Five senior judges found for the *Mirror* throughout the various hearings in this case, four for Naomi Campbell, yet she wins. If ever there was a less deserving case for what is effectively a back-door privacy law it would be Miss Campbell's.'[15] It is difficult to see how a number of hearings, all taking place in public courts, produced a privacy law 'through the back door', but clearly editors of popular newspapers were fearful of their power being diluted.

It could be said Fleet Street was defiant. The *News of the World*, whose stock in trade had always been sex-n-tell confessions or the shaming of celebrities, continued its journalistic traditions as if the Campbell case had never happened. In March 2008, it ran a story under the headline 'F1 boss has sick Nazi orgy with five hookers' followed by the sub-heading 'Son of Hitler-loving fascist in sex shame'. The son of the Hitler-loving fascist was Max Mosley, president of the Fédération Internationale de l'Automobile, and a well-known figure in motorsport. Mosley sued the newspaper on the grounds of breach of confidence and/or unauthorised disclosure of personal information. He won and obtained damages, as the paper's justification for the story, that there was a Nazi theme to sadomasochistic sexual activities between Mosley and a number of women, was untrue. This undermined the newspaper's defence of a public interest in running the story. Mosley admitted engaging in sadomasochism, but, as the judge said, 'The modern approach to privacy and sexual preferences and practices is very different from that of past generations ... Sexual conduct is a significant aspect of human life in respect of which people should be free to choose.' All the participants in events which the newspaper had described as an 'orgy' were willing parties and their behaviour was in private. In the absence of a Nazi theme, the *News of the World* exposure made no contribution to a debate of general interest.[16]

The Mosley case left open the possibility that there might still be circumstances when the sexual behaviour of celebrities would not remain private. In 2010, the *Sunday Mirror* splashed a story about the then England football captain, Rio Ferdinand, under the headline 'My Affair with England Captain Rio'. The source of the story was Carly Storey, a former girlfriend of Ferdinand before his marriage to Rebecca Ellison in 2009, whose relationship with Ferdinand continued after his engagement to Ms Ellison in 2007. Ferdinand had something of a wild reputation as football's bad boy, with driving convictions, a missed drugs test and, on his own admission in a newspaper interview with the *News of the World* in 2006, a history of womanising ('You do get girls coming on to you sometimes and I admit I have succumbed'). He had also written his autobiography to proclaim himself a reformed character. In 2008, the England manager, Fabio Capello, appointed Ferdinand captain of the national side, saying that his choice would be 'a symbol on and off the pitch'. This was a reference to the sacking of Ferdinand's predecessor, John Terry, for having had an extra-marital affair with a teammate's former partner while in charge of the England side. The transformation of Rio Ferdinand from one of football's wild boys to a responsible family man began with his engagement to Ms Ellison, the birth of his first child, his appointment as a patron of the Prince's Trust and the foundation of his own charity in 2008. The *Sunday Mirror* contended there was a public interest in reporting Ms Storey's exercise of her freedom of expression rights that she and Ferdinand continued their relationship until January 2010. There was an additional public interest in exposing Ferdinand's true character as the England captain had admitted he had tried to sneak Ms Storey into hotels where he and the England squad were staying.

The judge ruled that despite Ferdinand's reckless behaviour he did have a reasonable expectation of privacy, but he lost the case because, in the balancing exercise, the *Sunday Mirror* had a legitimate public interest in publishing the story. The paper's freedom of expression rights arose in view of Ferdinand's own press interview with the *News of the*

World and his autobiography. These pieces sought to promote an image of his character that was different from his previous wild times. 'Overall,' said the judge, 'the balancing exercise favours the Defendant's right to freedom of expression over the Claimant's right of privacy.'[17]

Privacy, or the misuse of private information, as judges now call the evolving civil wrong, does not trump freedom of expression. There is always a balancing exercise and the individual who claims a privacy right will not always win. But the new focus on privacy, which simply did not exist as recently as 1990 when Gorden Kaye brought his claim, has changed the climate in which the boundaries between personal autonomy and the public interest in exposing the lives of the rich and famous are drawn. Nowadays, judges will look with intense focus on the precise facts and circumstances which give rise to a privacy claim. Few hypocrites, liars or financial scoundrels will succeed in hiding behind flimsy claims to be left alone. By the same token, the press cannot simply cry 'it is in the public interest' to get the green light to publish from the judges.

In the early 1990s, there was no legal recognition of privacy and Gorden Kaye suffered the indignity of being photographed in the privacy of a hospital bed. There was no public interest at all in taking pictures of the ailing actor in hospital. Twenty-one years later, Naomi Campbell won a historic victory. She was also undergoing medical treatment and this fact trumped the public interest in reporting it, despite her previous denials of drug taking. English law has moved on in a civilised direction, but this does not mean celebrities can always hide behind a cloak of privacy. Rio Ferdinand came to grief as a result of his own promotion of his image. Celebrities cannot cease to be celebrities when they want to lose their status. In 2006, a photographer from the *Daily Mail* happened to catch sight of the celebrity singer and entertainer Sir Elton John arriving in a slightly dishevelled state at his London home having driven from his country home near Windsor. Sir Elton did not consent to being photographed on that occasion, but equally there was nothing in the circumstances of going towards his home from a car that had a reasonable expectation of privacy about it. English law did not require consent to be photographed and therefore his case fell at the first hurdle. Privacy did not arise, and therefore a balancing exercise was not necessary.[18]

The evolution and development of a law of privacy, called misuse of private information, from 1990 until the present day is most vividly illustrated in the excoriating judgment of the conduct of the BBC in relation to the singer and entertainer Sir Cliff Richard given in 2018.[19] The background to the privacy claim brought by Sir Cliff was the historical child sexual abuse scandals involving celebrities like Jimmy Savile, Rolf Harris and Gary Glitter. The Metropolitan Police had been investigating these cases in an operation called Yewtree. Among the complaints was an allegation that Sir Cliff had committed a sexual offence against an adolescent boy at an evangelical Christian rally in Sheffield in the 1980s. This was being handled by South Yorkshire Police. Sir Cliff has never been charged with this offence and has always vehemently denied any sexual interest in children. In the summer of 2014, when Sir Cliff was on holiday in Portugal, a reporter for the BBC received a tip-off that South Yorkshire Police were going to search one of Sir Cliff's properties in Sunningdale in Berkshire. The BBC mounted an operation using a helicopter to record the entry by police officers into the grounds of Sir Cliff's property. When told about this, Sir Cliff became close to physical collapse, but he issued a dignified statement acknowledging he had been aware of an allegation of historical impropriety being made against him, stating the allegation was completely false and promising to co-operate with any police investigation.

In contrast to Sir Cliff's calm denial, the BBC handled the story with what the judge described as 'breathless sensationalism' and depicting the search like a drama, with a reporter at the scene in front of shots of police cars outside the property. The story was a complete misjudgement by the BBC. Police protocol required that the names or identifying details of those suspected of crime should not be made public unless particular circumstances, not present in this case, applied. In their statement to camera, South Yorkshire Police's spokesman did not name Sir Cliff, nor did he identify the property. The BBC, however, identified Sir Cliff in their coverage. This simple and obvious point got Sir Cliff easily over the first hurdle: as a matter of general principle a suspect has a reasonable expectation of privacy in relation to a police investigation.

If Sir Cliff had a reasonable expectation of privacy before the search then it followed that the search itself should be carried out with due regard to it. The fact that neighbours might observe a police search going on does not automatically remove the suspect's privacy rights. There was nothing in Sir Cliff's public status as an entertainer or as publicly proclaimed Christian which deprived him of his legitimate expectation of privacy. On the contrary, the judge ruled, his public status emphasised his need for privacy. This was not removed just because information about a public person came into the hands of the media.

The BBC had argued that despite Sir Cliff's privacy rights there was a public interest in broadcasting the search as it was a contribution to a debate of public interest, namely the investigation of historical child abuse, which had occupied acres of newsprint and television coverage over the years. But this general justification had to be related to the individual in question. To know that Sir Cliff was under investigation added nothing to the genuine public interest in the existence of police inquiries into historical sex cases and the judge held that Sir Cliff's privacy rights were not outweighed by the BBC's rights to freedom of expression.

The case, which cost the BBC £2 million in legal costs and £850,000 in damages, was a costly mistake, but apparently Sir Cliff was out of pocket at the end of the exhausting proceedings. This reveals a disturbing feature of such cases: protecting one's privacy is the preserve of the rich, talented and famous. All the cases about privacy seem to be about singers, models, footballers, writers or entertainers. What they have in common is wealth and celebrity. Poor and vulnerable people did not seem to be benefiting from the new judicial recognition of privacy. When an ordinary mother from a deprived background, Mrs Wainwright, visited her son in prison in 1997 accompanied by her younger disabled son, they were both demeaningly strip-searched, which was permitted under prison regulations providing it was conducted humanely and with dignity. In the case of mother and son this stipulation was not observed as they were asked to remove their clothing in the same room and the son was assaulted by his penis being unnecessarily touched. Their real complaint, in an action against the prison authorities, was that their personal dignity and autonomy had been violated. The House of Lords declined, on the facts, to apply inventive reasoning to acknowledge the existence of a law which protected the mother and son from the real indignity, namely an intrusion into their private state of autonomy.[20]

The European Court of Human Rights in Strasbourg, however, has been prepared to uphold the privacy of ordinary people who are not celebrities. Late one night in August 1995 in Brentwood High Street in Essex, a man attempted to commit suicide by cutting his wrists with a knife. He was unaware that the council had installed CCTV footage in the high street which had helped alert the police, who disarmed him, detained him briefly under the Mental Health Act but did not charge him with any offence. Some months later, in an effort to publicise the usefulness of CCTV, the council published his photograph in a press release headed 'Defused – the partnership between CCTV and the police prevents a potentially dangerous situation'. A free paper, the *Yellow Advertiser*, also carried the story under the headline 'Gotcha'. The story and picture also featured on Anglia TV. At no time was the man's consent sought or obtained for the publicity exercise and his face was clearly visible. Many friends and family members had recognised him.

At this time, English law had not yet got to grips with privacy. Beyond expressing sympathy for the man involved and acknowledging that the arrival of CCTV to English high streets may on occasion cause undesirable invasion of privacy, the High Court judge put privacy rights to one side. The ruling concentrated on legislation covering local authority and police powers. These provided ample legal authority to publish the story and it was not an unreasonable use of their powers to promote the usefulness of CCTV in detecting and preventing crime. When the case was taken to the European Court of Human Rights in Strasbourg, the court ruled the publicity was lawful and pursued a legitimate aim of promoting public safety but that the council could and should have sought the man's consent before promoting the merits of CCTV using him as an example. He was not a criminal or a missing person and the effectiveness of CCTV in Brentwood could have been promoted without his identity being revealed, potentially, to thousands of readers and viewers. In addition, the council could have masked his identity. The extent of the ensuing publicity was not a proportionate curtailment of the man's privacy rights, as he could not have foreseen the large audience to whom his image, in distressing circumstances, was exposed.[21]

By 2010, English judges were starting to take privacy very seriously. Thirty years after Gorden Kaye was left without any remedy in privacy law, Lord Justice Laws explained why privacy matters:

The notion of the personal autonomy of every individual marches with the presumption of liberty enjoyed in a free polity ... An individual's personal autonomy makes him – should make him – the individual master of those facts about his identity, such as his name, health, sexuality, ethnicity, his own image; and also of the 'zone of interaction' between himself and others. He is presumed owner of these aspects of his own self; his control of them can only be loosened, abrogated, if the State shows an objective justification for doing so.[22]

This broad and refined statement has moved the law on from having to shoehorn notions of privacy into an equitable doctrine of confidence. By placing privacy within the territory of autonomy and personal liberty, the focus nowadays is to place privacy as a right and then to consider whether legitimate and proportionate curtailments of that right are necessary within a democratic community. The axis on which privacy now rotates is clear for all to see. A demonstrator at an event may not have his or her photograph taken by police and retained in police files just in case it might be needed to prevent crime sometime in the future. This would not be a proportionate intrusion into a privacy right.[23] A long-term prisoner who has correspondence in his cell which is protected by legal professional privilege cannot have that correspondence rifled through by prison officers searching his cell in his absence just because prison rules allow it.[24]

All these cases demonstrate privacy in modern Britain is not confined to a balancing exercise between a right to privacy and a right to free expression. That balancing exercise arises when celebrities take on the media when their own private space is invaded. Privacy for them may originate in the law of confidence and a culture of celebrity, but privacy for ordinary people is now recognised as important in its own right. Curtailing it must be lawful, necessary, legitimate and proportionate.

There has been a sea change in the outlook of the judiciary towards privacy in recent years. This was most vividly illustrated in the case brought by the Duchess of Sussex against the *Mail on Sunday*.[25] The duchess, Meghan Markle, had a difficult relationship with her father, who lived in California. Tom Markle did not attend his daughter's wedding in May 2018 and he had made this intention plain in the American media even though Prince Harry had texted Tom to ask him to stop talking to the Californian press. In August 2018, Meghan wrote to her father expressing her pain that it was only via the American media that she learned he had had a heart attack prior to the wedding. This became known as 'the letter'.

Some months later, *The People* newspaper in Britain published a piece putting 'the record straight' about Meghan's relationship with her father, quoting her close friends. It was in this article that the existence of the letter was first revealed to the public, though the article did not accurately state Meghan's reasons for writing it. Tom Markle was upset by the article and contacted the *Mail on Sunday* providing them with the contents of the letter. The *Mail* then published a 'world exclusive' on 'Meghan's shattering letter to her father' and using eighty-eight separate quotations from it. The editor's reasoning was that Tom Markle was entitled to have his side of the father–daughter relationship told and that Meghan had waived her right to privacy by allowing her friends to co-operate with *The People* and with a book about Meghan's life which was later published in 2020.

The English courts ruled that even though the duchess may have anticipated her father would reveal the contents of the letter to the British press, this did not override her reasonable expectation of privacy at the time the letter was written. As she had a reasonable expectation of privacy, it was reasonable for her to expect the *Mail on Sunday* to honour that expectation. It had not already entered the public domain via the *People* article as the contents of the letter were not an aspect of Meghan's celebrity status. The letter was a private communication between a daughter and father. The fact that the duchess chose on occasion to make aspects of her private life public did not impinge on the private nature of her method of communication with her father. Even if parts of the *People* article were inaccurate, it was not a proportionate journalistic response to publish virtually the entire contents of the letter to put Tom Markle's point of view before the public. Although the duchess received only nominal damages, her case was an important victory for privacy and confirmed the trend that had been fermenting in the English courts for some years.

That change has taken place over an era which began with Gorden Kaye's accident during the Burns Day storm in 1990. English judges were embarrassed when they had to rule that despite all the merits being on Kaye's side and all the wrongs being on the *Sunday Sport*'s side the law did not allow Kaye to win on privacy grounds. The law could not continue with such basic injustice going unrecognised. The case helped promote a culture of change when the intrusive behaviour of certain sections of the press started to sicken the public and judges used their erudition to create a law of privacy. Society as a whole has been the beneficiary.

Chapter 8

Democracy – The Miller Tales

W inston Churchill's well-known statement that democracy is the worst form of government except for all those other forms that have been tried from time to time is neither a description nor a definition. It is not surprising that even this statesman and historian failed in the attempt to describe the world's most elusive concept. A commendable effort to describe democracy comes from Bernard Crick, who calls it 'a recipe for an acceptable set of institutions ... allowing for peaceable compromises to be made between conflicts, values and interests'.[1] Democracy is, in reality, a process of evolution and organic growth within the political, cultural and sometimes religious history of a nation. David Runciman has described contemporary representative democracy as 'the default condition of politics, its virtues far outweighing its weaknesses'.[2] Democracies exist in Britain, the United States, most countries in the Commonwealth and in western Europe, but the political arrangements in each individual nation state are different. Democracies evolve when an absolute monarchy or dictatorship is broken, the hegemony of a single church disappears or the occupation by a colonial oppressor is driven away. Usually democracies take many generations to bed down to provide a system permitting equality before the law, a representative government elected by the people and broad civil liberties among citizens. Once these modern concepts are protected by a constitution, whether written or (as in Britain) unwritten, the existence of democracy is taken for granted. A return to absolutism or tyranny becomes unthinkable.

It seems almost trite to state these obvious points in modern Britain, but in two legal cases, initiated by a remarkably courageous woman called Gina Miller, senior judges were forced to confront the essence of constitutional democracy in the United Kingdom. The cases, *R (Miller) v Secretary of State for Exiting the European Union*[3] and *R (Miller) v The Prime Minister*,[4] have become famous for the political furore sparked by the decisions of the Supreme Court. Both cases had their origin in the febrile, hectic and unpleasant atmosphere in British politics following the 2016 referendum result which obliged politicians to start a process to leave the European Union. Both cases had the effect of halting the implementation of political decisions taken by the executive. The two Miller cases underlined important legal principles and the judgments provoked an unprecedented reaction from politicians and elements of the media. In each case, the judges who made the rulings had to suffer the scorn of some tabloid newspapers and rebuke from political leaders who had been chastened. It is tempting to conclude that now that 'Brexit has been done' and Boris Johnson still has a healthy, albeit discontented, parliamentary majority, the Miller cases will fade from the memory as being relevant only to a short and undignified part of modern political history, that period of difficulty when the country was divided and confused about the merits and the means of leaving the EU. Nothing could be further from the truth. The judgments of the Supreme Court will have a lasting effect when future generations begin to learn about the meaning of constitutional democracy in Britain. In essence, the first case, known as *Miller 1*, reaffirmed an important rule of law, first established in the reign of James I of England (James VI of

Scotland), that the royal prerogative cannot be used to stultify legisla-tion made in Parliament. The second, *Miller 2*, established that there were legal limits which the courts could impose on the power of the Prime Minister to close down Parliament. Each decision has huge rami-fications. Current attempts by the government to place its own limits on what it perceives to be 'judicial overreach' will have no lasting impact. The independence of the judiciary is too robust to bow to the will of the government of the day when years of history have defined its role in the constitutional business of the nation.

In her memoir, *Rise: Life Lessons in Speaking Out, Standing Tall & Leading the Way*,[5] Gina Miller described how she experienced an 'innate certainty' of the rectitude of taking legal action against the gov-ernment. It was a perceptive observation, as many of us harbour innate certainties about the democratic environment we live in. We assume that governments only govern because they enjoy the authority of the electorate who put them there and that our elected representatives in Parliament will make decisions on our behalf, applying in general terms the objectives on which they sought election. We are certain that the monarch acts on the advice of her ministers and that she wields no in-dependent power. We believe that if we land up in court, we will receive a fair hearing according to law. Such concepts are innate in the sense that they are imbued in us as we grow up and begin to experience our environment. When a referendum was called in 2016 to ask the elector-ate as a whole whether or not it wanted to leave the European Union, it was something of a novelty. Referendums are an exception to the gen-eral principle of representative democracy that Parliament is supreme. Referendums have only one winner: the majority, however small, who voted one way; those who voted the other way are discarded as losers. For those who welcomed the result, the referendum itself provided the democratic legitimacy for the government to implement the decision without further ado. 'The people' had made the decision, even though in 2016 it was evident that 48 per cent of 'the people' did not assent to the decision. Jacob Rees-Mogg MP spoke for many who had supported Brexit when he said in the House of Commons, 'Let us not use the word "respect" of the electorate any more; let us say "obey", for we will obey the British electorate.'[6]

Certainly it was the intention of the Prime Minister, Theresa May, to obey the electorate without reference to Parliament, many of whose members wanted to deliberate on the implications and consequences of the referendum result. She had told the Conservative Party conference in early October 2016 that she would trigger Article 50 of the Lisbon Treaty in time for negotiations to withdraw from the EU to commence by March 2017. Article 50 of the Treaty of the European Union provides that a member state may 'decide to withdraw from the Union in accordance with its own constitutional arrangements'. Gina Miller's 'innate certainty' about the British way of doing things gave her pause for thought. What exactly were the United Kingdom's own constitutional arrangements and who, precisely, should decide to withdraw?

These seemed sensible and important questions. After all, the United Kingdom had been a member of the European Community for over forty years when the referendum on continued membership was held. During that time, trade, travel, workers' rights and European law had become enmeshed within Britain's domestic arrangements. Forty years earlier, the United Kingdom had had to make big changes to make membership of the European Community a reality. Gina Miller's 'innate certainty' that Britain's democracy and constitutional arrangements were being undermined was a hunch on her behalf. It required lawyers and judges of the highest calibre to apply their learning to some fundamental principles to test whether Ms Miller's hunch was correct. In early July 2016, solicitors acting for Miller wrote to the government's lawyers to state that in their opinion the government did not possess any relevant prerogative power to trigger Article 50 as there had been no parliamentary authority providing the Prime Minister with the power.

Even before the case was heard, Miller suffered a torrent of vitriolic abuse including death threats on social media, such was the anger among some Brexiteers that she was seeking a judicial decision on the legality of the government's route to leaving the EU. In a rare pre-trial order, the High Court issued a warning that contempt of court proceedings would be initiated if the litigation Miller had started was interfered with by intimidation. There was a real risk that this would happen, as vehement Brexiteers were determined that neither Parliament nor the courts should become embroiled in a decision the British people had already made. In their view, there was a simplicity about the referendum result that neither law nor the legislature could question.

In reality, however, implementing the result of the referendum was not simple. The referendum was not, in itself, a decision to leave the EU, as Parliament had not, in the Referendum Act 2015, specified what would happen in the event of a 'yes' vote. Legally, the referendum was advisory only. While David Cameron, as Prime Minister, had promised that his government would honour the result, this declaration carried only moral and political weight and did not have the force of law behind it. If the vote in the referendum was not a 'decision' under Article 50 then who should actually make the decision to start the process of leaving the EU? Was this something the Prime Minister could do under executive powers or was it something only Parliament could authorise? The government, now led by Theresa May following Cameron's resignation, was confident the government itself would make the decision. This is exactly what the executive anticipated when Mrs May laid down her timetable for exiting at the Conservative Party conference in October 2016.

Mrs May was using a route permitting the exercise of power by way of the prerogative. Prerogative powers are those historically held by the sovereign but have not been abolished by parliamentary legislation over time. They include the making and ratifying of international treaties, conduct of diplomacy, the deployment of the armed services, appointment of ambassadors and in general terms the administrative power to carry on the ordinary business of government. In *Miller 1*, the government confidently argued that its decision to trigger Article 50, a decision to notify the EU that the United Kingdom proposed to leave the EU, was an administrative step in the field of international law. If this argument was legally sound then the decision to invoke Article 50 fell squarely within the use of the prerogative. If this was not legally sound, the government had a fall-back position: the decision to notify the EU of Britain's decision to exit Europe was a decision of high policy which was not capable of review by the courts.

These were powerful pragmatic arguments which had a moral force behind them as the government regarded the result of the referendum as decisive. In addition, there was no legal precedent explicitly forbidding the use of the prerogative in these circumstances. The counter-argument, and the one which held sway, was a much more fundamental one. It involved a consideration of how the United Kingdom constitution had developed and the principles upon which sovereign and parliamentary power rested. Britain has an unwritten constitution and understanding constitutional practice depends upon understanding how power in modern Britain is wielded. In short, the case of *Miller 1* was a case about democracy. The referendum could not obtain an instruction from the electorate about Britain's future relationship with the EU as the question was not on the ballot paper. It was not on the ballot paper as the answer could only be given by our parliamentary representatives as a whole. The process of disentangling the United Kingdom from its neighbours of forty years' standing involved representative government and therefore was an activity of democracy. The judges in *Miller 1* had to grapple with some core principles of our democratic arrangements to reach their decision, and this involved a little history.

Democracies do not grow from nothing. There has always been a pre-democratic period in all nations who become democracies. The institutions and practices that sustain democracies are created in reaction to what has gone before; democracies create structures to prevent a return to old ways. In Britain, that structure was an edifice to limit the power of the sovereign and it occurred in the seventeenth century.

James I of England acceded to the throne in 1603, having been King of Scotland since 1567. He ruled the two nations until 1625. It was during his reign that law ceased to be a collection of executive orders and directives and began to embody 'intangible and permanent values'. Now, as Robert Tombs has observed, 'the rule of law became central to English ideas of freedom and civilization'.[7] This development occurred when the powerful personality of the sovereign clashed with the learned and devout Chief Justice of Common Pleas, Sir Edward Coke. James had addressed Parliament in 1610 when he espoused the doctrine of the divine right of kings. Dressed in his elaborate ceremonial robes of delicate lace, his head adorned with an ornamental hat, James used his considerable erudition acquired from Calvinist schooling to lecture Parliament about his kingly responsibilities. A king was a god, he declared, who could raise or cast down his subjects as the people had given him the legal authority to do so by rogation. Unfortunately, the king had forgotten the unmentionable subject of money, which was vexing Parliament mightily. The gentry and property owners who comprised membership of the House of Commons wanted exclusive responsibility to levy taxes and to abolish purveyance, which allowed the king to raise money for himself.

While a power struggle between king and Parliament was simmering, a legal dispute, called the *Case of Proclamations*, was referred to the Privy Council for an opinion. The question involved a relatively minor matter of whether the king could use his authority to prohibit new buildings being erected in London by issuing a proclamation to that effect. Coke gave the judgment of the Privy Council: 'The King has no prerogative but that which the law of the land allows him.' Furthermore, Coke ruled that without Parliament the king could not change any part of the common law, nor create any offence which was not an offence before, by his proclamation. It was a ground-breaking and shattering legal opinion which was to inform the debates during the Civil War and lead to the wording of the Bill of Rights seventy-eight years later. In 1688, the Bill of Rights stated: 'The pretended power of suspending of laws or the execution of laws by regal authority without the consent of Parliament is illegal ... Levying money for or to the use of the Crown by pretence of prerogative without the grant of Parliament ... is illegal.'

The power of the sovereign had been curtailed, the powers of Parliament had been enhanced and the centrality of law to the practices of state institutions had been sown in the period 1610–88. At first sight, this seems ancient history. Could such events possibly be relevant to leaving the EU in the twenty-first century? Both the Divisional Court of the High Court and the majority in the Supreme Court decided the *Case of Proclamations* was highly relevant for one simple reason. The main decision involving Britain's relations with the European Union had been made by Parliament, with the historic decision to join the European Economic Community, later called the EU. The European Communities Act 1972 was a statute of profound importance. It provided that rights and duties derived from EU law should apply in the United Kingdom as part of domestic law. It also provided for the 'direct effect' of EU legislation when the legislation in question was necessary to accommodate Britain as a full member of the European Community. The doctrine of direct effect means, essentially, that if EU regulations are clear, unconditional, without reservation and not dependent on individual national circumstances, a member state must apply them and national courts must enforce them. The doctrine proclaims the place of regulations within the system of EU law. When Mrs May announced her intention to invoke Article 50, the European Communities Act 1972 had not been repealed and as a result important questions of democracy were thrown up. Could an existing parliamentary statute be ousted simply by a ministerial announcement? The government had given notice of its intention to put a Great Repeal Bill before Parliament, undoing the ramifications of membership of the EU, but this had not passed into law when Mrs May made her decision to invoke Article 50. She had not obtained the legislative permission of Parliament to embark upon such a wholescale change to British law. If she could do this of her own volition, relying on the referendum rather than the law as her mandate, then it followed that the executive could use a prerogative power to undo something Parliament had already decided upon in an earlier statute. This was something the *Case of Proclamations* had forbidden. The statute law on Britain's membership of the EU had been made by Parliament and the executive did not possess a prerogative power to change the law made in the 1972 statute.

Counsel for Gina Miller, Lord Pannick QC, had based his argument on the premise that invoking Article 50 was like pulling the trigger on a gun. Once the trigger was pulled and the bullet left the chamber, it was unstoppable until the target was reached. This meant that two years after the gun was fired Britain's legal relationship with the EU would automatically cease. Once this happened and the bullet hit its target, all legal rights enshrined in domestic law by virtue of our EU membership would come to an end. Such a course of events, started by the use of a prerogative power, would fly in the face of a constitutional and democratic principle that primary legislation cannot be displaced by the use of a prerogative power. The democratic principle in play was a fundamental one of Britain's constitutional democracy: that the Crown vested in Parliament is sovereign, and legislation enacted in Parliament is sovereign. The supremacy of Parliament cannot be diminished by the use of the prerogative because Parliament itself is supreme and its authority cannot be casually set aside.

Gina Miller's second argument was that the foundational principle of a constitutional democracy was the rule of law. Britain's constitutional democracy, like all mature democracies, is framed by legal rules and subject to the rule of law. The subordination of the Crown, the executive and the Prime Minister to law is the constitutional basis of our democracy. The prerogative may only be used if the law permits its use. These principles were established after a democratic struggle to constrain prerogative power and to enlarge parliamentary power which began in the *Proclamations Case*.

The High Court and the Supreme Court both decided that these matters of constitutional and democratic principle were vital in deciding whether Mrs May had the legal power to invoke Article 50 without prior parliamentary legislative approval. Leaving the EU was a constitutional change as fundamental to the law of the land as joining it had been. Joining the European Community was a change in kind as it involved changes in domestic law, laying down rights and duties derived from EU law. The Members of Parliament and peers who voted in Parliament for Britain to join the EU did not envisage that such a momentous decision could be undone by ministers at a future time without parliamentary approval. It was not enough for Mrs May and her Cabinet to rely on the referendum result. A referendum cannot be a constitutional way of changing existing law. Nor was it enough for the government to maintain that leaving the EU was simply withdrawing from an international treaty. Leaving the EU was more than simply cutting loose from a treaty; it had real *domestic* implications on the rights and duties of citizens under European directives Britain had incorporated in line with the doctrine of 'direct effect'. In short, it would be inconsistent with a longstanding and fundamental principle if such a far-reaching change to our democracy were brought about by ministerial decision alone.

The judgments in the High Court and in the Supreme Court are redolent with explanation about how the common law played its part in the evolution of parliamentary democracy. One could say the decision in *Miller 1* provided a powerful legal endorsement of the principle of parliamentary sovereignty and the democratic values such sovereignty protects. Given the historical importance of this reasoning, the reaction to the decision of the High Court in October 2016 was profoundly depressing. A section of the press, led by the *Daily Mail* and the *Daily Telegraph*, excoriated the judges who upheld Gina Miller's complaint with a venom that was reminiscent of Hitler or Stalin waging war on their opponents. Under a banner headline 'Enemies of the People', the paper went on to express their 'fury over out of touch judges who have "declared war on democracy" by defying 17.4 million Brexit voters'.[8] The character of this unprecedented attack on the independence of the judiciary was a consequence, in part, of the referendum process itself. As Jonathan Sumption has pointed out, referendums pose a threat to parliamentary democracy by the creation of a sense of entitlement in the majority that inhibits compromise and invites absolute outcomes.[9] Those who supported the referendum result interpreted it as a decision of the people as a whole, which, because it had been taken by the whole people, was inviolable and sacrosanct. Those who challenged it were 'enemies of the people' just like those who were guillotined in the reign of terror during the French Revolution for not being sufficiently revolutionary, or those communists who were shot in Russia for falling short of Stalin's strict standards of revolutionary zeal. But modern Britain should not be like revolutionary France or communist Russia. We are a democratic nation which prides itself on values including compromise between competing viewpoints and respect for people whose views we may not share. This is the shared political culture requiring the party achieving the majority of the seats in Parliament to follow certain conventions about the way politics should be conducted.

The most highly valued of these conventions is the importance of Parliament to the way decisions are reached. Procedures exist for a diversity of opinions to be expressed and no proposal by a government can be brought into law without the presentation of a Bill, an opportunity for amending the Bill, a close examination of the Bill in committee and voting on individual clauses. Finally, the consent of the House of Lords must be obtained. Although the upper chamber is unelected, it is where experts on proposed measures are often to be found. The upper chamber may also contribute to the discussion and sometimes insert improvements to a measure the House of Commons has approved. The whole process can be laborious, lengthy and frustrating, but it is the way our democracy actually functions. The practice of democracy can be hazardous if the government does not command a majority in the House of Commons. The combination of a government without a majority and the membership of our Parliament having a constitutional right to wield a power of its own led to the second legal case Gina Miller initiated.

Following the decision in *Miller 1* in January 2017, the government introduced the European Union (Notification of Withdrawal) Bill, a short, tightly worded document that empowered the Prime Minister to trigger Article 50 and which was passed into law quite quickly. The Supreme Court had said it was entirely a matter for Parliament how the legislation would be introduced and debated. The fact that the Bill was passed quite quickly was not the point. The important point was the constitutional principle that Parliament should make the decision. Constitutional principles are timeless and were not put aside when, less than three weeks after triggering Article 50, May called a general election. The majority that existed at the time of the referendum swiftly vanished and Mrs May had to form an administration with the support of the Democratic Unionist Party from Northern Ireland. But Parliament was sensing danger. The deadline for Britain's departure from the EU had been fixed, thanks to the decision to trigger Article 50, but the arrangements for exiting it had not, and the absence of a parliamentary majority meant the process of agreeing the arrangements was now fraught with difficulty. That meant there was a realistic possibility that Britain would leave the EU without any agreement about the nation's future relations with its European neighbours. This prospect alarmed many Members of Parliament on both sides. How was our supreme Parliament to assert itself in the face of this bleak prospect?

The short answer was by taking control of the business of the House of Commons. If a government does not command a majority and its approach is perceived to be reckless by a majority of MPs then the government is in trouble. This was the scenario that led to the judgment of the Supreme Court in *Miller 2*. Mrs May was struggling to get parliamentary approval for her European Union Withdrawal Bill, which was repeatedly defeated, and in March 2019 the House of Commons tied her hands by voting to prevent Britain leaving the EU without a deal. This led to the postponement of exit day and, in July 2019, the resignation of Theresa May. Boris Johnson succeeded her as Prime Minister, but by now there was fury in Downing Street about the behaviour of some Conservative members who had helped Parliament postpone the date for leaving the EU. Johnson was blaming many of his own MPs for the fact that exit day had been postponed twice, first from 29 March to 30 June and then until 31 October.

Without consulting his own party or giving advance notice to Parliament, the new Prime Minister was laying out plans to close Parliament down. While MPs were away from Westminster, Johnson was signing off arrangements to prorogue Parliament during the critical period when the timetable and the terms of Brexit would be at the forefront of MPs' minds. At the end of August, a deputation of privy counsellors, led by Jacob Rees-Mogg, went to Balmoral to tender to the Queen the Prime Minister's advice that she should prorogue Parliament for a period of five out of a possible eight weeks between the end of the summer recess and exit day on 31 October. Depending on your point of view, this bold and unusual move was either a necessary step to deal with the 'antics of parliamentary Remainers'[10] or 'an affront to democracy'.[11]

Each side was arguing in favour or against the prorogation advice entirely in political terms, whereas the decision was a challenge to a constitutional convention which placed the sovereignty of Parliament at the apex of our democracy. If this convention was important and had to be observed then it was the executive, not Parliament, that had disapplied convention. Looked at in these terms, the advice to prorogue engaged principles of parliamentary democracy, and this is how Gina Miller looked at it. She described the prorogation advice as a 'brazen attempt to prevent the executive from being held accountable for its conduct before Parliament'.[12] A similar legal challenge was initiated in Scotland by Joanna Cherry MP. The matter assumed great urgency in view of the cardinal disagreements among MPs and the looming exit day, 31 October. The Supreme Court heard the case in the middle of September 2019.

The frantic preparations in England and Scotland to mount a legal challenge to the prorogation decision took place during the parliamentary recess and the legal vacation. Lord Pannick QC received instructions to represent Gina Miller while he was on safari in Kenya. When parliamentary sittings resumed in early September, an opposition Member, Hilary Benn MP, was granted parliamentary time to enact legislation of his own. The 'Benn Act' forced Boris Johnson to seek yet a further extension of three months if MPs had not approved a deal in a meaningful vote (or approved leaving the EU without a deal) by 19 October. In those circumstances Parliament required the Prime Minister to formally request a further extension until 31 January 2020.

Mr Johnson, who had in the summer said he preferred death in a ditch to a postponement of exit day, was humiliated. He requested an extension with a diplomatic ill grace that demeaned his office. While these events were dramatic, innovative and for many as thrilling as any drama seen on television, they were for supporters of Boris Johnson the stuff of betrayal and an example of Parliament over-reaching itself. Yet the judges sitting in the High Court in London and the Court of Session in Edinburgh had to rule on the legality of the prorogation advice in purely legal terms. How could somewhat arid legal precedent possibly become separated from the torrid political hysteria that was beginning to characterise discussion about Brexit? And was the advice to the Queen even open to challenge in the first place?

In times past there has been a shared political culture which constrained the behaviour of political discourse within the boundaries constitutional evolution had placed on it. When acceptable conduct is observed, it is not necessary to explain why the practice exists nor to dig deep into law books to find out why elected representatives in Parliament behave as they do. The behaviour is ingrained within the shared culture. *Miller 1* and *Miller 2* are legal cases that made modern Britain because the English and Scottish courts and the Supreme Court, on appeal from both, were being asked to scrutinise the constitutional legal basis for modern political practice. The Brexit disputes had changed the shared culture: opinions became absolutist articles of faith, dialogue consisted of repetitious slogans, and implementing the 'will of the people' became an imperative that blocked out any consideration of how, sensibly, it could be done.

The judges hearing Gina Miller's arguments had to put that sound and fury to one side and rule on the legality of the advice Boris Johnson had tendered to the Queen. The Supreme Court delivered its unanimous judgment in September 2019. All eleven justices decided the Prime Minister was exercising a prerogative which was within his constitutional power to exercise, but they emphasised that in the past a Prime Minister has used the power in keeping with constitutional democratic practice. The Prime Minister has a constitutional responsibility as well as a political one. The Prime Minister is accountable to Parliament in terms of policy and the efficient despatch of government business, but he is accountable also to the courts of justice for the lawfulness of his decisions. Mr Johnson's counsel had argued that as the advice to the Queen to prorogue was an exercise of the Prime Minister's prerogative, the advice was not challengeable in the courts. This was a powerful argument, as there was no precedent for the courts interfering with the exercise of a lawful prerogative power. The argument, however, was flawed.

The existence of the prerogative power is lawful because the courts have recognised its lawfulness. The question raised in *Miller 2* was not the exercise of a lawful power but whether there were legal limits to the use of that power. The court was not concerned with legal generalities surrounding a prerogative power but with the use of it by Boris Johnson on this particular occasion. The court could not ignore the reality that on this occasion the effect of the use of the power had been to frustrate the constitutional role of Parliament in holding the government to account at an important time of deliberation about the details of withdrawing from the EU.

The Supreme Court concluded that Johnson had broken constitutional convention in seeking a prorogation for five out of a possible eight weeks from the end of the summer recess until exit day, which was then 31 October. The key question for the Supreme Court was whether, as well as breaking with convention, Boris Johnson's advice to the Queen was also outside the Prime Minister's own *legal* powers. Consideration of this question required the judicial eye to look into the deep recesses of English law and convention, the deep recesses that Lady Hale called the 'fundamental principles of constitutional law'. These principles embrace values, the most important of which is the principle of parliamentary sovereignty. This value would be undermined if the executive could decide to prorogue Parliament for as long as it pleased. As Lady Hale put it, 'The longer Parliament stands prorogued, the greater the risk that responsible government may be replaced by unaccountable government: the antithesis of the democratic model.' Our democracy, Lady Hale was saying, implies the use of a prerogative power which is compatible with the ability of Parliament to carry out its functions, which are constitutional and democratic functions.

The preservation of these functions, Lady Hale said, is within the province of the courts to uphold. This was the key point of the 1610 *Case of Proclamations* which was so important in *Miller 1* when it was established that a prerogative power is limited by statute and the common law. Having examined the fundamentals of our constitutional democracy, Lady Hale came to the nub of the case:

A decision to prorogue Parliament (or to advise the monarch to prorogue Parliament) will be unlawful if the prorogation has the effect of frustrating or preventing, without reasonable justification, the ability of

Parliament to carry out its constitutional functions as a legislature and as the body responsible for supervision of the executive. In such a situation, the court will intervene if the effect is sufficiently serious to justify an exceptional course.

The next stage in the reasoning of the Supreme Court was to examine the *effect* the advice had on the ability of Parliament to carry out its functions. The court decided that this was a question of fact which the courts routinely decide. The Supreme Court had absolutely no difficulty in deciding the factual effect of Johnson's advice. It prevented Parliament from carrying out its constitutional role for five out of a possible eight weeks in exceptional circumstances when a fundamental change to the constitution of the United Kingdom was due to take place, namely leaving the EU on 31 October. Parliament had already demonstrated its wish for Britain to leave the EU with a deal and as the deadline for leaving was fast approaching, it was especially important that Boris Johnson should face the House of Commons. It is Parliament which provides the legitimacy for the executive to act; the executive has no legitimacy in itself beyond the confidence it enjoys from the elected legislature, the House of Commons.

The language of the Supreme Court judgment was certainly robust, and some have argued the judgment strayed too far into the realms of politics. However, the foundation of the robust analysis of Johnson's actions lay in ancient constitutional law. It is hardly ground-breaking to say, in the twenty-first century, that the executive is the servant of Parliament, not the other way round. The judgment is clear that had Boris Johnson provided a reasonable explanation for his decision, the court would have considered it carefully. In the logical process of its reasoning, the Supreme Court had left a window of opportunity for the Prime Minister to say, despite the effect of prorogation, he had a reasonable explanation to offer as to the reason for it. The Prime Minister chose not to provide the court with his reasons. Instead he furnished documents from the director of legislative affairs in the Prime Minister's office which focused on the need for a new Queen's Speech in the week beginning 14 October but failed to explain why prorogation of five weeks was necessary. The only material provided to the court about how Downing Street prepares for a Queen's Speech was given by Sir John Major, whose unchallenged account was that never, in his experience, has a government needed as much as five weeks to put together its legislative agenda. The government failed to explain why it needed five weeks and ignored what Parliament might realistically have wanted to do in the fraught circumstances of Brexit. There was a realistic likelihood that Parliament might have approved a new withdrawal agreement or would have made time for the scrutiny committees of both Houses of Parliament to play their allocated role under the European (Withdrawal) Act 2018.

The Supreme Court was compelled to conclude that the Prime Minister was not complying with his constitutional responsibility in advising the Queen to prorogue and instead was focused on his role as leader of the government in promoting his own policies, which would be assisted if Parliament was silenced. As the Prime Minister had chosen not to furnish the court with any reason – let alone a good reason – the court could not speculate upon what reasons there might have been for his advice. It followed that the decision was unlawful.

Finally, the court had to rule on what legal consequences flowed from the ruling that the advice was unlawful. This was not straightforward, as Article 9 of the Bill of Rights Act 1688 forbade judges from questioning of impeaching any debate or proceeding in Parliament as this would challenge the supremacy of Parliament. This article upholds the supremacy of Parliament, but the general meaning of 'proceedings' in Parliament is the collective process of decision-making in debate, points of order, ministerial statements and so on. The Supreme Court decided that prorogation was not a 'proceeding' in Parliament as it was not something upon which Members can speak or vote. For that reason, the court was not prevented by the Bill of Rights from considering the validity of the prorogation itself, a process that began with the advice to the Queen. As the reasoning of the court had led to the conclusion that the advice was unlawful, this meant the advice was null and void and of no effect. Parliament was not prorogued and Parliament could decide what to do. There was no contest. The sittings resumed and the Speaker called the House to order.

The Supreme Court's decision was controversial politically and legally. Boris Johnson's immediate reaction was to announce that he disagreed with the decision, which he interpreted as an attempt to frustrate his Brexit plans. Gina Miller welcomed the decision as a victory for parliamentary sovereignty. Others picked up their cudgels and carried on as before. The Supreme Court had not changed minds. Instead it provoked a debate about the nature of the United Kingdom constitution and the values embodied within it. Academic experts took sides, some supporting, others criticising the reasoning of the United Kingdom's highest court. Unlike *Miller 1*, when the decision of the judges was upheld by the Supreme Court, in *Miller 2* the High Court had sided with the government, agreeing that Johnson's advice was not justiciable while, on appeal, the Supreme Court unanimously took the opposite view. In Scotland, the Inner House had come to the same conclusion as the Supreme Court on an earlier occasion, while the Court of Session had ruled the issue was not justiciable. Judicial, academic and political opinions differed. This is not entirely unsurprising since the Supreme Court was invited to rule on something that had not occurred before and, as Lady Hale emphasised, was unlikely to occur again. Despite the unique circumstances giving rise to the judgment, *Miller 2* cannot be consigned to a part of Brexit history which can be put behind us. The case raised profound questions about the nature of judicial law-making, our constitution and the democratic principles that underpin it.

In essence, the case forced Britain's highest court to examine the legal foundations of our democracy. In her memoir, *Spider Woman*, Lady Hale has emphasised the difference between legal power and political power. The Supreme Court in *Miller 2* was doing its job in deciding whether political power in our democracy had been used lawfully. As she says, 'The rights and freedoms of every individual and enterprise within our country depend upon those in political power acting within the powers which the law has given them. Otherwise is tyranny.'[13]

The Supreme Court was answering the legal question *Miller 2* posed: if our constitution permits prerogative power to be used, as it does, where does the justification for its use come from? The Supreme Court decided it was not an unlimited power and the limits to its use depended on its legality. Mark Elliott has argued that *Miller 2* articulated a principle that legality itself is sufficiently broad to enable the senior judiciary, as guardians of constitutional principle, to constrain the use of prerogative power. Behind the actual decision the Prime Minister took there must have been in existence the legal justification for it. The justification might have been the reasonableness of the decision in the circumstances, but this was something Boris Johnson failed to provide. The importance of *Miller 2* was the willingness of the Supreme Court to enter this political territory and make a ruling on reasonableness as legal guardians of our constitutional principles.[14] The irony is that while Johnson condemned the decision, he might have prevented it being handed down had he taken the trouble to provide the court with his reasons. While the Supreme Court was careful to say it would not speculate as to whether or not there were reasonable grounds, it is very tempting to conclude he had none that, objectively, could be called reasonable. If this conclusion is right, it simply reinforces the correctness of the Supreme Court ruling.

Judges did, to an extent, engage with politics in *Miller 2*, but only because their role as constitutional guardians permitted it. Guarding the constitution is one of the most important roles the Supreme Court can play in our democracy. The case therefore raised the whole question of the relationship between law and politics. The place of law in establishing the conditions for the conduct of politics was settled in the early seventeenth century in the *Case of Proclamations*, a decision which guided the reasoning of the Supreme Court in *Miller 1* and *Miller 2*. Sir Edward Coke had argued with the king in meetings of the Privy Council long before he delivered his *Proclamations* decision. Coke was at pains to point out to James I that while the sovereign was endowed with many gifts, he did not possess the knowledge to try causes in the courts, a process, Coke maintained, that protected the king in safety and peace. Coke was dismissed as Chief Justice in 1616, such was James's fury at the idea that law was above the king rather than that the king guarded and administered the law himself. This struggle between sovereign authority and the place of common law in the kingdom of seventeenth-century Britain laid the seeds of the modern concept of the rule of law in a democracy.

A persuasive explanation of the true relationship between the two has been made by Martin Loughlin in his book *Sword and Scales*,[15] in which he argues that the growth of democracy and the concept of the separation of powers coincided with the growth of commerce so that politics could only be conducted within a framework of laws. 'The sword of power, it might be said, should be wielded only in accordance with the scales of justice.' Loughlin's point is that law is not an assortment of customary practices nor simply commands of a sovereign power but a set of fundamental principles which exist to constrain and channel the conduct of politics. Loughlin developed this thesis in 2000 over a decade before the eruptions of Brexit overwhelmed politics in Britain. In Loughlin's conception, it was inevitable that judges as a constraining element within the body politic as a whole would be asked to perform their constitutional role when constitutional norms were being stretched to their limits. As Loughlin has put it, while there is a jurisdictional division between the practice of law and politics, they are united in the common venture of 'keeping the show on the road'.

This is what Gina Miller's 'innate certainty' told her when she instructed lawyers to challenge the government in her two cases. The country was in a state of complete constitutional confusion after the referendum, as the Diceyean doctrine of parliamentary supremacy was inconsistent with the sovereignty of 'the people', who had given a yes or no answer to a complex question. It is not surprising that those who supported the result should have regarded the vote as providing an instruction to the executive, bypassing Parliament in the process. This muddle was articulated by Liam Fox MP, a leading supporter of Brexit, who said:

> Parliament has not got the right to stop the Brexit process because Britain has a 'leave population' and a 'remain' parliament. This parliament made a contract with the people that the people will make the decision and we (Parliament) will honour it ... Parliament sub-contracted its sovereignty on the issue of whether we stayed in the EU to the people. Parliament gave sovereignty to the people.[16]

Parliament could not sub-contract or give away something which was absolute, and the authority of Parliament could not be diminished simply because there had been a referendum. Yet this constitutional nonsense was espoused by a minister of the Crown as the justification for the government to leave Europe by any means possible.

Gina Miller and her supporting litigants were using their constitutional rights to ask the courts to answer the legal questions which arose when Mrs May invoked Article 50 and when Boris Johnson advised the Queen to prorogue Parliament. It should be stressed that the Supreme Court in each case were ruling on the powers of the executive as they exist within a democracy which embraces parliamentary sovereignty. The fact that the reality of a sovereign Parliament is difficult to recognise at a time when power in modern Britain is diffused within a tightly controlled party system, devolved administrations and extragovernmental corporate conglomerates is not the point. The Supreme Court was ruling on the legal framework of our democracy as it is, not as some might like it to be. The Diceyean concept of parliamentary sovereignty still survives even though Dicey saw it through the lens of loose party discipline where a handful of grandees from wealthy families spent a lot of time in the chamber of the House of Commons and were not answerable to a full franchise. Parliament is now a completely different place from the institution it was in the late nineteenth century. The Supreme Court was upholding a constitutional rule that exists, not a system that is necessarily fit for purpose in modern times. The Supreme Court has no role in making a system suitable for modern times; that is exclusively a decision for Parliament.

The judgment of the Supreme Court in *Miller 2* was a legal judgment, pure and simple. It ruled on an event, the prorogation of Parliament in order to stifle democratic debate, which is unlikely ever to occur again. This legal ruling did not engage at all with the ideas from all shades of opinion about the state of modern democracy. Those are within the arena of politics. Nowadays there are intense political discussions on the merits of a proportional voting system or the need for the House of

Lords to be abolished or the reasons why we need a written constitution or why a federal structure to give the regions of England similar powers to the devolved nations of Scotland and Wales is necessary. Democracy is in a state of flux, but the Supreme Court in the two Miller cases provided a clear reminder of the historical foundational strength to our system of government. Britain's highest court provided some ballast to the ship of state's journey into choppy waters. In giving the two *Miller* judgments, the Supreme Court applied the law our democratic evolution has provided us with. The intensity of the Brexit disagreements reached such a pitch following the referendum that democracy seemed irrelevant to their resolution. After the decision in *Miller 2*, when the Speaker ordered parliamentary sittings to resume, the Attorney General, Geoffrey Cox QC, who was the government's chief legal adviser, declared that Parliament, of which he was a member, was 'dead', 'a disgrace' and had 'no moral right to sit'.[17] If representative democracy can die if there is a conflict between it and direct democracy, there is a real risk to the long-term survival of parliamentary democracy. The Supreme Court in the two Miller cases applied a brake to a movement that appeared to be accelerating in the direction of weakening our democratic traditions.

Institutions can grow tired and become less vigorous as time goes by and many saw the institution of Parliament as being irrelevant to accomplishing the withdrawal from the European Union. Boris Johnson and his advisers in Downing Street were so dissatisfied with the views of over twenty Conservative Members of Parliament that he expelled them from the Parliamentary Conservative Party in September 2019. This meant they had virtually no chance of being elected again to Parliament as Conservative candidates. It was a ruthless exercise of executive power over members of the elected legislature. In Johnson's view, the will of the individual Prime Minister of the day had to prevail. The composition of Parliament which the electorate had voted for did not have sufficient Conservative members who would obey the objectives of the executive. The remedy was to punish them and bring their careers to a halt. In pure democratic terms the hung parliament had as much legitimacy as the Prime Minister, chosen by members of his own party. All members of the 'dead' parliament, as Geoffrey Cox called it, had been elected by the franchise. Until December 2019, when he led the Conservative Party to a decisive election victory, Boris Johnson as Prime Minister had no mandate from the electorate.

These fractures to the edifice of our democratic traditions opened up during the frenetic Brexit process and it is tempting to believe that now that episode is over there will be an orderly return to democracy as we have always known it. This is by no means certain. The failure of our democratic institutions to keep pace with a rapidly changing world was identified in 2006 by a Commission of Inquiry, funded by the Joseph Rowntree Charitable Trust. They identified the main problem to be the decline in trust between elected politicians and the electorate, and a growing lack of faith in the efficiency and accountability of our democracy.[18] It recommended a concordat should be drawn up between the executive and Parliament indicating where key powers lie and providing significant powers of scrutiny and initiation for Parliament. In addition, it recommended greater powers for Parliament to initiate legislation, launch public inquiries and act on public petitions. It further suggested a loosening of the power of the whips and enhancing the powers of select committees.

When these recommendations were published in the spring of 2006, Facebook did not exist in its current global form. It was opened to the wider public in the autumn of that year with modest ambitions. Fifteen years later, Facebook had over 20 million users. David Runciman has called the extraordinary growth and popularity of Facebook and Twitter 'network power', a new form of corporate power which challenges democracy. Network power has been harnessed by authoritarians to interfere with the processes of democracy, distribute misinformation and promote conspiracy theories. But it does not require determined authoritarians to make use of network power. It is freely available to anybody, and malicious individuals can harness its power and outrun the influence of opinions expressed through traditional media outlets. Cynicism about democratic solutions to endemic problems play into the hands of network power whose often anonymous users can foster hatred and identify culprits on a whim. These are challenges to democracy in modern Britain.[19]

David Runciman argues that modern democracy is going through something of a midlife crisis. A principal reason for this, Runciman argues, is the change technology has made to the way society operates. Communication used to be from the top down, with powerful proprietors owning a small number of newspapers with huge circulations. Political discourse was also tilted towards the top when politicians found it easy to speak to us but we did not have the means to talk back. This has all changed as a result of technological developments that were unthinkable twenty years ago.

In their different ways, the Power to the People Commission and the author David Runciman have identified the wear and tear in the fabric of our democracy and have suggested ways in which it can and should be patched up. But the patching has a single central aim, which is to preserve and improve the garment that is our democracy. Changing from democratic rule to some other sort of rule would almost certainly be worse than what we have at the moment. The Supreme Court in *Miller 1* and *Miller 2* gave mature legal consideration to what, historically, has given rise to our present arrangements. The Supreme Court was not altering the clothing of our democracy: on the contrary, it was identifying the threads that make up the clothing. The strongest thread, the one that binds all the others together, is our parliamentary democracy, where Parliament is supreme. There is little support, beyond the imagination of extremists of left or right, for a change to that principle. In the hectic and often hysterical period of Brexit fervour, however, rhetoric which did attack that principle entered the currency of political debate. The Supreme Court put a lid on that rhetoric, restored some order to political discourse and upheld constitutional principles that were being forgotten in the heat and fury of the referendum aftermath. In a sense, the excrescence that infected the language of debate after the referendum became so intense it demanded a balm of good sense to quieten things down. This happened in the reasoning in *Miller 1* and *Miller 2*, despite the press reaction at the time to *Miller 1* and the ill grace with which the Prime Minister greeted *Miller 2*. It seems highly likely that *Miller 1* and *Miller 2* will be remembered as the two great constitutional cases of the twenty-first century long after the hysteria of Brexit is forgotten.

Chapter 9

Sovereignty – Spanish Ships and Metric Martyrs

This is the story of how a few Spanish fishing boats and some market traders in Sunderland and Hackney created a legal and constitutional storm in the wake of Britain's entry into the European Economic Community. Their activities were reported widely across the media and they taxed the minds of Britain's cleverest lawyers. It is a story of courage, cunning, obstinacy and cussedness as well as some legal hard truths handed down by judges.

The Spanish fishing boats belonged to an Anglo-Spanish fishing company, Factortame Ltd. The case initiated by this obscure company was the most ground-breaking in legal terms and the most controversial in political ones of all the legal cases that made modern Britain. The so-called metric martyrs were stallholders who stubbornly refused to display both imperial and metric scales, as the law required, on their stalls. This was the most minor of offences, but their principled stand against European regulations made them national heroes in the minds of some who disliked Europe. The two cases involved a clash between political objectives on the one hand and a need to observe international legal obligations on the other. They compelled judges to think anew about exactly what parliamentary sovereignty meant once Britain had made the decision to join the European Community and thus was obliged to apply EC law to a domestic legal dispute. They also provoked a mood of anger about a foreign nation trespassing on fishing rights and long-standing customs among market traders. The Factortame case took nearly fifteen years of legal wrangling in United Kingdom courts and in the European Court of Justice to resolve. In the end, the British tax-payer had to foot a bill of £55 million in compensation to Spanish fish-ermen. Despite the technical and legal complexities of the case, the facts of which are mostly forgotten, the legal judgments in *Factortame* played a part in instilling the mood of suspicion and dislike of the European Union which contributed to the 2016 referendum result when Britain voted to leave the bloc.

In order to understand the ramifications of this important legal case, known as *R (Factortame Ltd) v Secretary of State for Transport, 1, 2, 3, 4 and 5* (the case went on for so long the separate stages were given different numbers), it is necessary to know something about fishing in the north Atlantic before and after Britain joined the European Economic Community, as it was then called, in 1973.[1] The general principles of fishing rights for nations within the European Community were established in the Treaty of Rome in 1957. In essence, this provided for a freedom of 'establishment', meaning mobility of businesses within the Community and a ban on discrimination based on nationality. In keeping with these broad principles, a free trade area for fishing was created for the six nations who then comprised the Community: France, Germany, Belgium, the Netherlands, Italy and Luxembourg. Only France had a significant interest in fishing in the north Atlantic. This principle of equal access, created before Britain joined the Community, treated fish as a mobile resource; food in the sea was deemed to be the common property of all Community member states. At that time, the main European maritime nations, in addition to France, were Britain, Ireland,

Denmark, Greenland, Iceland, Norway and Spain. If any of these nations were to join the Community, as Britain did in 1973, that nation
would sign up to the Treaty of Rome and would have to obey the equal
access principle on fishing.

While Britain dithered and debated whether or not to join the Community in the early 1960s, there was trouble looming for Britain's fishermen, who had become used to catching boatloads of cod in the waters
around Iceland. In 1958, Iceland took a unilateral decision to extend
its territorial waters to 12 nautical miles, which deprived, at a stroke,
UK fishermen from lucrative stocks they had become used to catching.
Then, in 1972, Iceland ratcheted up the protection of their waters by
further extending their own fishing limits to 50 nautical miles, patrolled
by cable-cutting boats to sabotage the nets of Britain's trawlermen. The
might of Britain, it appeared, was being ordered about by a tiny island.
The United Kingdom became locked in what was, in effect, a war with a
small and puny nation. The Royal Navy found itself embroiled in active
service protecting British boats. The episode ended in humiliation
for Britain when the United Kingdom eventually accepted a 200-mile
exclusion zone around Iceland and accepted also the responsibility to
compensate thousands of fishermen and their families who had lost
their livelihoods in the 'cod wars'.

During the course of this acrimonious and demeaning encounter
with Iceland, Britain was negotiating to become a member of the European Economic Community for reasons that had little to do with fishing, even though deep-sea commercial fishing was a sensitive and difficult topic for Britain's self-esteem. By joining the European Economic
Community, Britain had to accept that all member states of the Community should have equal access to each other's national fishing waters.
Until January 1973, the United Kingdom controlled its own waters,
which under international law was called the exclusive economic zone

of a nation state. Before joining the EEC, this zone extended for 200 nautical miles around the UK coastline. When Britain joined the European Community, it was reduced to just 12 miles, with the remaining part of Britain's waters becoming part of the exclusive economic zone of the European Community as a whole. This zone had nothing to do with the concept of territorial waters, with which it is often confused. The term territorial waters relates to activity on the surface of the sea, not activity beneath the waves.

During the period of Britain's humiliating tussle with Iceland, from 1958 until 1976, the six European nations were forging ahead with a bold and imaginative approach to fishing. It was called the Common Fisheries Policy and it was created in 1970, three years before Britain joined the Community. It established that individual nation states would no longer control their own waters but everything to do with fish, including quotas, catches, subsidies and so on, would be directed centrally by the European Commission. Nations with coastlines, like Britain, would have to share their waters with other members of the Community. The idea was that all vessels belonging to an individual member state could fish anywhere in Europe's fishing zone, providing that nation held a quota allocation for the stock of fish they wanted to catch.

In 1983, the European Community put in place the principle of total allowable catches for the European economic zone as a whole and then divided the whole by allocating to each member state fishing quotas to implement the Common Fisheries Policy. Fishing communities in Britain wanted an element of local control over the national allocation of quotas. Local and regional fish producer organisations, such as the North Atlantic, the Anglo-Scottish and the Cornish Fish Producer Organisation were set up by government and administered by the Department for Agriculture and Fisheries and Food with power to control the distribution of quotas to fishing companies. These POs, as they were called, were powerful producer organisations who did not necessarily have the interests of small fishing communities at the heart of their commercial considerations. The United Kingdom government was content to treat quota allocations as quasi-property rights which could be bought and sold over the heads of fishing communities.

Spain, which imported most of its fish and was outside the bloc, was forced to make bilateral agreements with the EEC to enable its fishermen to make even a small use of fishing waters controlled by the Community. Spanish fishermen then thought of an easier way to gain access to lucrative Community fishing waters. The plan was to register a vessel as British and become eligible for a UK quota, which the UK was entitled to by virtue of membership of the Community. This practice became known as 'quota-hopping': fishing companies would re-flag their vessels onto a member state's register in order to obtain some of their quota allocation. In the case of Spain, if such a registration took place, it would enable companies which were in reality Spanish to obtain a licence from the Ministry of Agriculture, Fisheries and Food in Whitehall and a quota allowance to fish in Community waters. Quota-hopping was particularly important for Spain if it was to gain access to the Great Sole Bank of the Atlantic Ocean, which traditionally had been an important area for the Spanish fleet. The area could be opened up again for Spanish trawlers without the need for specific negotiation with Brussels if Spanish vessels became UK registered. Using quota-hopping for your own advantage in this way was perfectly legal, made possible under an Act of Parliament passed in Victorian times. The Merchant Shipping Act 1894 had not been at the forefront of the minds of British diplomats who negotiated Britain's accession to the European Community in 1972. By 1983, there were over sixty Anglo-Spanish vessels on the UK register.

While Spain was doing all it could to expand its ability to exploit rich fishing opportunities, Britain was belatedly doing its best to protect its domestic fishing industry. A hastily introduced Fishing Boats Act of 1983 required 75 per cent of the crew of a vessel fishing under UK quota limits to be EEC nationals. This hit Spain hard, theoretically, but the restriction was difficult to enforce as the boats were on the high seas and hardly ever docked in British ports.

When Spain joined the Community on 1 January 1986, the European Commission laid down limits to fishing for Spanish-registered boats in Spain's Treaty of Accession, but this did not affect Anglo-Spanish vessels, Spanish fishing companies who had registered in Britain under quota-hopping. By now, the United Kingdom government was waking up to the fact that Spain was posing a threat to Britain's maritime pride, just as Iceland had done a decade or two earlier.

The Fishing Boats Act 1983 effectively placed a ban on Spanish crews, but it did not outlaw completely Spanish companies from continuing to register fishing fleets in the United Kingdom so as to become Anglo-Spanish companies. By the end of 1986, there were fifty registered Anglo-Spanish vessels and just over twenty Spanish vessels whose fishers had bought quotas from British fish producer organisations. This had been a purely commercial decision by domestic bodies to sell unwanted quota allocations to companies owned and controlled overseas.

The intention of the British government to squeeze Spanish fishermen out of competition with British crews had not worked. The government now wanted to ban Spanish fleets altogether from waters that British fishermen regarded as their fishing territory. The Conservative Party included in their manifesto for the 1987 general election a promise to make policing the Common Fisheries Policy more effective and to 'introduce legislation to ensure that UK quotas are reserved for UK fishermen'. It was a little-noticed challenge to the ethos of Community fishing, but the promise of legislation was honoured. After the election, Parliament enacted the Merchant Shipping Act 1988, which confined the registration of fishing vessels as British to those managed, directed and controlled from within the UK. Seventy-five per cent of shareholders in British-registered fishing companies had to be either British citizens or citizens who were resident and domiciled in the UK. The Spanish were, in reality, now locked out of being able to register any fishing vessels in the entire United Kingdom. By being unable to register, their access to a UK fishing licence was blocked.

But was it? The European Court of Justice in Luxembourg was already embroiled in a legal challenge to the regulations the British government had introduced. The court had ruled that it was contrary to Community law for Britain, as a member of the EEC, to require 75 per cent of the crew of a British-registered vessel to be resident in the United Kingdom.[2] It was in direct conflict with a principle of the European Economic Community which required a freedom of establishment in member states. But what remedy did Spanish fishermen have if Community law said one thing and the British Parliament said another? A legal ruling about an incompatibility between English law and Community law would not, in itself, bring victory for the Spanish fishers unless the United Kingdom Parliament bowed its head and changed the regulations. This was not something the British government was prepared to do. On the contrary, Britain had gone further by enacting stringent exclusion provisions in the Merchant Shipping Act 1988. Battle royal had been joined. It was a dispute that would shake traditional certainties about the supremacy of the British Parliament to their core and instil a culture of anti-Europeanism in Britain that would lead, in the end, to Brexit.

The story of how these momentous events unfolded begins with one Spanish fisherman. John Couceiro was a brave and determined fisheries businessman from Galicia and the Basque country who had been educated in England and understood the English well. He was the managing director of Factortame Ltd. He was perplexed and frustrated that the United Kingdom Parliament could, apparently, pass a law which contradicted Community law and discriminated against Spanish citizens purely on grounds of their nationality. He sought advice from England's leading expert in European law, David Vaughan QC. With bravery matched only by Couceiro himself, Vaughan and his team prepared to challenge the most important tenet of the entire United Kingdom constitution: the place of Parliament within the body politic to make law, which has the status of supremacy. Vaughan wanted that supremacy temporarily suspended and disapplied until the European Court of Justice gave a ruling on the discriminatory nature of the Merchant Shipping Act 1988.

Couceiro was the lead spokesman for ninety-five companies whose directors and shareholders were mostly Spanish. They had registered perfectly legally under the 1894 Act but were now precluded from re-registering under the 1988 Act due to the nationality discrimination deliberately inserted into that Act. They were undoubtedly 'quota-hoppers' and for that reason the government wanted to stop the fleets registering their vessels as British in order to fish under a British quota allocation.

This argument threw down a challenge to traditional, British constitutional verities. In essence, what the Anglo-Spanish fisherman wanted a court of law to decide was whether a British law limiting the ability to fish to those whom Britain deemed British was in breach of the Treaty of Rome. Britain had signed up to obeying the Treaty of Rome when the United Kingdom joined the European Economic Community in 1973. If the Spanish fishermen were right, it would appear that an Act of Parliament passed by a democratically elected legislature could be overridden by unelected Community officials in Brussels. The point was of such fundamental importance that the High Court in London refused to make a decision until an opinion was given by the European Court of Justice.

While awaiting this opinion, the High Court disapplied the part of the 1988 Act affecting the Spanish fishermen and imposed an injunction on the British government to allow the Anglo-Spanish vessels to remain on the register pending the verdict from the European judges. This decision was, in itself, fiercely contested by the British government and an appeal went as far as the House of Lords. Could our membership of the European Community allow a situation whereby the government of the country could be ordered to desist from applying a law Parliament had enacted? It seemed, to some, preposterous. The House of Lords drew back from upholding the injunction against an elected government and referred the correctness of this decision to the European Court of Justice in Luxembourg. The European Court of Justice gave its preliminary opinion that the Spanish fishermen were quite right: Parliament's legislation in 1988 did indeed breach Community law and as a consequence the fishermen did have a remedy against the UK's elected government. Couceiro and his supporters were banging on the doors of the citadel of power in Britain and a legal case of huge constitutional importance was looming when *Factortame* went back to the House of Lords for a second time.

In the course of the House of Lords hearing, Lord Bridge, the leading Law Lord, gave a speech which, for some, was entirely obvious, logical and correct; for others, it was contentious, provocative and revolutionary. Lord Bridge said this:

Some public comments on the decision of the European Court of Justice, affirming the jurisdiction of the courts of member states to override national legislation if necessary to enable interim relief to be granted in protection of rights under Community law, have suggested that this was a novel and dangerous invasion by a Community institution of the sovereignty of the United Kingdom Parliament. But such comments are based on a misconception. If the supremacy within the European Community of Community law over the national law of member states was not always inherent in the EEC Treaty it was certainly well established in the jurisprudence of the European Court of Justice long before the United Kingdom joined the Community. Thus, whatever limitation of its sovereignty Parliament accepted when it enacted the European Communities Act 1972 was entirely voluntary. Under the terms of the Act of 1972 it has always been clear that it was the duty of a United Kingdom court, when delivering final judgment, to override any rule of national law found to be in conflict with any directly enforceable rule of Community law. Similarly, when decisions of the European Court of Justice have exposed areas of United Kingdom statute law which failed to implement Council directives, Parliament has always loyally accepted the obligation to make appropriate and prompt amendments. Thus there is nothing in any way novel in according supremacy to rules of Community law in those areas to which they apply and to insist that, in the protection of rights under Community law, national courts must not be inhibited by rules of national law from granting interim relief.[3]

Lord Bridge made three points, each of which was important. First, when Britain joined the EEC, Parliament knew what it was doing and did so voluntarily; secondly, it was clear at the time that if a directly enforceable rule of Community law conflicted with national law, national courts would uphold Community law; and third, that there was nothing novel in according supremacy to rules of Community law where they protected rights which a national court should have the ability to protect also.

Although so far the British courts were involved in preliminary issues about the legality of their jurisdiction, *Factortame* had created a storm. Most of the press, reflecting no doubt the views of their readers, thought Lord Bridge was taking a step too far. *The Times* suggested the Senior Law Lord was inventing new law in its headline 'Landmark ruling gives EC power over UK law'.[4] Sir William Wade, the country's most eminent constitutional academic, thought Lord Bridge's few sentences had shattered the doctrine of parliamentary sovereignty and heralded a revolution.[5]

There was certainly a body of distinguished opinion that regarded Britain's decision to join the EEC in 1972 as a turning point in Britain's constitutional evolution. In one case, manufacturers of British cider had produced and then advertised something called 'champagne perry'. The producers of Bollinger, James Bond's favourite champagne, took a case in the English courts, claiming their labelling rights had been infringed by a British company daring to label their ersatz product Babycham as 'champagne'. Lord Denning, who gave the ruling, said of Community law: 'The Treaty is like an incoming tide. It flows into the estuaries and up the rivers. It cannot be held back. Parliament has decreed that the Treaty is henceforward to be part of our law. It is equal in force to any statute.' He added that English sovereignty had been taken away by the European Court of Justice.[6]

Lord Denning had struck a chord with elements of the public. Long before Brexit had entered the lexicon of familiar expressions in Britain, public opinion was becoming accustomed to the fact that the United Kingdom had enemies when it came to fishing. As the political commentator Alan Watkins put it in 1995, 'Spain has replaced Iceland as the enemy. The villains are the Spanish fishermen. They have even been to the House of Lords in their judicial capacity, and won their case.'[7] In 2013, the same journalist put the point that was troubling those who were suspicious of European interventions: 'The sovereignty of Parliament was ended with the European Communities Act 1972 ... The several cases involving the Spanish fishermen known as Factortame demonstrated that'.[8] There were many who agreed with him.

Alan Watkins was quite right to focus on sovereignty. It is the kernel of the point raised by the Spanish fishermen, but the word 'sovereignty' is opaque and not always easy to understand. The word sovereignty means different things to different people. The most basic meaning of sovereignty is the inherent understanding by people of the fundamental authority residing in the institutions of the nation state where they reside. It is the political and legal foundation for the sort of government that makes a nation state function.[9] In the United Kingdom, where we have an unwritten constitution and a political and legal foundation which has evolved over time, our sovereignty is usually expressed as 'parliamentary sovereignty' or the fundamental authority of our nation state residing in the 'supremacy of Parliament'. The greatest exponent of Britain's unique system of government, the constitutional monarchy, was the constitutional theorist A. V. Dicey. He described the secret source of strength of the British system as the 'absolute omnipotence, the sovereignty of Parliament ... at bottom nothing less than unlimited power'. He went on: 'Parliament under the English Constitution has the right to make or unmake any law whatever ... No person has the right to override or set aside the legislation of Parliament.'[10]

These emphatic and unqualified pronouncements have seeped into the psyche of the British people and have become a justification for the power of Parliament, which has endured long after Dicey's death in 1922. Fifty years later, when Parliament was debating how Britain's arrangements would fit into the new European ones of the EEC, Dicey was largely forgotten as parliamentarians struggled to find a way to keep our traditions intact while at the same time incorporating Community law into English law. The Treaty of Accession, signed by Edward Heath, stated that Community law should be treated as a legal system which domestic courts had to apply whenever Community law had a direct effect in trade and business in the United Kingdom. This is exactly what happened in the Factortame case. Lord Bridge was accurate when he said Parliament had made the necessary constitutional adjustments voluntarily when Britain joined the Community.

Despite this obvious legal and political fact, the full implications of accession to the European Economic Community were not properly understood at the time. Parliament approved a mechanism for all Acts of Parliament in the future to be construed and have effect subject to the Treaty of Accession. If any dispute were to arise about this, the matter could be referred to the European Court of Justice and then domestic courts would make a ruling in accordance with the principles laid down in decisions of the European Court. Once again, this is exactly what happened in the Factortame case. For a time, the constitutional necessity of Britain having to adapt its view of sovereignty from the rigid certainties that Dicey had formulated was not fully grasped. Politicians and the people, through the confirmatory referendum of 1975, seemed united in the belief that the advantages to trade, ease of travel and commercial opportunities were more important than arcane constitutional niceties.

Despite the many economic, strategic and diplomatic benefits of being part of a European community of nations, the vivid and powerful image conjured up by Lord Denning of an unstoppable incoming tide of European law seeping into the fabric of Britain's sovereignty was hard to shake off. He later moderated this view considerably, but

Lord Denning had brilliantly articulated a simmering scepticism about Europe among the British people. In the 2016 referendum, the topic of sovereignty or 'taking back control' was one of the most important factors which persuaded the British people to vote to leave the EU. In polls conducted at the time of the referendum in 2016, the most frequently cited reason among Leave voters for their choice was 'to strike a better balance between Britain's right to act independently in its co-operation with other countries'. In a similar poll conducted two years later, asking for the reason people had actually cast their vote, Leave voters cited a wish for the EU to have no role in UK law-making as the second most important reason, falling just short of a wish to regain control over immigration.[11] During the referendum campaign, Boris Johnson stated that if Britain remained in the EU, it would mean 'the steady and miserable erosion of parliamentary democracy in this country'.[12] He even resurrected the Factortame case by declaring, 'The EU pinch our fish.'[13] The narrative some politicians placed in the public mind, that membership of the European Union allowed disreputable practices to overwhelm us with the sinister intent of eroding our home-grown democracy, was difficult to dislodge. Within ten years of Britain joining the EEC, the television comedy *Yes Minister* was reducing the nation to helpless laughter by depicting a government minister trying to vanquish 'Brussels bureaucrats' in their attempt to rename the British sausage 'emulsified high-rate offal tube'.

A narrative was developing that the United Kingdom could either retain its historical sovereignty or it could remain in the European Union; there was no halfway house. As the journalist Ambrose Evans-Pritchard put it during the referendum, there was a stark choice either to continue living under a supranational regime in Europe or to restore full self-government to the British nation.[14] Another journalist reminded readers of the *Daily Telegraph* that the Factortame case was one of the most important rulings in our legal history, as it was 'the moment when the penny really dropped about how much power we had ceded in joining the Common Market'.[15] Even the United Kingdom government itself believed membership of the European Union had diminished parliamentary sovereignty. In the 2017 White Paper mapping a possible future for Britain outside the EU, the government stated that 'whilst Parliament has remained sovereign throughout our membership of the EU, it has not always felt like that'.[16]

Here, the anonymous author of a government White Paper was putting into elegant English the rather more innate feelings of some of Britain's traditional market traders. This was because the perception of the European Community as a sinister institution threatening the British way of life had extended to the relatively obscure subject of metrification. Historically, Britain had always regarded itself as an imperial power using imperial units of measurement in shops, but the United Kingdom was out of step with Europe on this, as Europe used kilos and not pounds for displaying the weight of products in shops. Nowadays, this is taken for granted, but it was seen as a sinister development by some when, in January 2000, the EC issued a new directive requiring goods sold loose by weight, mainly fresh food, to be sold by grams and kilograms. The directive prohibited traders from displaying loose food *only* in imperial measurements. Traders could continue to express the weight in pounds and ounces as well if they wished; the directive only required that the metric equivalent was also displayed so there was uniformity to enable consumers to compare prices between shops.

This was hardly the stuff of revolution. The government used powers given to it by Parliament in the 1972 Act to incorporate the directive in a regulation amending the Weights and Measures Act 1985 to give effect to the metrification directive. Despite the latitude given to market traders to continue to display goods in both units of measurement, one trader in Sunderland, supported by others in different parts of the country, decided to disobey the new law and to display and sell his vegetables *only* by imperial weight and to refuse to use metric scales. He was warned by a trading standards officer that his weighing machines did not comply with the regulations, but the trader took no notice and refused to alter them. When the officer visited a second time, the local authority took enforcement action to require him to amend his practice and abide by the regulation. The trader in question, Steve Thoburn, then became dubbed a 'metric martyr' by the tabloid press, who printed lurid stories about the possibility of the British pint being banned in pubs or the Queen being put in the dock if she sold wood from her Sandringham Estate in feet rather than metres. A case in the Sunderland magistrates' court where Mr Thoburn was given a conditional discharge (the lowest penalty in the calendar) was now a *cause célèbre* and went to the High Court, where two senior judges had to ponder on some important points about sovereignty.[17]

Despite the furore over Mr Thoburn's market stall in Teesside resembling an episode of *Yes Minister*, this market trader case raised important constitutional issues. Thoburn's counsel had argued that powers given by the European Communities Act 1972 to ministers could not be used to make changes to a *future* Act of Parliament like the Weights and Measures legislation, as this would allow Parliament to bind its successors. One of the cardinal principles of the sovereignty of Parliament is that no parliament can tie the hands of a future parliament. An Act of Parliament which is inconsistent with an earlier one is deemed to have repealed, impliedly, the earlier Act. If this principle is not honoured, parliamentary sovereignty is diminished. The contrary argument, put forward by Sunderland City Council, was that by joining the European Community, Parliament allowed Community law to become entrenched into English law as it was a unique legal order in itself and supreme above all the individual systems in member states. Curiously, both sides of the argument were reinforcing British scepticism of the European Union by adopting rather extreme positions.

Lord Justice Laws subjected the decision of the United Kingdom to join the European Community to a cerebral legal evaluation and concluded that the foundation of the edifice that permitted Community law to take precedence when it had direct effect on domestic law was Parliament itself. European law had not become entrenched into English law, as Parliament was supreme and was therefore incapable of giving up its own sovereignty. In agreeing to obey substantive Community law when it had direct effect domestically, Parliament did not agree to give up its own constitutional preconditions upon which sovereign legislative power rested. By joining the EEC in 1973, Parliament did not allow the European Court of Justice or any other institution ('Brussels bureaucrats', for example) to touch or qualify the *conditions* of Parliament's legislative supremacy in the United Kingdom. The law, which recognised the existence of parliamentary sovereignty, could not allow such an encroachment on a sovereign Parliament. The British Parliament does not, of itself, possess the foundational authority to allow its foundational conditions to be qualified. 'Being sovereign,' Lord Justice Laws pronounced, 'it cannot abandon its sovereignty.' It is the common law which recognises and obeys that sovereignty that does not permit Parliament to abandon its own sovereignty.

When Britain joined the European Community, there came into existence two supremacies: the supremacy of European law and the supremacy of Parliament. Substantive Community rights, such as the freedom of establishment (to undertake business without discrimination based on nationality), which occurred in the Factortame case, do prevail over express terms of domestic law and legislation. But substantive law does not abrogate a foundational constitutional principle, the supremacy of

Parliament principle, as it was Parliament that permitted that law. Lord Justice Laws likened the European Communities Act 1972 which took Britain into the EEC as a constitutional statute akin to Magna Carta, the Act of Union, the Great Reform Act or the Human Rights Act. These Acts, in themselves, did not contemplate *implied* repeal. Such limitations on sovereignty as membership of the European Community requires means that member states have the sovereign power to override national legislation but only if it is necessary to protect rights granted under Community law.

This scrutiny is a far cry from the unstoppable incoming tides of European law drowning out our sovereignty described by Lord Denning in 1974 or the strident complaints of much of the British media. *Factortame* and the 'metric martyr' cases had compelled English judges to return to first principles in analysing what exactly parliamentary sovereignty meant and how it is sovereign under law. While judges pondered issues of constitutional law, the nuts and bolts of *Factortame* were far from over. One could say the grinding machinery had hardly warmed up. If you are a claimant, what matters in law is establishing a fault and winning a remedy, and John Couceiro and his colleagues were interested in that, not arcane constitutional debates. If the United Kingdom had discriminated against Couceiro and the Spanish fishermen on grounds of nationality, how serious was this? Could a nation state, the United Kingdom, be held liable, and what loss, if any, had the Spanish suffered? These were important questions which touched on European and domestic law, so the Factortame case continued its course both in Luxembourg and in the High Court, the Court of Appeal and the House of Lords in London.

For the next ten years the legal disputes in *Factortame* rumbled on. European Community law was vague on the subject of available remedies, as the cause of the breach was usually a nation state. European judges had so far drawn back from ruling that a nation state could be required to pay damages to a company or an individual. *Factortame*, however, was forcing the issue and the European Court in Luxembourg could not avoid a ruling any longer. The court ruled that if a nation state concluded that a breach of Community law was sufficiently serious and there was a direct causal link between the breach and the damage sustained then a judge in Britain could decide those questions. The ball was now back in the British court and the government took the opportunity to argue the breach depriving Spanish-owned vessels from registering under the UK flag was not really a serious one.

The High Court, the Court of Appeal and the House of Lords were all of the same opinion, and it was not a comforting one for the government, who were strenuously attempting to uphold the consequence of the 1988 Act for Spanish fishermen even though it was discriminatory. The government maintained that until *Factortame* went to the House of Lords the first time, the law was unclear, and it had not intended to break the law or harm Spanish fishermen. These arguments cut no ice with the judges. First, the clear effect of the domicile and residence requirements for registration of vessels was discrimination on the grounds of nationality. Community law forbidding such discrimination was understandable and important since the whole point of the European Community to trade as a common organisation was to exclude discrimination between producers and consumers. The United Kingdom had deliberately flouted this principle when enacting the Merchant Shipping Act 1988. Parliament had not acted inadvertently when it introduced this legislation. It was obvious that the 1988 Act would cause loss and damage to many fishermen. It was a manifest breach of the treaty the United Kingdom had entered into when it joined the Community.

The point was clear. It was the United Kingdom Parliament, by bringing into force the discriminatory legislation in 1988, that was the root cause of the long-running controversy, not the laws of the European Community trespassing upon national sovereignty. The *Factortame* litigation had been long and arduous. The first legal ruling given in the High Court in London was in March 1989 and the last hearing in the House of Lords was more than a decade later in October 1999. By now the case was called *Factortame No. 4*. It was still not over even though the government had lost comprehensively before all the tribunals it had appeared in. The amount of damages to be paid by the United Kingdom to the Spanish was still unresolved. Theoretically, this would be a judicial decision unless the parties came to an agreement. Finally, in March 2000, the ninety or so Anglo-Spanish fishing companies *Factortame* had represented reached an agreement to accept £55 million in compensation – but this included a sum of around £26 million in interest. Had the British government recognised its errors earlier and compensated the fishermen sooner, much of this sum of public money would have been saved. It was another humiliation for Britain when it came to fishing. While the Icelandic cod wars had been fought and lost on the high seas, this time the United Kingdom government had fought and lost in the law courts.

Factortame will remain long in the British memory for this reason alone, but it is the constitutional consequences of the case that qualify it as one of the legal cases that made modern Britain. For Eurosceptics, the case placed fairly and squarely before the British people the impression that European law was a threat to the sovereignty of the United Kingdom Parliament. The fact that the Spanish won was plain to see, and it demonstrated beyond argument, they held, that our constitution was diminished in some way. This bold assertion, one which undoubtedly helped the Eurosceptic case in the 2016 referendum, needs some critical appraisal.

The United Kingdom is a nation without a written constitution, and traditionally we have relied on scholars, historians and constitutional theorists to tell us what our unwritten, invisible constitution actually says. The most notable and eminent of all these is A. V. Dicey, a Vinerian Professor of Law at the University of Oxford. Dicey's depiction of parliamentary sovereignty is crisp and forthright: 'Parliamentary sovereignty is an undoubted legal fact.' Authority must reside somewhere and the English Civil War extinguished the power of a despotic sovereign and replaced it with two Houses of Parliament, the Commons and the Lords. It was in Parliament where the sovereign, being subservient to Parliament, resided.

In this way, Dicey argued, the sovereign's supremacy was replaced by Parliament's supremacy. The word 'sovereignty', Dicey maintained, means a power to make law, unrestricted by any legal limit. Defined in this way, sovereign power, according to Dicey, exists in Parliament. This is subject only to the electors exercising their power to elect a sovereign Parliament.[18] This description ignores the reality of politics in the late nineteenth and early twentieth centuries. Sovereignty was the cloak behind which land-owning and business power dealt with the Crown. Once power shifts, whether towards trade unions, grassroots party-political members, lobbying organisations or even Europe, Dicey's explanations begin to look quaint and somewhat irrelevant.

Dicey's explanations are historical. They do not analyse *why* Parliament is supreme and who, in law, vested in Parliament the unlimited authority to 'make or unmake any law whatever'. Dicey asserted unequivocally that 'no person or body is recognised by the law of England as having a right to override or set aside the legislation of Parliament'. Plainly, this was not the case once Britain entered the European Community, as the *Factortame* legal judgments categorically established. *Factortame* demonstrated, among other things, the need for a fundamental reappraisal of Dicey.

Lord Justice Laws reconciled the Diceyean concept of parliamentary sovereignty with British membership of the European Union in his reasoning in the 'metric martyr' case. He said it was the law itself which would not and could not dilute the supremacy of the United Kingdom Parliament. Put simply, supremacy of Parliament is an aspect of law, and Parliament could not abandon the sovereignty the law provided it with. It was the law which provided the conditions for an elected legislature to be supreme. Parliament was supreme because the common law created and recognised it. For this reason, the European Court of Justice did not possess any authority to elevate European law to a status within the body of English law that English law could not itself aspire to. As English law recognised the supremacy of Parliament, it followed this could not be diminished by European Community law.

This is a sophisticated and highly persuasive analysis, even if it did not penetrate into the minds of those, like Boris Johnson, who said during the referendum campaign that Britain was in thrall to Brussels to the extent that Europe was dictating the shape of our bananas.[19] *Factortame*, and its humiliation for the British government, had done much to foster this mindset but in doing so opened up for further examination traditional justifications for parliamentary sovereignty. While populists banged the drum for a plucky Britain trying to break out of a Brussels straitjacket, academic lawyers were drawing the opposite constitutional lessons from the Factortame case.

What, exactly, gave the United Kingdom Parliament its supremacy and how, exactly, did Parliament give power to Community law? After all, the United Kingdom Parliament had the supremacy to leave the EU in the same way it had used its supremacy to join it. Community law played no part in limiting Britain's unilateral decision to leave. At heart, something happened in 1972 when Parliament passed the European Communities Act 1972 to add a new criterion to the validity of laws passed by Parliament in the future. Henceforward, Parliament entrusted UK courts to recognise the validity of Community law where it had direct effect. Parliament did so by giving the Treaty of Accession to the EEC a rule-making power and obliged domestic courts to recognise it. This was not a decision to diminish or reduce Parliament's sovereignty; it was simply creating a further norm empowering judges to decide cases according to law. In 1972, Parliament decided that once Britain became a member of the EEC there would be laws which Parliament incorporated in the Treaty of Accession.[20] What *Factortame* compelled lawyers to think about was the part our common law, the law applied by judges, played in our constitution. Dicey had completely overlooked this in his magisterial account of why Parliament is supreme.

Unlike Dicey, modern constitutional theorists began describing the British constitutional framework as 'pragmatic, ambiguous, opaque and subtle'.[21] There was a flexibility within our constitution that allowed an accommodation, domestically, of law made within Europe providing Parliament intended that result. When Parliament passed legislation to join the EEC, this intention was signalled by a desire to bring about an innovation which the pragmatic flexibility of our constitution permitted. Parliament decided of its own free will to accord some priority to European law. This was plainly stated in the wording of the European Communities Act 1972. Mark Elliott has argued that domestic courts are perfectly entitled to take account of this plain parliamentary objective when determining the extent to which later law enacted by Parliament has overridden, repealed or displaced earlier legislation. There was an element of constitutional fundamentality about the decision to join the EEC, but this did not entrench the decision. Entrenchment would be contrary to parliamentary sovereignty. However, a signal to judges that Parliament did not expect the implications of joining the European Community to be disturbed by subsequent legislation would not. Viewed in this way, the decision in *Factortame* was as inevitable as the defeat of the 'metric martyr' from Sunderland was predictable.

While the British government fought a valiant rearguard action over the course of a decade in *Factortame*, the longer it went on, the more fragile the flexible and pragmatic foundations of our constitution appeared to be. In Dicey's conception, the supremacy of Parliament was an unquestionable established fact which was immoveable and static. After *Factortame* and the 'metric martyr' cases, it became increasingly clear that parliamentary sovereignty was a legal and dynamic concept. While trying to preserve the Diceyean version of sovereignty, the British government had unwittingly revealed some holes in the fabric of our body politic. It was malleable and not always as strong in some parts as it was in others.

If Dicey's description of parliamentary sovereignty is taken at its face value, what is to stop a supreme Parliament from enacting thoroughly unjust and objectionable statutes: 'to deprive Jews of their nationality, to prohibit Christians from marrying non-Christians, to dissolve marriages between blacks and whites', for example? Lord Bingham, one of the nation's most outstanding judges, provided these examples, and his explanation for the utter unlikelihood of Parliament contemplating such things is that the public would not accept it. In addition, the civil rights of the Queen's subjects have been preserved, traditionally, by the trinity of the Crown, the elected chamber of the Commons and the revising chamber of the Lords acting powerfully and independently before legislation is enacted. This explanation, as Lord Bingham admits, is now fraying at the seams as Britain undergoes a period of unparalleled constitution change.[22]

The question that arises is simple. If Dicey's explanations about sovereignty are out of date, what exactly does the word 'sovereignty' mean in modern Britain? Dicey would have difficulty in recognising the law of the constitution he spent a lifetime examining and explaining. The Crown plays no part, nowadays, in the legislative process and the House of Lords has no independent power apart from delaying legislation approved by the Commons. Devolution in Scotland, Wales and Northern Ireland has given rise to a commitment by Parliament not to legislate on devolved matters without the consent of the devolved assembly. The Human Rights Act obliges judges to read and give effect to legislation enacted by Parliament in a way which is compatible with Convention rights, and the whipping system in the House of Commons makes the chamber far less independent of the executive than Dicey ever experienced. The decision to entrust the British people with a decision of difficulty and complexity, namely to remain in the European Union or to leave it, is a further example of the weakness of the Diceyean concept of sovereignty. All these developments mean the constitution functions very differently now than it did in Dicey's time.

These are all serious changes to the classical justification for the sovereignty of Parliament, but they have nothing to do with Britain's membership of the European Union. Yet in the popular imagination – spurred on by sections of the press, Nigel Farage, UKIP, Boris Johnson, Michael Gove and countless others – it has been the EU that has posed the greatest threat to British sovereignty. For them, *Factortame* provided the most vivid example of how Europe was encroaching on the nation's heritage of a supreme Parliament, and the refrain 'Take Back Control' became a slogan to proclaim pride in our home-grown institutions.

In the cold light of day, the United Kingdom having exited the EU, it is easier to view parliamentary sovereignty through a more objective prism. It was hardly surprising that in *Factortame* the House of Lords did not give effect to the Merchant Shipping Act 1988, which flouted the nation's international obligations. The United Kingdom constitution was flexible enough to permit an accommodation of European law over

257

domestic legislation that conflicted with it. Lord Bridge and his judicial brethren recognised this when they used unwritten norms, the innate aspects of our constitution, to permit the temporary disapplication of the discriminatory legislation in the 1988 Act, pending a ruling from the European Court of Justice. The unwritten norms give ample space for legislative authority to be restrained within 'multilayered and common law constitutionalism'.[23] This means our flexible constitution contains opaque and unwritten rules where there is a responsibility for all organs of the state to sustain a democracy so that it functions efficiently. An efficient modern democracy is upheld by mutual respect being accorded by each constitutional pillar providing a strength to the edifice as a whole. Parliament is not absolutely supreme, nor does the highest court (the House of Lords at the time of *Factortame*, the Supreme Court now) have the status of a constitutional court.

There are two great paradoxes about *Factortame* which occupied the time of judges in Britain and in Europe for a period of over ten years. The first is that for the reasons just set out, *Factortame* was not a constitutional revolution which demolished parliamentary sovereignty and allowed the tides of Europeanism to overwhelm us. It did not deserve the acres of newsprint and the vitriolic commentary it received, though the circumstances surrounding it undoubtedly fired the popular imagination. It evoked elements of Britain's past maritime sea power when Sir Francis Drake became a national hero by opposing Spain, Nelson conquered the French at Trafalgar and in general Britannia ruled the waves. *Factortame* threw light on the real nature of our parliamentary sovereignty in a modern age and it forced judges to give effect to nascent elements of our flexible constitution following Britain's membership of the European Union. As with so much of current discourse on topics of national importance, opinions about *Factortame* are unlikely to shift. For those who disliked the European project all along, it will be etched in the memory as an event that demonstrated the sinister motives of those who wanted a European superstate. For those who were more disposed to the merits of joining the European Community and who now regret our departure, *Factortame* hardly changed their opinions at all.

The second paradox is the result of *Factortame* in purely fishing terms. The Conservative government elected in 1987 under Margaret Thatcher's leadership vowed to put into law a principle that allowed UK fishing quotas to be allocated to UK fishermen, a commitment that dismally failed after the Factortame cases. The litigation played an important part in fostering a desire of the British people to leave the EU, but when Britain finally did leave, the aspiration of the ill-fated Merchant Shipping Act 1988 was still not realised. The British consumer was simply not eating the fish UK fishermen caught. Around 80 per cent of UK fish landings were being exported. Quota-hopping was advancing apace and half of England's EU quota, £160 million in value, was in the hands of Icelandic, Spanish or Dutch vessels flying British flags. This is, in reality, economically sensible as those crews catch species of fish not popular with the British consumer. Nonetheless, when Britain embarked on a mission to 'take back control', the omens for fishing were not good. The political declaration and the withdrawal agreement of November 2019 promised a new fishing agreement on access to waters and a share of quotas. The final document Boris Johnson commended to Parliament hardly lived up to these grandiose expectations. There would be a phased transfer of the fishing rights of EU boats in UK waters, but this would involve only a quarter of Europe's fleet being transferred over a period of five years and a reduction of EU quotas in UK waters of only 15 per cent in the first year and then gradual further reductions of 2.5 per cent in succeeding years. This adjustment period lasts only until 2026, when talks will once again resume to attempt to settle what quantity of fish can be caught in UK waters.[24] For Scottish fishermen who rely on large exports to the EU, the burden of paperwork that exiting the EU required became unbearable. The conclusion to the fraught negotiations that led to the United Kingdom leaving the EU was a bitter disappointment to the fishing industry as a whole. It was summed up by the American news channel NBC News. Quoting the Prime Minister, Boris Johnson, who had promised he would achieve full control, stating, 'For the first time since 1973, we will be an independent coastal state with full control of our waters,' a reporter re-interviewed fishermen who had voted to leave the EU in the referendum. They were bitterly disappointed by the agreement and felt let down and betrayed by promises that far exceeded the actual result.[25]

In the final analysis, *Factortame* has meant different things for different people. For some, the Spanish claims were nothing less than a seditious attack on the fortress of the British constitution that kept Britain secure, independent and beholden to no one, an attack that forced judges into surrender. For others, it provided a treasure chest of legal, political and constitutional puzzles to work out. In its impact, however, there is no doubt that *Factortame* was one of the legal cases that made modern Britain.

Chapter 10

Death – To Cease Upon the Midnight Without Pain

L ife, the experience given to us by nature, is precious and inviolate. Intentionally ending the life of another human being is, for every civilised society, a crime of wickedness meriting the highest punishment. Death, on the other hand, is inevitable at some stage in our lives and it is often anticipated with fear, dread or unhappiness. In between life and death there is, for many, an intermediary stage of dying, the approach of death under the eyes of loved ones or medical practitioners where a person is helpless and dependent for survival on those around them. Sometimes, the condition of dying is unbearably painful and distressing. People have felt that to be alive under these conditions is not living, and an easeful death would be a better option. Yet, to provide an easeful death to a patient who requests it and whose mental faculties are functioning while the body is wasting away may involve an act of murder by the person who causes it. Mercy killing is not a concept most nation states, including Britain, recognise. In the past twenty years, Britain's highest courts have been presented with heartbreaking cases when an applicant suffering from an incurable and irreversible health condition has sought legal guidance on who might break the law if their wish to die were granted. One such case was that of Tony Nicklinson.

Tony Nicklinson was a fit and health man until a catastrophic stroke in 2005 caused him to become paralysed from the neck down. He could move only his head and his eyes. He had lived like this for seven years, a life he regarded as 'dull, miserable, demeaning, undignified and intolerable'. For many years, he had wanted to end his life, but he could not do so without assistance, other than by self-starvation, a protracted, painful and distressing exercise. He wanted someone to kill him by injecting him with a lethal drug, but if necessary he was prepared to kill himself by means of a machine invented by an Australian doctor which, after being loaded with a lethal drug, could be digitally activated by Mr Nicklinson, using a pass phrase, via an eye-blink computer. He had been a campaigner for a 'right to die with dignity' since his paralysis and he was bitterly disappointed when the High Court refused his application. He then refused food and died of pneumonia in August 2012. His wife, Jane, pursued an appeal to the Court of Appeal, as a spouse or partner may continue legal proceedings if it involves a denial of an Article 8 right of the European Convention (the right to a private and family life) of a deceased person. The High Court and the Court of Appeal had refused to make a legally binding declaration that it would be lawful for a doctor to kill him or to assist him in terminating his life. In addition, he wanted a declaration that the current state of the law in that connection was incompatible with his right to a private life under Article 8 of the European Convention on Human Rights. This would have forced Parliament to reconsider the law on assisted suicide.

In the same proceedings, which had begun in 2012, another applicant, known only as Martin, wished to end his life by travelling to Switzerland to make use of the Dignitas service, which, under Swiss law, enabled people who wish to die to do so. Martin had suffered a brain-stem stroke in August 2008 rendering him completely unable to move; his condition was incurable. Martin wanted a legal order to require the

Director of Public Prosecutions to modify the 'Policy for Prosecutors in respect of Cases of Encouraging or Assisting Suicide' to clarify the risk that responsible people such as carers might face if they assisted a patient like Martin to commit suicide through Dignitas, a Swiss self-determination group.

When the Supreme Court began to hear Nicklinson and Martin's appeal, a panel of nine Supreme Court judges were convened to hear the case. Normally, only five would be needed. The nine justices pondered their ruling over a period of nearly six months before delivering their judgment. Every member of the panel delivered a reasoned decision, but there was no unanimity. The moral, ethical and legal problems were acute and difficult. In essence, the subject of assisting dying engages a debate between private morality and public policy. In addition to deciding where the boundary lay between these two competing values, Tony Nicklinson's case raised a constitutional point of great importance. Parliament had enacted an apparently unambiguous prohibition on assisting or encouraging another to commit suicide. In the Suicide Act 1961 (re-enacted in 2009), any person who intentionally does an act capable of encouraging or assisting the suicide or attempted suicide of another commits an offence, punishable with up to fourteen years' imprisonment. If Parliament, in legislation, has laid down this public policy, did judges have any role to play in altering it? Only, it would seem, if the Act was incompatible with a human right of private morality provided for in the European Convention on Human Rights, which Britain had incorporated in the Human Rights Act 1998.

But the Human Rights Act did not, of itself, provide the Supreme Court with an easy route to acceding to Tony Nicklinson's request to die at the time of his choice. Human rights under the European Convention are not, in the main, unqualified rights. In general, the machinery for giving citizens their protection under the Convention lies with domestic legislatures. These legislatures have discretion to restrict exercise of a right if it is necessary in a democratic society for one or more of the purposes specified in that article. The United Kingdom Parliament had prohibited assisting suicide to protect health or morals and to protect the rights and freedoms of others. This was entirely lawful under the European Convention. The legal language for this general principle is called 'the margin appreciation'.

Strasbourg judges had made it clear that in relation to suicide the United Kingdom Parliament had a wide margin of discretion to regulate through its own criminal law activities which are detrimental to the life and safety of others. Assisting another to commit suicide was one such activity. By making assisting or encouraging suicide a crime, Parliament was not flouting any human right guaranteed in the Convention.

A preliminary question for the Supreme Court to decide was whether the blanket ban on assisting suicide was even within the power of the court to rule on in the first place. It was only if the court had constitutional authority to consider this that the court could go on to decide whether the Suicide Act 1961 was, in fact, compatible with the overarching principles of the European Convention. Put simply, was the Supreme Court entitled to rule on the moral basis for permitting an applicant before them to have his wish to die carried out without offending a general policy principle to protect the sanctity of human life for everybody else? Should judges become embroiled in morality if there is a law made by Parliament which makes assisting suicide a crime?[1]

There was certainly a respectable argument for saying the Supreme Court should not try to reopen questions which had been argued and ruled upon in earlier cases. United Kingdom judges first became seriously engaged in the morality of assisted suicide when Diane Pretty attempted to obtain an undertaking from the Director of Public Prosecutions that her husband would not be prosecuted if he helped her to die. Diane Pretty suffered from motor neurone disease and had only a short time to live before she anticipated a humiliating and painful death. She was mentally alert and wanted to choose the time of her death so that with the help of her husband she could die peacefully. Her husband was willing to provide help for her to end her life. In response to her application, the DPP gave no undertaking that her husband would not be prosecuted. Ms Pretty challenged the lawfulness of this refusal. When the case came before the House of Lords in 2001, Lord Bingham had no difficulty in dismissing her claim on the grounds that principles 'deeply embedded in English law' respected the sanctity of life, which was inviolate even if the person in question consented to its violation. Lord Bingham rejected any claim that Diane Pretty's case engaged any human rights guaranteed by the European Convention.[2]

She appealed this decision to the European Court of Human Rights in Strasbourg, where she argued that the prohibition on assisted suicide in English law flouted her human rights under Article 8 of the Convention. This is a person's right to respect for his or her private and family life, home and correspondence. Judges at Strasbourg interpreted this to mean, in the context of a right to die, a right to autonomy in making end-of-life choices. In this limited respect, Strasbourg judges corrected a misapprehension by Lord Bingham that Article 8 simply did not apply to an end-of-life decision. But what sort of right was Article 8 in assisted dying applications? In reality, it was really only a right to immunity from state interference with a settled decision of a person to kill himself, *unless* the interference was justified. Most Convention rights can be qualified if it is considered necessary in a democratic society. A member state may qualify a Convention right in a way prescribed in the law of the state in question. When the Strasbourg judges interpreted Article 8 to include a right of autonomy in taking end-of-life decisions, they were ruling that it was a right only to the extent that no justification for restricting it existed under *human rights* law. It was not an explicit, unqualified right to commit suicide. European Convention law was clear thar if a nation state concluded that it was necessary for reasons of public policy to limit the exercise of the right, it may legislate to do so. The United Kingdom Parliament had done so in the blanket ban on assisting suicide in the 1961 Act.

When the Supreme Court in *Nicklinson* analysed the principles that lay behind the Strasbourg decision in *Pretty*, the justices could not agree. What, exactly, had Strasbourg meant when devolving the responsibility for autonomy to choose a time of death to the UK Parliament under the 'margin of appreciation' principle? One thing, at least, was clear. The whole topic was not one that Strasbourg wanted to take on themselves and attempt to give human rights guidance which would be applicable in all member states. The majority of the Supreme Court justices in *Nicklinson* decided that in the circumstances of assisted suicide, Strasbourg had given to each member state a wide margin of appreciation to decide for themselves how Article 8 rights could be accommodated in their domestic law. Within each member state there are independent courts of law and elected legislatures. The Strasbourg judges were dropping a big hint that the United Kingdom court should first interpret the meaning of Article 8, the relevant article in question. Having done so, UK courts could go on to decide where the division should lie between the law-making powers of Parliament and those of the courts. By advising domestic courts to adopt this approach, Strasbourg was not questioning the supremacy of the United Kingdom Parliament, as Parliament had given the courts power to decide whether or not there was an infringement of a Convention right under the Human Rights Act 1998.[3] The Supreme Court took the hint from Strasbourg and decided that it was the work of judges not to shy away from decision-making which is separated from considerations of what is just or fair. This is especially so when the court is considering the balancing of interests required under the Human Rights Convention. In cases of suffering, it was a judicial responsibility to weigh social risks to the wider public and their moral convictions with the values of human autonomy and human dignity advocated by others.[4] This meant, according to the majority, that on the preliminary constitutional point the Supreme Court had institutional competence to reopen the prohibition Parliament had imposed on assisting suicide.

The minority view was articulated by Lord Sumption. He focused on the constitutional consequence of the decision of the UK to enact the Human Rights Act. What constitutional difference did it make? For Lord Sumption, the European Convention did not alter a fundamental constitutional principle that there were certain issues that Parliament, exclusively, should decide. This is because suicide and assisted suicide involve choices between mutually inconsistent moral values about which there is no consensus. These choices, he maintained, were essentially legislative in nature as the decision-makers represent the community as a whole. Lord Sumption repeated these views in his first Reith Lecture, 'Law's Expanding Empire'.[5]

The gulf existing within the Supreme Court on the institutional competence of the court to even start examining the moral questions raised by Tony Nicklinson's application lies in the sensitivity of the subject of assisted death. There are strongly held views about the ethics of allowing a person to choose the time of their death which are difficult to reconcile. Certainly, European and domestic judges have traditionally steered away from becoming embroiled in the topic. The majority in Tony Nicklinson's case were prepared to make a move away from this judicial shyness. For the justices in the majority, the time had come for the judiciary to begin to get to grips with the ethics of assisted death. Two justices, Lady Hale, who later became president of the Supreme

Court, and Lord Kerr, were prepared to go further and declare UK law on assisted dying incompatible with a guaranteed Convention right.

Having successfully mounted the constitutional hurdle, the justices moved on to the moral obstacles, which involved considerations of patient autonomy, medical ethics and the moral purpose of our laws of suicide and assisting suicide. In the decade before the Supreme Court heard Tony Nicklinson's case, a debate was taking place in Britain and around the world which posed one simple question: is death always so bad that it must, in all circumstances, be worse than life? During this time, campaigners for and against changing the law on assisted death were gathering pace in Britain. Those who wanted change were focusing attention on laws in the state of Oregon in the United States and in the Netherlands and Belgium. Campaigners argued there was little evidence from those places that voluntary euthanasia was being used to exploit the vulnerable. On the contrary, laws in those places respected the dignity of the dying who had made a cogent, rational choice to end their suffering with the assistance of another. On the other side of the argument, campaigners from the established church, Roman Catholics and doctors specialising in palliative care argued that the law as it stood protected the vulnerable without prejudicing the rights of others. Palliative care could involve the withdrawal of life-prolonging treatment and therefore there was no pressing need to change the law to one which permitted the active hastening of death. There is no doubt that all nine of the justices who heard Tony Nicklinson's arguments in December 2013 were fully aware of these competing arguments.

The background to the Nicklinson case was the application Debbie Purdy had made to the House of Lords (then Britain's highest court) five years earlier. The two cases had similarities. Debbie Purdy suffered from primary progressive multiple sclerosis, which was incurable. She wanted to know if her husband, Omar Puente, would be prosecuted by the Director of Public Prosecutions if he helped her to go to Switzerland to die under Swiss law, which permitted suicide in defined clinical conditions.[6] Debbie Purdy and her husband were in a state of uncertainty. If she was allowed to die at Dignitas by her own hand under Swiss law, would her husband be branded a criminal for helping her make the journey? By 2010, 115 UK residents had been accompanied to Dignitas for the purpose of ending their lives and eight visits had been reported to the DPP for advice on prosecution. No relatives or friends who made the journey were actually charged with assisting suicide, but this was mainly for lack of evidence. The publicity surrounding Ms Purdy's application might mean the evidence was only too clear and her husband's compassionate intentions might still place him at risk of a prosecution.

At the time, the DPP had no settled policy on prosecuting people who helped others to die. Parliament had enacted a law in 1961 which decriminalised the act of suicide undertaken by a person, thus removing any threat of prosecution against anybody who failed in an attempt to kill themselves. However, the Act went on to make it an offence for any other person to do an act capable of encouraging or assisting suicide if that person intended to assist another to die. As this topic was a sensitive one, it required the consent of the Director of Public Prosecutions before anybody could be charged with assisting another to commit suicide.

There was, under this law, something of an anomaly. Parliament had made it a crime to assist somebody to do an act which was not, in itself, a crime. This held even if the assister was requested to assist by the person wishing to die. In addition, the assister would be guilty even if he or she were acting with motives of compassion, not of evil intent. By enacting the Suicide Act, Parliament was wrestling with somewhat contradictory objectives. On the one hand it was holding firm to the interests of society in protecting life, while on the other it was pulling back from making a criminal out of someone who was exercising autonomy and personal choice and committed suicide alone. Logically, this was a difficult distinction to justify. If the Suicide Act was mainly intended to reinforce the principle that human life is sacred then why was the failed suicide attempt not retained as a crime, as it was prior to 1961? It would seem that the cardinal 'sanctity of life' principle did not prevent the legislators in 1961 from removing the label of criminal from somebody who wished voluntarily to end his or her life. When a law itself does not appear to have clear objectives, the discretion vested in a prosecutor to decide when to press charges became, after 1961, very important.

The House of Lords, in 2009, unanimously decided that the Code for Crown Prosecutors was not sufficiently clear on this offence-specific factual scenario. The House of Lords thought there was a substantial risk that the acts Ms Purdy wanted her husband to do in helping her travel to Switzerland would give rise to a prosecution. The way out of this difficulty for Omar Puente was for the House of Lords to order the Director of Public Prosecutions to publish prosecution guidance in relation to the factors weighing in favour or against prosecuting those who assist the suicide of others. The House of Lords was prepared to take this step and the DPP responded straight away. In February 2010, guidance was published so that the risk could, to a considerable extent, be predicted. Ms Purdy and her legal team believed a significant victory had been obtained for those who wanted help to die.

This ruling was borne out by experience. By the time the *Nicklinson* application reached the Supreme Court in December 2013, 215 people had gone to Dignitas from the United Kingdom and not a single person had been prosecuted under the Suicide Act 1961.

When Tony Nicklinson's case reached the Supreme Court, therefore, two small steps towards accommodating the desires of those who wished to end their lives had been taken: the topic had been found to fall within the bounds of Convention law and the Director of Public Prosecutions had been compelled to provide guidance on the sort of case which would fall foul of English law. The Supreme Court at least had these steps to lead them further towards shaping the law on assisted dying if they chose that path. The steps led in two directions, constitutionally. Either the court could rule that the Suicide Act 1961 *was* incompatible with Tony Nicklinson's Convention rights, as the Pretty case had opened that window of opportunity. Alternatively, it could decide that Parliament should not be asked to reconsider the law of assisting suicide. It all turned on whether the Supreme Court were prepared to make a declaration of incompatibility. Under the Human Rights Act, a senior court in the United Kingdom could rule that a particular piece of legislation was not, in law, compatible with a Convention right or that limitations on that right were not lawfully prescribed. This is called a 'declaration of incompatibility', which obliges Parliament to reconsider the offending legislation. As Parliament is supreme, no court may order Parliament to legislate in a particular way. Here the Supreme Court could not agree.

Three justices thought the law on assisted suicide, taking into account *Pretty* and *Purdy*, was now in a satisfactory state. For them, the 1961 Act was not an anomaly leading to inhumane prosecutions. This point of view was articulated adroitly in the judgment of Lord Sumption. He acknowledged that *Nicklinson* had raised the complex moral dilemma of our law in having to uphold the principle of autonomy and the principle of the sanctity of life at the same time. For Sumption, personal autonomy is a fundamental value but so also is sanctity of life. The Suicide Act 1961 was a pragmatic solution to the moral dilemma of reconciling the two by *decriminalising* the lone suicide attempt. This was not a moral point as it did not provide a legal right to take one's own life. It simply stated that the extreme state of mind that induces suicide should no longer be a legal wrong. In this respect, Parliament was upholding the principle of autonomy which the law has always recognised. By contrast, the assister in suicide cases does not act under any principle of autonomy but only under compassion if the assistance is compassionate. In Lord Sumption's opinion it is difficult, if not impossible, to legislate in advance for compassionate circumstances that may arise from time to time, but the duty of legislators is to protect the vulnerable. If assisting suicide were to be legalised, even in tightly defined circumstances, there was a danger that those, like Nicklinson, who contemplated death with a settled and intelligent perception would encourage others to do the same. These others were very likely to be the vulnerable in need of protection, as their own circumstances might cause them to believe they were becoming a burden on their carers. This is conventionally called the 'slippery slope' or 'thin end of the wedge' argument as the vulnerable may be persuaded to be allowed to be put to death with the help of those who did not have compassionate motives. Six justices disagreed, but importantly they all agreed on the jurisdictional role they possessed as judges in Britain's highest court. They all held that the Supreme Court did have the institutional competence to rule on whether the Suicide Act 1961 fell within the 'margin of appreciation', that is to say whether it fell within Parliament's responsibility to decide how to balance private morality with public policy. The parting of the ways in the Supreme Court was *how* their institutional jurisdiction should be exercised. This decision involved considerations of morality.

Lord Sumption's view on the moral argument raised by Nicklinson was that autonomy and sanctity of life must always be in conflict and it was for Parliament to resolve the conflict. But this starting point for resolving the moral issues in the case was, itself, controversial. Until her death in 2019, Mary Warnock was one of Britain's foremost moral philosophers. She wrote about the evidence given by specialists in palliative care and geriatric psychology to a House of Lords select committee in 2004. They described the suffering of people under their care who were once able to exercise free will but who were now trapped in an 'enforced intimacy of severe illness'. Such people, the experts testified, are distinctive personalities who want, as death is foreseen, to be in charge of their fate. This state of mind was a species of 'existential autonomy', an experienced condition, not an abstract right. Warnock argued that it was this autonomy, far from standing in opposition to the sanctity of life, that actually made life 'sacred', at least for the person who lived it.[7] The select committee described the state of affairs of those who want to be in charge of their fate but who are denied that choice as a horror. It involved, the committee concluded, a loss of dignity and control.

Mary Warnock and Elisabeth Macdonald, a former specialist in cancer treatment, argued that it is not always helpful to categorise all human motivation as having obvious moral imperatives guiding it. Moral sentiment, compassion and pity arise in situations that present themselves and are not easily converted into generalisations with universal application. When we read of the distress of people like Tony Nicklinson, we are more likely to support their claim to be able to choose the time of their death because of our sympathy, not because of a principle. Warnock and Macdonald maintain that a resolution to cases like Nicklinson are, philosophically, acutely difficult. It is not just a consideration of autonomy versus sanctity of life; it is the task of fashioning law to permit the relief of suffering for those who want to die without endangering others who do not want to be in charge of their fate. Unlike Lord Sumption, Warnock did not believe the law must err towards protecting the vulnerable. Instead, she argued for a law which acknowledges that each human life, including those who wish to die, has a value which must be respected. From her philosophical standpoint, she saw merit in legal systems like those in the Netherlands or the state of Oregon in the United States, which have laws permitting assisted suicide in legally defined circumstances.

When the justices of the Supreme Court began their task of weighing the competing arguments in Tony Nicklinson's case, the respective cases for and against a law on assisted dying were hotly debated in Britain. In the heat of the argument some claims had become somewhat extreme on both sides. Ilora Finlay is a crossbench peer in the House of Lords and an expert in palliative medicine. She is also a strong opponent of any change to the present law on assisted dying. In her book *Death by Appointment: A Rational Guide to the Assisted Dying Debate*, co-authored with Robert Preston, she rightly acknowledges that it should be permissible in law and in medical ethics for a doctor to increase dosages of medication to relieve pain and distress. She further acknowledges that such medical treatment may involve a risk of hastening the patient's death. Such medical practices are ethically and legally sound, she admits, because the doctor's intention is to kill the pain, not the patient. This is called the 'doctrine of double effect', which will be discussed and explained later. Suffice to say, it is a doctrine which applies in English law.

Baroness Finlay then continues with a somewhat extravagant claim. Administering medication under the 'double effect' principle, she says, is 'radically different from acting with the deliberate intention of bringing about a patient's death ... The Rubicon would be crossed if doctors were to be licensed to supply lethal drugs to some of their patients.' But what does she mean by 'bringing about' a patient's death? If a drug addict living in a squat asks his friend to give him 'something to go to sleep' and the friend prepares a syringe of heroin ready for injection and the drug addict injects himself and later dies, has the friend 'brought about' the addict's death? It is perfectly possible to argue that morally the friend is culpable, but in English law he is not. As *R v Kennedy* found in 2007, the friend supplied the heroin, the 'lethal drug', but he did not cause the addict's death. The cause of death was the inhalation of gastric contents while acutely intoxicated by opiates and alcohol. The drug addict had made a voluntary decision to inject himself with the heroin and it was this decision that killed him.[8]

There is no mention of autonomy in the scenario Baroness Finlay paints after the law crosses the Rubicon, as she would put it. Her picture is of a law where doctors are 'licensed' to kill their patients. Here, she conjures the image of the notorious Dr Kevorkian, an avowed advocate of assisted suicide in the United States, who administered voluntary euthanasia to fifty-two of his patients. He was convicted of second-degree murder and sentenced to a lengthy term of imprisonment. The spectre of licensed killers working in the National Health Service would be alarming, if it were true. No advocate of a change in the law has proposed such a thing.

Some on the other side of the argument go too far in their rejection of established legal convention. L. W. Sumner is a Canadian moral philosopher who has dissected from a philosophical viewpoint the ethical distinction between two scenarios. In the first scenario, a doctor gradually withdraws life-sustaining treatment to a patient who has made known a wish to die. In the second, the doctor administers a lethal injection to the same patient who has expressed the same wish. Under English law, as in other common law jurisdictions, the former is legal but the latter is not. The ethically legal justification for the distinction is that in the first scenario the doctor is fulfilling a duty to act in the best interests of the patient under his or her care. Secondly, in the first scenario the law is recognising the patient's right to self-determination. By contrast, in the second scenario the doctor is embarking on an active step which he knows will kill the patient and which is not taken to relieve suffering.

The distinction is justified in English law as our law maintains a dividing line between foreseeing an outcome and intending it. If palliative care is administered, the doctor intends to palliate pain and discomfort. He does not intend the patient to die even if it is foreseeable in the doctor's experience and knowledge that the palliative treatment will hasten the patient's death.

This is an understandable distinction to most people brought up with a moral compass or religious conviction. Most people instinctively recoil from the thought that a power over life and death should be held by a medical practitioner who has access to lethal drugs, and the very word 'euthanasia' wreaks of wrongdoing. Relieving suffering, on the other hand, connotes compassion, sympathy, love, duty and responsibility. Professor Sumner, however, has embarked on a cerebral philosophical analysis of the concept of causation to argue that there is no real difference between palliative medicine which a doctor can foresee will shorten life and a lethal injection that will certainly shorten life.[9] Perhaps in philosophical academic circles the distinction may not demonstrate the logic a philosophical discipline demands, but it is a sensible and reasonable distinction which commands public confidence in the eyes of the law.

The Supreme Court avoided philosophical hair-splitting and concentrated instead on core general principles: what ethical questions arise when a patient says, 'My best interests are to die'? The question was posed in 2002 in the tragic case of a young woman known only as Ms B. She was an able and talented woman who had suffered a serious haemorrhage of her spinal cord for which surgery was needed to stop further bleeding. This would probably result in severe disability. Ms B then made a living will giving instructions that treatment should be withdrawn if she were to suffer from a life-threatening condition, permanent mental impairment or permanent unconsciousness. About a year later, her condition in hospital deteriorated and she developed a cervical spine cavernoma, rendering her a tetraplegic, and soon needed a ventilator to breathe. She was confined to an intensive care unit in the hospital. Three months later, she asked a consultant anaesthetist to turn the ventilator off. She remained in this state of total immobility, breathing through a ventilator. She could only be transferred to a hospice on the condition that a ventilator was maintained.

Her request to be allowed to die came before the Family Court.[10] The judge applied principles of law which were clearly established. First, English law goes to great lengths to protect a person of full age and capacity from interference with his or her personal liberty. Second, the right to determine what shall be done with one's own body is a fundamental right encompassing the principles of self-determination and autonomy. Third, a mentally competent person has an absolute right to refuse consent to medical treatment for any reason. Fourth, the principle of the sanctity of life is not an absolute one. It does not compel a doctor to treat a patient who will die if he does not continue the treatment if the express wish of the patient is not to be treated. Fifth, these principles entitle a patient of sound mind to require that life-supporting measures should be stopped.

The conclusion the judge reached in Ms B's case was that there is a presumption in English law that a patient has a mental capacity to make decisions. Ms B did have the capacity to consent or refuse medical or surgical treatment when under the care of a doctor. The doctor has a corresponding duty and obligation to comply with the patient's choice. Ms B was allowed to obtain a transfer to a hospital where physicians would agree to withdraw the ventilator.

In his judgment in the Nicklinson case, the president of the Supreme Court, Lord Neuberger, drew a moral conclusion from Ms B's case that went beyond principles of autonomy and self-determination. Lord

Neuberger posed the question that if sanctity of life is the principle that makes it legitimate to prohibit assisting or encouraging suicide, why is it lawful for a person, exercising autonomy, to end his or her life? Parliament decriminalised suicide and, in moral terms, was sending a signal that to take one's own life was not a moral wrong. If suicide is not a moral wrong, why should the law prevent a person from seeking assistance from someone else to achieve that moral end?

Resolving this moral problem is difficult. In order to comply with existing law, Tony Nicklinson could only be helped to die if the law held onto the clear dividing line between the principle of autonomy, the right to end one's own life, on the one hand and the right not to be killed on the other. Such a dividing line also engages difficult questions about the interests that society in general has on the need to protect life and the duty of doctors to treat patients in accordance with their best interests.

In one sense the moral questions raised by Tony Nicklinson are, by their nature, too subjective and too personal to expect even the wisest and most cerebral judges in the country to agree upon. This is what happened in the nine separate judgments handed down by the Supreme Court, who divided three ways. The task of the court was to decide whether the objective Parliament wanted to achieve by prohibiting the act of assisting another to die was sufficiently important to justify a limitation on the Article 8 right. Was a blanket ban on assisting suicide a rational limitation and was it the minimum necessary to accomplish the objective? Did the prohibition strike a fair balance between the right of the individual on the one hand and the interests of the wider community on the other? These were legal questions, but answering them necessarily involved considerations of morality.

The boldest approach was in the judgments of Lady Hale and Lord Kerr, who concluded that the blanket ban on assisting suicide under the 1961 Suicide Act was incompatible with a Convention right. In their judgment the Supreme Court should make a declaration of incompatibility, which was within the power of the court to do under the Human Rights Act. This would have required Parliament to revisit the 1961 Act and to decide how to respond to the declaration. Under our constitution, it is Parliament which is supreme and the higher courts of the nation cannot declare any law unconstitutional. Lady Hale and Lord Kerr's reasoning was that Parliament had not struck a fair balance by legislating for a blanket ban on assisting another to die. They questioned what the justification was for the view that the interests of the community *must*, in all circumstances, prevail over the desire by one person to end his life. Does the sanctity of that life require that person to endure untold misery until a 'natural' death takes over? If passive assistance, withholding life-sustaining care, is permitted, why is active assistance not? It appeared to Lady Hale and Lord Kerr that the passive and active assister are both acting under the same moral and conscientious foundations. There was no obvious logical reason why those who in the future may want to commit suicide should feel more vulnerable because a law would exist permitting those who cannot do so from getting help. Yet, the only justification for the blanket ban was to protect the vulnerable. Strasbourg had ruled this was a legitimate aim but left the responsibility of achieving this aim to the UK Parliament. In rulings on assisted dying handed down by Strasbourg judges, the court has judged that any person should be capable of exercising free will at an end-of-life stage. Strasbourg did not elaborate and rule that this autonomy was confined only to those who were physically capable. The principle of autonomy applied equally to those who were capable of freely acting to die at their own hand and to those who required assistance. If the assister was acting responsibly and was fully informed about the circumstances and the reason for the person's decision to die then, morally, the assister was no different from the person exercising autonomy. Lady Hale and Lord Kerr gave judgment that by exercising autonomy a person is exercising the right not to be condemned to a life bereft of pleasure or quality.

Plainly, Lady Hale and Lord Kerr were influenced by their own moral compass when stating their legal reasons for favouring a declaration of incompatibility in respect of that part of the 1961 Suicide Act which prohibited every act of assisting suicide without exception. Yet, according to Lord Sumption, articulating a moral compass is exactly why judges should not become embroiled in the morality of assisted death. His view is that judges are not equipped to make judgments about morality when there is no general consensus on the rights and wrongs of the issue at hand. Judges are not appropriately equipped to arbitrate. Being a judge does not allow them to impose their personal opinions into their judgments. If such opinions were imposed, they would lack all constitutional legitimacy.

In essence, Lord Sumption viewed Tony Nicklinson's case as one engaging a complex moral dilemma of which autonomy was only one moral value in play. There are others of which the state, in this instance the UK Parliament, should be the guardian. When a state performs this function there may not be a rational or utilitarian justification (the focus of the criticism of Lady Hale and Lord Kerr), but the state may act in a way to preserve values which are fundamental to our humanity. By enacting the Suicide Act 1961, Parliament was not attempting to reconcile the two conflicting principles of autonomy and sanctity of life. It was acting pragmatically. The pragmatism was the recognition in 1961 that it was inhumane to make a failed suicide attempt a criminal offence. Experience had shown that criminalising suicide did not deter those who had a settled intention to end their lives, but Parliament was not legislating to signal that suicide was not a *moral* wrong.

Three other justices also took this view. Judges may interpret a law made by Parliament but they may not usurp the legislative function. They thought the law made by Parliament was clear and unambiguous. Once judges venture on an inquiry about whether the Suicide Act is compatible with the Convention, they embark on trying to decide complex questions of social policy and moral questions about which there is not consensus. When Parliament passed the Suicide Act 1961, it did so because the institution of Parliament is democratically accountable and representative. Judges do not have a democratic mandate in the opinion of Lord Sumption and three other justices.

These judgments, two on one side and four on the other, take polar opposite views on the limits to be placed on the court's deference to Parliament's judgment. Lady Hale and Lord Kerr stated that the Suicide Act made no conceptual sense, was illogical and disproportionate in pursuing its aim of protecting the vulnerable; it was incompatible with human rights principles. The differing view of Lord Sumption and three other justices was that great respect and deference should be accorded to Parliament in accordance with well-known constitutional principles. This difference of view also encapsulated unbridgeable differences on the moral legitimacy of assisted suicide. Had the matter rested there, the judgments of four would have prevailed over the judgments of two. The law would have remained in the same place as it was after Ms Purdy's appeal in 2009. Tony Nicklinson would not have started a case that made modern Britain.

It did not end there. There were nine justices and three others, the president, Lord Neuberger, Lord Wilson and Lord Mance, took an interesting midway position which pointed the law in a new direction. This middle way was set out in powerful reasoning by Lord Neuberger, who argued that the present law was in an unsatisfactory state both morally and in its application. He thought there might come a time when a future Supreme Court would declare the Suicide Act 1961 to be incompatible with the Convention. He did not think it was appropriate in Tony Nicklinson's case, but only because the factual basis for this step was not sufficiently clear.

Lord Neuberger scrutinised the argument that the blanket ban on helping another to kill himself was necessary and proportionate to protect the vulnerable. Who were the vulnerable on this argument? Were they people like Tony Nicklinson or were they others who might feel a duty to die to avoid burdening friends and family? If they were the former then Lord Neuberger thought the protection argument especially weak. He cited evidence which showed that some people with a progressive degenerative disease felt forced to end their lives before they became incapable of committing suicide. In these cases, the blanket ban impinged adversely on their personal autonomy as they died before they needed to. The moral arguments for keeping the law as it is were not, in Lord Neuberger's opinion, particularly strong. The moral arguments for changing the law to allow Tony Nicklinson to die then become quite strong if the focus is on autonomy. The particular circumstances affecting Nicklinson were that he hoped to be able to use a machine which he could activate with an eye-blink. This could set in motion the administration of a lethal dose to end his life. Lord Neuberger thought this scenario was potentially moral as it did not engage the services of another to provide the immediate cause of death.

Secondly, Lord Neuberger pointed out that the application of the present law was unsatisfactory. It was plain, from the evidence, that the Director of Public Prosecutions did not prosecute friends and family accompanying their desperately afflicted relative to Switzerland so their loved one could die with dignity, under the Dignitas regime. This impacted adversely on those who may prefer to die at home without the upheaval and expense of travelling to Switzerland. The evidence demonstrated that assisted suicide was tolerated in certain circumstances under existing law. The blanket ban was not consistent in its application. It would be preferable, he thought, if the weak and vulnerable were protected not by an *ex post facto* review by a prosecutor after a suicide had taken place but by a judge or an assessor beforehand so that a responsible and impartial person could know of the proposed plan. The arrangements could be approved if the person contemplating suicide did, in fact, make a voluntary, clear, settled and informed wish to die. This would allow the act of suicide to be organised in an open and professional way.

In Tony Nicklinson's case, the arrangements that had been proposed before his death were not sufficiently precise or necessarily administratively feasible. Tony himself had envisaged using the Australian machine, but as he had died through starvation before the Supreme Court heard his plea to use it, the reliability and workings of the machine could not be investigated. It was therefore not appropriate to declare the Suicide Act incompatible with his human rights at this stage. However, Lords Neuberger, Wilson and Mance gave a clear and unambiguous warning to Parliament. The legislature must address in a satisfactory way the predicament faced by Tony Nicklinson and others in similar distress. They urged Parliament to get to grips with the issue of assisted suicide and to debate whether there should be further legislation, and if so, what the content of that legislation should be. Parliament was the appropriate forum for this exercise. There might be another case coming before the courts when an opportunity would present itself for the Supreme Court to consider again the acute issues raised by Tony Nicklinson.

The judgment of these justices in deciding it was not exclusively for Parliament to keep or to change the law on assisted suicide was decisive. There was now a majority, five justices, who ruled that the Supreme Court did possess the constitutional authority to make a declaration that the blanket prohibition on assisted suicide was incompatible with Article 8 of the Convention. The difference between them was only the occasion for a declaration to be made. Lady Hale and Lord Kerr wanted Tony Nicklinson to be the legal case in which it was done. Lords Neuberger, Wilson and Mance thought Parliament should be given one more chance to consider whether the Suicide Act 1961 really was the last word on the morality of assisted suicide.

Tony Nicklinson's application for an immediate declaration of incompatibility therefore failed, as did his application for a ruling that if a doctor assisted him to die his actions would be lawful. In that sense Tony Nicklinson lost and so did Martin, the second claimant. He failed in his application for the DPP's guidance on prosecuting policy, issued after Debbie Purdy's case, to be further modified. However, in a real and substantive sense, both had succeeded. The case placed before the Supreme Court strong constitutional and moral arguments that could not lightly be pushed aside. Only four out of the nine Supreme Court justices were content to leave to Parliament the exclusive responsibility to make law on assisted suicide. The other five believed a judicial involvement was both necessary and legally permissible. Their judgments continued the slow and gradual steps towards change that had begun in Strasbourg with Diane Pretty and continued in the House of Lords with Debbie Purdy. The law on assisted suicide was not standing still; it was moving in a new direction. The question remaining is whether it will be Parliament or the courts which will take the process of review a step further forward.

The majority in the Supreme Court were in step with public opinion on the morality of assisted death. A YouGov poll conducted in August 2021 found that 73 per cent of respondents now think the law should be changed to allow doctors to assist in the suicide of people suffering from a terminal illness, including 74 per cent of Conservative voters and

76 per cent of Labour voters. There was less support for a change for people like Tony Nicklinson who suffer from a painful and incurable condition but not terminal illness: 50 per cent backed such a move with 23 per cent opposed.[11] The distinction in the public's mind between the morality of assisting the terminally ill to die compared with the distress of those who are incapacitated but not terminally ill was one also made in a commission chaired by Lord Falconer which reported in 2012.[12] It took evidence from many individuals and organisations and concluded there was strong support for the law providing a choice to die with assistance for the terminally ill. However, there was no consensus for such a choice being available for those who are profoundly incapacitated through a catastrophic life-changing event. In 2014, Lord Falconer introduced a Bill in the House of Lords in an attempt to put into law the conclusions of his commission, but the attempt failed. It reached committee stage before running out of time in the session. In February 2020, members of the British Medical Association were polled on whether the BMA should reverse its opposition to a change in the law prohibiting the administration of a drug to assist an eligible patient to die. Opinion was divided, with 40 per cent opposed to a change but 30 per cent supportive and 23 per cent undecided. The BMA has described the survey as one of the biggest that has ever been undertaken on the issue.[13] As a result, the British Medical Association now take a neutral stance on assisted dying, a move away from their previous opposition. This change removes a central plank of the arguments of those opposed to any change in the law: the claim that the medical profession in Britain are opposed.

The perceptible but gradual change that is taking place on the way sanctity of life should be honoured and respected in modern Britain has arisen mainly through the huge advances made by medical science. Dr Haider Warraich is a physician and cardiologist and a professor at the Harvard Medical School in Boston, USA. He has extensive experience of treating patients in intensive care and has observed death and dying throughout his medical career. He has concluded that while 'in innumerable ways, medicine has made life better and certainly longer, death is more harrowing and prolonged today than it has ever been before'.[14] Cardiopulmonary resuscitation (CPR) did not exist until the 1950s, liver transplants were unknown until 1963 and the first heart transplant did not take place until 1967. It is only in the latter part of the twentieth century that the electroencephalogram (ECG) was invented. The increase in life expectancy has risen by a third since 1969 and doubled in the course of the past 150 years. When it comes to death, those who die in hospital usually do so following the withdrawal of life-sustaining treatment. Surgical procedures when the end of life is approaching rarely provide any meaningful benefit to the patient in prolonging life significantly or in relieving distress. Modern medicine, Warraich states, can only postpone death as its inevitability approaches. It cannot save life.

This frankness about the realities of death among those who are seriously ill in hospital is nowadays increasingly shared by lawyers, judges and philosophers. Their focus is on the procedures that, ethically, should be in place to protect the vulnerable if the dying are to be granted their wish to die. L. W. Sumner has suggested that there are ethical bottom lines before a physician can help a patient to die. First, the patient must agree or disagree to end-of-life treatment at a certain moment in time by a named physician. Second, the patient must have capacity, the competence to make a reasoned decision for or against the treatment. Third, before making the decision, the patient must have disclosure; this means he or she must have enough information about the proposed treatment to be able to make a decision. The information should be as complete as a reasonable person, in the condition of the patient, would regard as sufficient. Finally, there must be, medically, a diagnosis. This means the patient's illness or condition must be serious enough to warrant an option of hastening death. Sumner argues this may, but need not, be terminal. The patient must be experiencing a degree of suffering which he regards as intolerable and one that cannot be alleviated to the patient's satisfaction by a treatment option that will not also have the effect of hastening death. The diagnosis must involve a medical assessment that all purely life-prolonging options have been exhausted.

The extent of the safeguards that should be put in place to protect the vulnerable was considered by the Supreme Court in *Nicklinson*. Lady Hale thought it was well within the wit of a legal system to devise a process to identify the few people who would be allowed to end their life with assistance. The requirements, she suggested, were capacity, lack of undue influence, disclosure and an understanding of the consequences if a decision to die was not made. These are similar to the conditions mooted by L. W. Sumner. Lord Wilson suggested nearly twenty safeguards which included, in addition to the above, an assessment of the patient's ability to tolerate continued suffering. He also wanted consideration to be given to the motive of the individual proposing an end-of-life solution. This should include any financial or other benefit that would be likely to be received by a person assisting the death. Lord Neuberger thought it was premature, in the *Nicklinson* appeal, to speculate too much on the details of future safeguards.

In October 2021, Baroness Meacher introduced a new Assisted Dying Bill in the House of Lords. It was the third attempt to change the law. In the new Bill the conditions for exercising a choice to die would be that the patient was a mentally competent adult aged eighteen or over who was terminally ill with a life expectancy of less than six months, certified by two independent doctors. The safeguards would be that the close relatives of the patient making a choice to die would be inter-viewed to check their motivations, if any, and finally the process would have to be approved by a High Court judge of the Family Division. The House permitted the Bill to proceed to the committee stage. During the debate, Lord Mance, who was in the majority in the Nicklinson case, spoke in support of the Bill's safeguards, describing them as carefully limited and balanced.[15]

The second reading of Baroness Meacher's Assisted Dying Bill demonstrated the powerful emotions that exist in proponents and op-ponents of assisted dying. Members spoke of their own illnesses and suffering as well as those of relatives and parents who had died in dis-tressing circumstances. Others spoke of the illogicality of the present law, which does not forbid suicide, only assisting someone else to die. Opponents stressed the ability of palliative care to reduce end-of-life suffering and the central importance of the sanctity of life to civilisation. One thing was abundantly clear. The legislature would not be debating the issue at all were it not for people like Tony Nicklinson who took the whole question of choice and autonomy as their death approached for a decision by judges in Britain's highest court.

The Tony Nicklinson case is perhaps the most vivid example of all those discussed in this book of the role senior judges play in raising, discussing and often resolving contemporary social, moral and political problems that arise in modern Britain and are tested in the courts. In this case, as in the first chapter, Life, senior judges had to apply analyti-cal reasoning to a novel legal problem. In another, Sovereignty, Britain's highest court had to show bravery in disapplying an Act of Parliament in the legal confusion that had arisen when European Community sovereignty was in conflict with traditional ideas about British sover-eignty. The nation's top judges also delved into history to find the true foundations for the concept of the supremacy of Parliament in the cases discussed in Chapter 8, Democracy. In others, judges had to be flexible and pragmatic in applying old ideas about the equitable notion of confidence in order to develop a modern law of privacy. Taken together, the cases in this book demonstrate that judges, in their fidelity to law, can be adaptable, ingenious, logical and inventive in their decisions; judgments, all of them, that made modern Britain.

Notes

Introduction

1 Andrew Marr, *Elizabethans: How Modern Britain Was Forged* (London: William Collins, 2020).

2 Ronald Dworkin, *Taking Rights Seriously* (London: Duckworth, 1981), pp. 110–13.

3 Allan C. Hutchinson, *Is Eating People Wrong? Great Legal Cases and How They Shaped the World* (New York: Cambridge University Press, 2011), p. 11.

4 A. W. Brian Simpson, 'The Study of Cases' in *Leading Cases in the Common Law* (Oxford: Clarendon Press, 1995), pp. 1–12.

5 Allan C. Hutchinson, *Is Eating People Wrong?*, op. cit., p. 10.

6 Kenan Malik, *The Quest for a Moral Compass: A Global History of Ethics* (London: Atlantic Books, 2014), p. 340.

7 See, for example, James Slack, 'End of human rights farce', *Daily Mail*, 3 October 2014; Martyn Brown, 'Fury at European Court as terrorists win human rights', *Daily Express*, 19 August 2015; and Theresa May MP, speech to the Conservative Party conference October 2011 in her capacity as Home Secretary: https://www.politics.co.uk/comment-analysis/2011/10/04/theresa-may-speech-in-full-2/

8 *Ghaidan v Godin-Mendoza* [2004] UKHL 30.

9 Anthony King, *Who Governs Britain* (London: Pelican Books, 2015), p. 273.

10 Anthony Sampson, *Anatomy of Britain* (London: Hodder & Stoughton, 1962), p. 159.

11 Anthony Sampson, *Who Runs This Place? The Anatomy of Britain in the 21st Century* (London: John Murray, 2004), p. 173.

12 *Attorney General v Jonathan Cape Ltd* [1976] QB 752.

13 *Attorney General v Observer Ltd* [1990] 1 AC 109.

Chapter 1: Life – Jodie and Mary, the Conjoined Twins

1 *Re A (Conjoined Twins: Surgical Separation)* [2000] EWCA Civ 254.

2 Lord Justice Hoffman in *Airedale NHS Trust v Bland* [1993] 1 All ER 821.

3 George J. Annas, 'Siamese Twins: Killing One to Save the Other' (*The Hastings Center Report*, vol. 17, no. 2, April 1987).

4 *R v Dudley and Stephens* [1884] 14 QBD 273.

5 For a full account of the case of *Dudley and Stephens* see Allan C. Hutchinson, *Is Eating People Wrong?*, op. cit. and A. W. Brian Simpson, *Cannibalism and the Common Law* (Chicago: Chicago University Press, 1984).

6 J. C. Smith, *Justification and Excuse in the Criminal Law*, Hamlyn Lecture 1988 (London: Stevens & Sons, 1989).

7 *R v Bourne* [1939] 1 KB 687.

8 For a full account of the trial of Dr Adams see Patrick Devlin, *Easing the Passing: The Trial of Dr Bodkin Adams* (London: Bodley Head, 1985).

9   For a full account of the trial of Dr Moor see Anthony Arlidge QC, 'The Trial of Dr David Moor'
    (*Criminal Law Review*, vol. 31, 2000), pp. 31–40.
10 *Perka et Al v The Queen* [1984] 13 DLR (4th) 1.

Chapter 2: Sex – Lady Chatterley Goes on Trial
1   Bernard Levin, *The Pendulum Years: Britain and the Sixties* (London: Jonathan Cape, 1970),
    p. 282.
2   Christopher Booker, *The Neophiliacs: A Study of the Revolution in English Life in the Fifties and
    Sixties* (London: Collins, 1969), p. 86.
3   Arthur Marwick, *British Society Since 1945* (London: Penguin Books, 1996), p. 61.
4   Geoffrey Robertson, *Obscenity* (London: Weidenfeld & Nicolson, 1979), p. 41.
5   *R v Martin Secker & Warburg Ltd* [1954] 1 WLR 1138.
6   John Sutherland, *Offensive Literature: Decensorship in Britain, 1960–1982* (London: Junction
    Books, 1982), pp. 10–11.
7   Kenneth Tynan, *The Observer*, 6 November 1960.
8   Faramerz Dabhoiwala, 'Repression and Control' in *The Origins of Sex: A History of the First Sexual
    Revolution* (London: Penguin Books, 2012), pp. 350–60.
9   Alan Travis, 'The Hounding of D. H. Lawrence' in *Bound and Gagged: A Secret History of Obsceni-
    ty in Britain* (London: Profile Books, 2001), pp. 128–65.
10 Dominic Sandbrook, *Never Had It So Good: A History of Britain from Suez to the Beatles* (London:
    Abacus, 2006), p. xxi.
11 A summary discussed in Jeffrey Weeks, *The World We Have Won* (Abingdon: Routledge, 2007),
    p. 61.
12 Paul Addison, *No Turning Back: The Peacetime Revolutions of Post-War Britain* (Oxford: Oxford
    University Press, 2010), p. 202.
13 Hera Cook, 'Truly it felt like year one' in *The Long Sexual Revolution: English Women, Sex, &
    Contraception 1800–1975* (Oxford: Oxford University Press, 2004), pp. 271–95.
14 Sheila Rowbotham, *Promise of a Dream: Remembering the Sixties* (London: Verso, 2001), p. 23.
15 Arthur Marwick, *The Sixties* (Oxford: Oxford University Press, 1998), p. 803.

Chapter 3: Race – The Cricketer and the Hotel
1   *Short v Poole Corporation* [1926] Ch 66.
2   Peter Fryer, *Staying Power: The history of black people in Britain* (London: Pluto Press, 2018).
3   David Olusoga, *Black and British: A Forgotten History* (London: Pan Books, 2017). For a detailed
    account of the indignities suffered by Caribbean people see Anthony H. Richmond, *Colour Prej-
    udice in Britain: A Study of West Indian Workers in Liverpool, 1941–1951* (London: Routledge &
    Kegan Paul, 1954) and Kenneth Little, *Negroes in Britain: A study of Racial Relations in English
    Society* (London: Routledge & Kegan Paul, 1948).
4   Peter Mason, *Learie Constantine* (Oxford: Signal Books, 2008), p. 80.
5   Jeffrey Hill, *Learie Constantine and Race Relations in Britain and the Empire* (London: Blooms-
    bury Academic, 2020), pp. 105–7.
6   Learie Constantine, *Colour Bar* (London: Stanley Paul, 1954), p. 138.
7   David Olusoga, *Black and British*, op. cit., p. 487.
8   See generally David Olusoga, 'Swamped' in *Black and British*, op. cit., pp. 489–519, and Dominic
    Sandbrook, 'The Newcomers' in *Never Had It So Good*, op. cit., pp. 308–47.
9   *In re Lysaght* [1966] Ch 191.
10 Quoted in Arthur Marwick, *British Society Since 1945*, op. cit., p. 164.
11 Frank Birbalsingh, quoted in Jeffrey Hill, *Learie Constantine and Race Relations in Britain and the
    Empire*, op. cit., p. 113.
12 Sir Rabinder Singh, 'What Magna Carta and the Race Relations Act Mean To Us Today', Runny-
    mede Trust conference, 29 July 2015.

13 Andrew Pilkington, 'Migration, race and ethnic diversity' in *Racial Disadvantage and Ethnic Diversity in Britain* (Basingstoke: Palgrave Macmillan, 2003), pp. 29–50.

14 *R (Begum) v Governors of Denbigh High School* [2007] 1 AC 100.

15 *Azmi v Kirklees Metropolitan Borough Council* [2007] ICR 1154.

16 'Creating the conditions for integration' (London: Department for Communities and Local Government, 2012).

17 Matthew d'Ancona, *Identity, Ignorance, Innovation: Why the Old Politics is Useless and What to Do About It* (London: Hodder & Stoughton, 2021), p. 20.

18 David Lammy, *Tribes: How Our Need to Belong Can Make or Break Society* (London: Constable, 2021), p. 166.

19 Jenny Bourne, 'The Race Relations Act 1965 – blessing or curse?', Institute of Race Relations, 13 November 2015.

20 'Commission on Race and Ethnic Disparities: The Report', March 2021: https://assets.publishing. service.gov.uk/government/uploads/system/uploads/attachment_data/file/974507/20210331_-_ CRED_Report_-_FINAL_-_Web_Accessible.pdf.

21 Simon Woolley, 'Despite the Sewell report, No 10 can no longer remain in denial about racism', *The Guardian*, 1 April 2021.

22 David Olusoga, 'The poisonously patronising Sewell report is historically illiterate', *The Guardian*, 2 April 2021.

23 Reni Eddo-Lodge, *Why I'm No Longer Talking to White People About Race* (London: Bloomsbury, 2018), p. 64.

24 Hashi Mohamed, *People Like Us: What it Takes to Make it in Modern Britain* (London: Profile Books, 2020), p. 74.

25 Trevor Phillips, *Race and Faith: The Deafening Silence* (London: Civitas, 2016), p. 4.

26 Trevor Phillips, 'The march of wokeism is an all-pervasive new oppression', *The Times*, 7 November 2020.

27 Afua Hirsch, *Brit(ish): On Race, Identity and Belonging* (London: Vintage, 2018), p. 83.

28 David Olusoga, *Black and British*, op. cit., pp. 1–28.

Chapter 4: Power – The Pilot Officer and the Home Secretary

1 *Liversidge v Anderson* [1942] AC 206.

2 The narrative in this chapter is based on the Home Office and security services files on Liversidge. They are HO 382/410/1, HO 382/410/2 and KV 2/3717 and KV 2/3718 held at the National Archives. The other sources on which this narrative is based are A. W. Brian Simpson, *In the Highest Degree Odious: Detention Without Trial in Wartime Britain* (Oxford: Clarendon Press, 1992) and Peter and Leni Gillman, *Collar the Lot!: How Britain Interned and Expelled its Wartime Refugees* (London: Quartet Books, 1980).

3 A full account of the changes made to the original regulation and the legal issues which arose in *Liversidge v Anderson* is given by Tom Bingham in 'Mr Perlzweig, Mr Liversidge, and Lord Atkin' in *The Business of Judging: Selected Essays and Speeches* (Oxford: Oxford University Press, 2000), pp. 211–22.

4 A. W. Brian Simpson, *In the Highest Degree Odious*, op. cit., pp. 29–32.

5 Geoffrey Lewis, *Lord Atkin: A biography* (Oxford: Hart Publishing, 1999), p. 138

6 The Evershed Memorandum, 23 January 1950, National Archives, LC02, 3827.

7 Anthony King, *Who Governs Britain*, op. cit., p. 14.

8 Anthony Sampson, *Anatomy of Britain* (London: Hodder & Stoughton, 1962), p. 159.

9 Sir William Wade, quoted in Tom Bingham, *The Business of Judging*, op. cit., p. 207.

10 *Magor and St Mellons Rural District Council v Newport Corporation* [1952] AC 189.

11 *Padfield v Minister of Agriculture, Fisheries and Food* [1968] AC 997.

12 *R v Commissioners of Inland Revenue ex p Rossminster Ltd* [1980] AC 952.

13 *A v Secretary of State for the Home Department* [2004] UKHL 56.

14 Anthony Sampson, *Who Runs This Place?*, op. cit., p. 173.

15 Anthony King, *The British Constitution* (Oxford: Oxford University Press, 2007), p. 138.
16 A. W. Brian Simpson, *In the Highest Degree Odious*, op. cit., p. 421.

Chapter 5: Free Speech – The Thalidomide Scandal

1   Timothy Garton Ash, 'Post Gutenberg' in *Free Speech: Ten Principles for a Connected World* (London: Atlantic Books, 2016), pp. 1–4.
2   The factual information in the account of the thalidomide tragedy is taken substantially from the book *Suffer the Children: The Story of Thalidomide* (New York: The Viking Press, 1979) by Phillip Knightley and the Insight team of the *Sunday Times*, who undertook extensive research into the events surrounding the manufacture and marketing of the drug, the medical consequences and the legal actions that followed.
3   A. V. Dicey, *An Introduction to the Study of the Law of the Constitution*, 10th edition, p. 239.
4   *The Sunday Times v United Kingdom – application 6538/74* [1979] ECHR 1, 26 April 1979.
5   *McCartan Turkington Breen v Times Newspapers Ltd* [2001] 2AC 277.
6   *Sunday Times v United Kingdom (No. 2)* [1992] 14 EHRR 229.

Chapter 6: Protest – We Shall Overcome Some Day

1   *Ziegler and Others v DPP* [2021] UKSC 23.
2   Sir Leslie Scarman, 'The Red Lion Square Disorders of 15 June 1974', Report of Inquiry, 1975, Cmnd 5919, and Lord Scarman, 'The Brixton Disorders, 10–12 April 1981', Report of Inquiry 1981, Cmnd 8247.
3   *Beatty v Gillbanks* [1882] 9 QBD 308.
4   K. D. Ewing and C. A. Gearty, *The Struggle for Civil Liberties: Political Freedom and the Rule of Law in Britain, 1914–1945* (Oxford: Oxford University Press, 2000), p. 31.
5   *Duncan v Jones* [1936] 1 KB 218.
6   *Hubbard v Pitt* [1976] QB 142.
7   *Moss v McLachlan* [1985] IRLR 76.
8   *Nagy v Weston* [1966] 2 QB 561.
9   *Hirst and Agu v Chief Constable of West Yorkshire* [1987] 85 CR App R 143.
10 Tony Thompson, 'Twenty years after, mystery still clouds Battle of the Beanfield', *The Observer*, 12 June 2005.
11 *DPP v Jones (Margaret) and Another* [1999] UKHL 5.
12 *R (Laporte) v Chief Constable of Gloucestershire* [2006] UKHL 55.
13 *Redmond-Bate v DPP* [1999] EWHC Admin 733.
14 *Munim Abdul v DPP* [2011] EWHC 247.
15 *R v Jones (Margaret) and Others* [2006] UKHL 16.
16 *City of London Corporation v Samede and Others* [2012] EWCA Civ 160.
17 *Tabernacle v Secretary of State for Defence* [2009] EWCA Civ 23.
18 Police, Crime, Sentencing and Courts Act 2022, s. 73.

Chapter 7: Privacy – The Actor and the Redtop

1   *Kaye v Robertson* [1990] EWCA Civ 21.
2   *The Times*, 28 November 1989.
3   *Blackstone's Commentaries*, 17th ed. (1830), Book IV, 151, quoted in Raymond Wacks, *Privacy and Media Freedom* (Oxford: Oxford University Press, 2013), p. 45.
4   Quoted in Andrew Marr, 'What is News?' in *My Trade: A Short History of British Journalism* (London: Pan Macmillan, 2005), pp. 50–116.
5   Fred Inglis, *A Short History of Celebrity* (Princeton: Princeton University Press, 2010).
6   Fred Inglis, 'The Performance of Celebrity' in *A Short History of Celebrity*, ibid., pp. 11–12.
7   Samuel D. Warren and Louis D. Brandeis, 'The Right to Privacy' (*Harvard Law Review*, vol. 4, no. 5, 15 December 1890), p. 193.

8   Raymond Wacks, 'Personal Information' in *Privacy and Media Freedom*, op. cit., pp. 6–19.
9   Jules Stewart, *Albert: A Life* (London: I. B. Taurus, 2012).
10 *Prince Albert v Strange* [1849] 41 ER 1171.
11 *Duchess of Argyll v Duke of Argyll* [1967] 1 Ch 302.
12 *Malone v Metropolitan Police Commissioner* [1979] 1 Ch 344.
13 *Douglas v Hello! Ltd* [2005] EWCA Civ 595, [2003] EWHC 786, [2007] UKHL 21 are the main reported occasions of the lengthy litigation.
14 *Campbell v MGN Ltd* [2004] 2 AC 457.
15 'Naomi Campbell wins privacy case', *The Guardian*, 6 May 2004.
16 *Mosley v News Group Newspapers Ltd* [2008] EWHC 1777.
17 *Ferdinand v MGN Ltd* [2011] EWHC 2454.
18 *John v Express Newspapers* [2006] EWHC 1611.
19 *Richard v British Broadcasting Corporation* [2018] EWHC 1837.
20 *Wainwright v Home Office* [2003] UKHL 53.
21 *Peck v United Kingdom* [2003] 36 EHRR 41.
22 *Wood v Commissioner of Police for the Metropolis* [2010] EMLR 1 (CA).
23 *Wood v Commissioner of Police for the Metropolis*, ibid., although Laws LJ dissented on this point.
24 *R (Daly) v Secretary of State for the Home Department* [2001] UKHL 26.
25 *Duchess of Sussex v Associated Newspapers* [2021] EWCA Civ 1810.

Chapter 8: Democracy – The Miller Tales

1   Bernard Crick, *Democracy: A Very Short Introduction* (Oxford: Oxford University Press, 2002), pp. 9, 93.
2   David Runciman, 'Something Better?' in *How Democracy Ends* (London: Profile Books, 2018), pp. 165–206.
3   *R (Miller) v Secretary of State for Exiting the European Union* [2017] UKSC 5.
4   *R (Miller) v The Prime Minister* [2019] UKSC 41.
5   Gina Miller, *Rise: Life Lessons in Speaking Out, Standing Tall & Leading the Way* (London: Canongate, 2018).
6   Hansard, House of Commons Debate, 7 December 2016, vol. 618, col. 301.
7   Robert Tombs, *The English and Their History* (London: Allen Lane, 2014), p. 206.
8   *Daily Mail*, 3 November 2016.
9   Jonathan Sumption, 'Brexit and the British Constitution' in *Law in a Time of Crisis* (London: Profile Books, 2021), p. 188.
10 *Daily Telegraph*, 29 August 2019.
11 *Financial Times*, 29 August 2019.
12 Lisa O'Carroll and Severin Carrell, 'Gina Miller's lawyers apply to challenge Boris Johnson's plans', *The Guardian*, 28 August 2019.
13 Lady Hale, *Spider Woman: A Life* (London: Bodley Head, 2021), p. 243
14 Mark Elliott, 'Constitutional Adjudication and Constitutional Politics in the United Kingdom: The *Miller II* Case in Legal and Political Context' (*European Constitutional Law Review*, vol. 16, no. 4, January 2021).
15 Martin Loughlin, *Sword and Scales: An Examination of the Relationship Between Law and Politics* (Oxford: Hart Publishing, 2000).
16 BBC Television, *The Andrew Marr Show*, 20 January 2019.
17 Hansard, House of Commons Debate, 25 September 2019, vol. 664, col. 660.
18 'Power to the People: The report of Power, an Independent Inquiry into Britain's Democracy', 2006. House of Commons Library: https://commonslibrary.parliament.uk/research-briefings/sn03948/.
19 David Runciman, *How Democracy Ends*, op. cit., pp. 120–64.

Chapter 9: Sovereignty – Spanish Ships and Metric Martyrs

1   The source for much of the history and development of fisheries policy within the European

Economic Community is taken from Robin Churchill, *EEC Fisheries Law* (Stockholm: Martinus Nijhoff, 1987). The source for more recent developments is Aaron Hatcher, Julian Frere, Sean Pascoe and Kate Robinson, '"Quota-hopping" and the foreign ownership of UK fishing vessels' (*Marine Policy*, vol. 26, no. 1, 2002), pp. 1–11.

2   *R v Ministry of Agriculture, Fisheries and Food, ex p. Agegate Ltd* [1990] 2 QB 151.

3   *R v Secretary of State for Transport, ex p. Factortame (No. 2)* [1991] 1 AC 603.

4   *The Times*, 20 June 1990.

5   H. W. R. Wade, 'Sovereignty – Revolution or Evolution? (*Law Quarterly Review*, vol. 112, 1996), pp. 568–75.

6   *HP Bulmer Ltd v J Bullinger SA and others* [1974] EWCA Civ 14.

7   Alan Watkins, 'Mr Major is a slippery fish but can he get away with it?', *The Independent*, 24 December 1995.

8   Alan Watkins, 'Legal lords a-leaping to my Lord of Derry's air', *The Independent*, 23 April 2013.

9   Robert Jackson, *Sovereignty: The Evolution of an Idea* (Cambridge: Polity Press, 2007), pp. 78–112.

10 A. V. Dicey, *An Introduction to the Study of the Law of the Constitution* (London: Macmillan, 1959).

11 Economic and Social Research Council, 'CSI Brexit 4: People's Stated Reasons for Voting Leave or Remain', report by the Centre for Social Investigation, Nuffield College, Oxford, April 2018: https://ukandeu.ac.uk/wp-content/uploads/2018/07/CSI-Brexit-4-People%E2%80%99s-Stated-Reasons-for-Voting-Leave.pdf.

12 Macer Hall, 'Boris Johnson urges Brits to vote Brexit to "take back control"', *Daily Express*, 20 June 2016.

13 ITV News, 16 June 2016: https://www.facebook.com/itvnews/videos/boris-and-the-lobster-the-eu-is-pinching-our-fish/10153831517442672/.

14 Ambrose Evans-Pritchard, 'Brexit vote is about the supremacy of Parliament and nothing else', *Daily Telegraph*, 13 June 2016.

15 Philip Johnston, 'EU membership broke our constitution by giving British judges too much power at the expense of Parliament', *Daily Telegraph*, 8 November 2016.

16 'The United Kingdom's exit from and new partnership with the European Union' (London: HMSO 2017, Cmnd 9417).

17 *Thoburn v Sunderland City Council* [2002] EWHC 195.

18 A. V. Dicey, *Introduction to the Study of the Law of the Constitution*, op. cit.

19 Jon Henley, 'Is the EU really dictating the shape of your bananas?', *The Guardian*, 15 May 2016.

20 Neil MacCormick, 'A Very British Revolution?' in *Questioning Sovereignty: Law, State, and Nation in the European Commonwealth* (Oxford: Oxford University Press, 1999), pp. 79–96.

21 Mark Elliott, 'Sovereignty, Primacy and the Common Law Constitution: What has EU Membership Taught Us?' in Mark Elliott, Jack Williams and Alison L. Young (eds), *The UK Constitution After Miller: Brexit and Beyond* (Oxford: Hart Publishing, 2018), pp. 221–48.

22 Tom Bingham, 'The Rule of Law and Sovereignty of Parliament' in *The Rule of Law* (London: Allen Lane, 2010), pp. 160–70.

23 Mark Elliott, 'The Parliamentary Sovereignty in Legal, Constitutional and Political Perspective' in Jeffrey Jowell, Dawn Oliver and Colm O'Cinneide (eds), *The Changing Constitution*, 8th edition (Oxford: Oxford University Press, 2015), pp. 38–66.

24 The UK in a Changing Europe, 'Fisheries and Brexit' (June 2020): https://ukandeu.ac.uk/research-papers/fisheries-and-brexit-3/.

25 Saphora Smith, 'They voted for Brexit. Now many UK fishermen feel betrayed', NBC News, 30 January 2021: https://www.nbcnews.com/news/world/they-voted-brexit-now-many-u-k-fishermen-feel-betrayed-n1255986

Chapter 10: Death – To Cease Upon the Midnight Without Pain

1   *R (on the application of Nicklinson and another) v Ministry of Justice* [2014] UKSC 38.

2   *R (on the application of Pretty) v DPP* [2009].

3   Ibid., Lord Neuberger.

4   Ibid., Lord Mance.
5   Jonathan Sumption, 'Law's Expanding Empire' in *Trials of the State: Law and the Decline of Politics* (London: Profile Books, 2019).
6   *R (Purdy) v DPP* [2009] UKHL 45.
7   Mary Warnock and Elisabeth Macdonald, *Easeful Death: Is There a Case for Assisted Dying?* (Oxford: Oxford University Press, 2008), pp. 7–10.
8   *R v Kennedy* [2008] 1 AC 269.
9   L. W. Sumner, *Assisted Death: A Study in Ethics and Law* (Oxford; New York: Oxford University Press, 2011).
10 *Re B (Consent to Treatment; Capacity)* [2002] 1 FLR 1090.
11 Harriet Sherwood, 'Three in four Britons back assisted dying for terminally ill – poll', *The Guardian*, 4 August 2021.
12 'The Commission on Assisted Dying' (London: Demos, 2011): https://demosuk.wpengine.com/files/476_CoAD_FinalReport_158x240_I_web_single-NEW_.pdf?1328113363.
13 British Medical Association, 'Physician-assisted dying survey': https://www.bma.org.uk/advice-and-support/ethics/end-of-life/physician-assisted-dying/physician-assisted-dying-survey.
14 Haider Warraich, *Modern Death: How Medicine Changed the End of Life* (London: Duckworth Overlook, 2018).
15 Lord Mance had been created a life peer in 2005 when he was appointed a Lord of Appeal in Ordinary as a member of the judicial committee of the House of Lords, then the United Kingdom's highest court. He was automatically transferred as a justice of the Supreme Court when the court was created in 2009. He retired as a justice of the Supreme Court in 2018 and was therefore free to speak in his capacity as a life peer.

Select Bibliography

Addison, Paul, *No Turning Back: The Peacetime Revolutions of Post-War Britain* (Oxford: Oxford University Press, 2010).

Baker, Dennis J. and Horder, Jeremy (eds), *The Sanctity of Life and the Criminal Law: The Legacy of Glanville Williams* (Cambridge: Cambridge University Press, 2015).

Barendt, Eric, *Freedom of Speech* (Oxford: Clarendon Press, 1985).

Bedford, Sybille, *Would You Let Your Wife Read This Book? The Trial of Lady Chatterley's Lover*, 2nd ed. (London: Daunt Books, 2016).

Bhopal, Kalwant, *White Privilege: The myth of a post-racial society* (Bristol: Policy Press, 2018).

Bingham, Tom, *The Business of Judging: Selected Essays and Speeches* (Oxford: Oxford University Press, 2000).

——, *The Rule of Law* (London: Allen Lane, 2010).

Blick, Andrew, *Stretching the Constitution: The Brexit Shock in Historic Perspective* (Oxford: Hart Publishing, 2019).

Bogdanor, Vernon, *Beyond Brexit: Towards a British Constitution* (London: I. B. Taurus, 2019).

Booker, Christopher, *The Neophiliacs: A Study of the Revolution in English Life in the Fifties and Sixties* (London: Collins, 1969).

Bourne, Stephen, *Under Fire: Black Britain in Wartime 1939–45* (Cheltenham: The History Press, 2020).

Burk, Kathleen (ed.), *The British Isles Since 1945* (Oxford: Oxford University Press, 2003).

Churchill, Robin, *EEC Fisheries Law* (Stockholm: Martinus Nijhoff, 1987).

Cook, Hera, *The Long Sexual Revolution: English Women, Sex, and Contraception 1800–1975* (Oxford: Oxford University Press, 2004).

Doyle, Andrew, *Free Speech and Why It Matters* (London: Constable, 2021).

Driver, Julia, *Ethics: The fundamentals* (Oxford: Blackwell, 2007).

Dunt, Ian, *How to Be a Liberal* (Kingston-Upon-Thames: Canbury Press, 2020).

Dworkin, Ronald, *Taking Rights Seriously*, 3rd ed. (London: Duckworth, 1981).

Eddo-Lodge, Reni, *Why I'm No Longer Talking to White People About Race* (London: Bloomsbury, 2017).

Elliott, Mark; Williams, Jack; and Young, Alison L. (eds), *The UK Constitution after Miller: Brexit and Beyond* (Oxford: Hart Publishing, 2018).

Evans, Geoffrey and Menon, Anand, *Brexit and British Politics* (Cambridge: Polity Press, 2017).

Evans, Harold, *My Paper Chase: True Stories of Vanished Times – An Autobiography* (London: Abacus, 2010).

Ewing, K. D., *Bonfire of the Liberties: New Labour, Human Rights, and the Rule of Law* (Oxford: Oxford University Press, 2010).

— — and Gearty, C. A., *The Struggle for Civil Liberties: Political Freedom and the Rule of Law in Britain, 1914–1945* (Oxford: Oxford University Press, 2000).

Feldman, David, *Civil Liberties and Human Rights in England and Wales*, 2nd ed. (Oxford: Oxford University Press, 2002).

Fenwick, Helen, *Fenwick on Civil Liberties and Human Rights*, 5th ed. (London: Routledge-Cavendish, 2016).

Finlay, Ilora and Preston, Robert, *Death by Appointment: A Rational Guide to the Assisted Dying Debate* (Newcastle Upon Tyne: Cambridge Scholars Publishing, 2020).

Fryer, Peter, *Staying Power: The history of black people in Britain*, 3rd ed. (London: Pluto Press, 2018).

Garton Ash, Timothy, *Free Speech: Ten Principles for a Connected World* (London: Atlantic Books, 2016).

Gillman, Peter and Gillman, Leni, *Collar the Lot! How Britain Interned and Expelled its Wartime Refugees* (London: Quartet Books, 1980).

Goldsworthy, Jeffrey, *The Sovereignty of Parliament: History and Philosophy* (Oxford: Clarendon Press, 1999).

Gostin, Larry (ed.), *Civil Liberties in Conflict* (London: Routledge, 1988).

Grayling, A. C., *Democracy and Its Crisis* (London: Oneworld, 2017).

— —, *The Good State: On the Principles of Democracy* (London: Oneworld, 2020).

Hale, Lady, *Spider Woman: A Life* (London: The Bodley Head, 2021).

Hall, Lesley A., *Sex, Gender and Social Change in Britain since 1880* (Basingstoke: Palgrave Macmillan, 2012).

Hill, Christopher, *The Century of Revolution, 1603–1714* (Abingdon: Routledge Classics, 2002).

Hill, Jeffrey, *Learie Constantine and Race Relations in Britain and the Empire* (London: Bloomsbury Academic, 2018).

Hirsch, Afua, *Brit(ish): On Race, Identity and Belonging* (London: Vintage, 2018).

Holmes, Stephen, *Passions and Constraint: On the Theory of Liberal Democracy* (Chicago: Chicago University Press, 1995).

Hutchinson, Allan C., *Is Eating People Wrong? Great Legal Cases and How They Shaped the World* (Cambridge: Cambridge University Press, 2011).

Inglis, Fred, *A Short History of Celebrity* (Princeton: Princeton University Press, 2010).

Jackson, Robert, *Sovereignty: The Evolution of an Idea* (Cambridge: Polity Press, 2007).

Jowell, Jeffrey; Oliver, Dawn; and O'Cinneide, Colm (eds.), *The Changing Constitution*, 8th ed. (Oxford: Oxford University Press, 2015).

King, Anthony, *The British Constitution* (Oxford: Oxford University Press, 2007).

— —, *Who Governs Britain* (London: Pelican Books, 2015).

Knightley, Phillip, *Suffer the Children: The Story of Thalidomide* (New York: The Viking Press, 1979).

Lee, Simon, *Law and Morals: Warnock, Gillick and Beyond* (Oxford: Oxford University Press, 1987).

Lester, Anthony, *Five Ideas to Fight For: How our freedom is under threat and why it matters* (London: Oneworld, 2017).

Levin, Bernard, *The Pendulum Years: Britain and the Sixties* (London: Jonathan Cape, 1970).

Lewis, Geoffrey, *Lord Atkin: A biography* (Oxford: Hart Publishing, 1999).

Lively, Jack and Lively, Adam (eds), *Democracy in Britain: A Reader* (Oxford: Blackwell, 1994).

Loughlin, Martin, *Sword and Scales: An Examination of the Relationship between Law and Politics* (Oxford: Hart Publishing, 2000).

MacCormick, Neil, *Questioning Sovereignty: Law, State, and Nation in the European Commonwealth* (Oxford: Oxford University Press, 1999).

Malik, Kenan, *The Quest for a Moral Compass: A global history of ethics* (London: Atlantic Books, 2014).

Manchester, A. H., *A Modern Legal History of England and Wales 1750–1950* (London: Butterworths, 1980).

Marquand, David and Seldon, Anthony, *The Ideas That Shaped Post-War Britain* (London: Fontana Press, 1996).

Marr, Andrew, *A History of Modern Britain*, 10th anniversary ed. (London: Pan Books, 2017).

— —, *Elizabethans: How Modern Britain Was Forged* (London: William Collins, 2020).

Marwick, Arthur, *British Society Since 1945* (London: Penguin Books, 1996).

— —, *The Sixties* (Oxford: Oxford University Press, 1998).

Mason, Peter, *Learie Constantine* (Oxford: Signal Books, 2008).

Matthew, Colin, *Nineteenth-Century Britain* (Oxford: Oxford University Press, 2000).

Miller, Gina, *Rise: Life Lessons in Speaking Out, Standing Tall & Leading the Way* (London: Canongate, 2018).

Mohamed, Hashi, *People Like Us: What it Takes to Make it in Modern Britain* (London: Profile Books, 2020).

Olusoga, David, *Black and British: A Forgotten History* (London: Pan Books, 2017).

Phillips, Trevor, *Race and Faith: The Deafening Silence* (London: Civitas, 2016).

Pilkington, Andrew, *Racial Disadvantage and Ethnic Diversity in Britain* (Basingstoke: Palgrave Macmillan, 2003).

Richmond, Anthony H., *Colour Prejudice in Britain: A Study of West Indian Workers in Liverpool, 1941–1951* (London: Routledge & Kegan Paul, 1954).

Robertson, Geoffrey, *Obscenity* (London: Weidenfeld & Nicolson, 1979).

— —, *People Against the Press: An Enquiry into the Press Council* (London: Quartet Books, 1983).

Rolph, C. H. (ed.), *The Trial of Lady Chatterley: Regina v Penguin Books Ltd* (Harmondsworth: Penguin Books, 1961).

Rozenberg, Joshua, *Trial of Strength: The Battle between Ministers and Judges over Who Makes the Law* (London: Richard Cohen Books, 1997).

— —, *Privacy and the Press* (Oxford: Oxford University Press, 2004).

Runciman, David, *How Democracy Ends* (London: Profile Books, 2018).

Sandbrook, Dominic, *Never Had It So Good: A History of Britain from Suez to the Beatles* (London: Abacus, 2006).

— —, *White Heat: A History of Britain in the Swinging Sixties* (London: Little, Brown, 2006).

Sandel, Michael, *Justice: What's the Right Thing to Do?* (London: Penguin Books, 2010).

Sampson, Anthony, *Anatomy of Britain* (London: Hodder & Stoughton, 1962).

— —, *Who Runs This Place? The Anatomy of Britain in the 21st Century* (London: John Murray, 2004).

Sedley, Stephen, *Ashes and Sparks: Essays on Law and Justice* (Cambridge: Cambridge University Press, 2011).

— —, *Law and the Whirligig of Time* (Oxford: Hart Publishing, 2018).

Simpson, A. W. Brian, *Cannibalism and the Common Law* (Chicago: Chicago University Press, 1984).

— —, *In the Highest Degree Odious: Detention Without Trial in Wartime Britain* (Oxford: Oxford University Press, 1992).

— —, *Leading Cases in the Common Law* (Oxford: Clarendon Press, 1995).

Stevens, Robert, *The English Judges: Their role in the changing Constitution* (Oxford: Hart Publishing, 2002).

Sumner, L. W., *Assisted Death: A Study in Ethics and Law* (Oxford; New York: Oxford University Press, 2011).

Sumption, Jonathan, *Trials of the State: Law and the Decline of Politics* (London: Profile Books, 2019).

— —, *Law in a Time of Crisis* (London: Profile Books, 2021).

Sutherland, John, *Offensive Literature: Decensorship in Britain, 1960–1982* (London: Junction Books, 1982).

Thornton, Peter, *Decade of Decline: Civil Liberties in the Thatcher Years* (London: National Council for Civil Liberties, 1989).

Tombs, Robert, *The English and Their History* (London: Allen Lane, 2014).

Travis, Alan, *Bound and Gagged: A Secret History of Obscenity in Britain* (London: Profile Books, 2001).

Wacks, Raymond, *Privacy and Media Freedom* (Oxford: Oxford University Press, 2013).

Warnock, Mary, *An Intelligent Person's Guide to Ethics* (London: Duckworth, 1998).

— — and Macdonald, Elisabeth, *Easeful Death: Is There a Case for Assisted Dying?* (Oxford: Oxford University Press, 2008).

Warraich, Haider, *Modern Death: How Medicine Changed the End of Life* (London: Duckworth Overlook, 2018).

Weeks, Jeffrey, *The World We Have Won* (Abingdon: Routledge, 2007).

Williams, Glanville, *The Sanctity of Life and the Criminal Law* (London: Faber & Faber, 1958).

Wootton, Sarah and Riley, Lloyd, *Last Rights: The Case for Assisted Dying* (London: Biteback Publishing, 2020).

Acknowledgements

First and foremost, I must acknowledge the brave people who made this book possible, the nine people and one hospital who initiated or defended their legal cases with tenacity and courage. In doing so, they made the cases for this book. Learie Constantine, John Couceiro, Harold Evans, Gorden Kaye, Sir Allen Lane, Robert Liversidge, St Mary's Hospital Manchester, Gina Miller, Tony and Jane Nicklinson and Nora Ziegler all contributed to making Britain what it is today. With the exception of Sir Allen Lane, founder of Penguin Books, and Nora Ziegler, all were claimants who at risk to their own reputations and resources embarked on risky litigation with no guaranteed prospect of success. Penguin Books and Nora Ziegler were defendants in criminal prosecutions brought against them. They stood their ground and in challenging the prosecuting bodies each established a point of principle. I owe them all a debt of gratitude. It has been a privilege to reveal their legal battles to a wider audience.

I must also thank the librarians who have assisted me so much. The staff at the Inner Temple and Middle Temple libraries as well as those at the London Library and the British Library have all found books and law reports with alacrity and efficiency as well as providing congenial writing conditions when I have needed it. I owe a special debt of gratitude to the staff at the National Archives who responded to my

Freedom of Information request to see all the files on Robert Liversidge with courtesy and proficiency. Thanks to them, previously embargoed files were made available, enabling me to tell the full story of Robert Liversidge's detention without trial in 1940.

My editor, Olivia Beattie, encouraged this project from the start at Biteback and has assisted me greatly in putting the book together and seeing it through the press. My grateful thanks go to her.

Finally, I must extend loving thanks to my wife Mary, who read drafts with a critical eye and provided much needed advice and suggestions for improvement. Errors and omissions which remain are, of course, down to me.

Inigo Bing
June 2022

Index

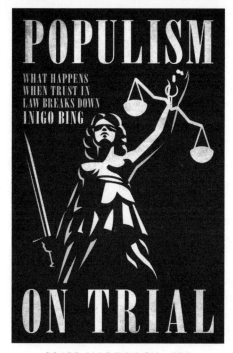